Women of Color

Women of Color

Mother-Daughter Relationships in 20th-Century Literature

Edited by

ELIZABETH BROWN-GUILLORY

University of Texas Press Austin

Printed in the United States of America

First University of Texas Press edition, 1996

∞ The paper used in this publication meets the minimum requirements of American National Standard for Information Sciences—Permanence of Paper for Printed Library Materials, ANSI Z39.48-1984.

Library of Congress Cataloging-in-Publication Data

Women of color : mother-daughter relationships in twentieth-century literature / edited by Elizabeth Brown-Guillory. — lst University of Texas Press ed.

p. cm.

Includes bibliographical references and index.

ISBN 978-0-292-70847-1

1. American literature—Minority authors—History and criticism. 2. Women and literature—United States—History—20th century. 3. American literature—Women authors—History and criticism. 4. American literature—20th century—History and criticism. 5. Mothers and daughters in literature. 6. Ethnic groups in literature. 7. Motherhood in literature.

I. Brown-Guillory, Elizabeth.

PS153.M56W66 1996

810.9'9287'08693—dc20 96-15697

To

LEO BROWN,
my father, who is devoted to my mother and to us all

MARJORIE SAVOIE BROWN,
my mother, who gives me courage

LUCIA ELIZABETH GUILLORY,
my daughter, who is the miracle of my life

LUCIUS M. GUILLORY,
my husband and my best friend,
who supports me unconditionally

Contents

Acknowledgments

The University of Texas Press welcomed my proposal for this book and accepted my vision for this project. I thank especially Frankie Westbrook, who was my initial contact with the Press, and Tayron Tolley Cutter, who guided me through the process.

Abundant accolades go to the scholars who contributed essays to this volume. I am thankful for their interest, enthusiasm, and cooperation as we progressed through the various stages of the project.

I am immensely grateful to Tora L. Cureton, my graduate research assistant at the University of Houston, for her outstanding and invaluable services. Tora, a Clemson University graduate, came to the University of Houston to earn a master's degree in English. I chose to mentor her and, in return, she has shown exceptional commitment to me on this and other projects.

I am appreciative of the support I received from the University of Houston while working on this project. Portions of this book were written and edited while I was on sabbatical in the spring of 1995. I am also grateful for the Limited-Grant-in-Aid from the Office of Sponsored Programs at the university. I cherish my relationship with my colleagues and friends in the English Department. I value deeply their continued support of my work.

I hold in high regard the encouragement from my dear friend Dr. Violet Harrington Bryan of Xavier University of New Orleans, who served with me as co-organizer of the "Women of Color: Mother-Daughter Relationships in Twentieth-Century Literature" session at the annual convention of the South Central Modern Language Association in 1987.

DeLinda Marzette Moon, a Texas Southern University graduate student in English, deserves recognition for clerical assistance during the preparation of the first draft of the manuscript.

I am most indebted to my husband, Lucius M. Guillory, for his unconditional love and support during this and every project I undertake. He is my steady ship and, as a character in my play *Just a Little Mark* says, he is "the sugar in my coffee." I also feel compelled to thank my daughter, Lucia, who motivates me to model for her that she can and will do great things with her life.

Contributors

Elizabeth Brown-Guillory is a playwright and Associate Professor of English at the University of Houston, where she teaches African American literature and American drama. Among the seven plays she has written are *Bayou Relics, Snapshots of Broken Dolls, Just a Little Mark, Saving Grace,* and *Missing Sister*. She is the author of *Their Place on the Stage: Black Women Playwrights in America,* editor of the anthology *Wines in the Wilderness: Plays by African American Women from the Harlem Renaissance to the Present,* and currently is working on a book about Alice Childress.

Charlene Taylor Evans is Professor of English and Chairperson of the Department of English, Foreign Languages, and Reading at Texas Southern University. She is the principal author of *I Say What I Mean,* a developmental writing text, and former review editor of *The Houston Defender*. She has published articles on James Baldwin, E. M. Forster, and Toni Morrison.

M. Marie Booth Foster is Professor of English and Vice President for Instruction at Central Florida Community College. The author of *A Bibliography of Southern Black Creative Writers, 1829–1953,* she also has published articles on Ernest Gaines and Naomi Madgett Long and has lectured on Black Southern writers throughout the United States and in Ankara, Turkey.

Lucille P. Fultz is Assistant Professor of English at Rice University. She is the coeditor of *Double Stitch: Black Women Write About Mothers and Daughters* and has published articles on Toni Morrison. She serves as Associate Editor of *SAGE: A Scholarly Journal on Black Women.*

Maria C. Gonzalez, Associate Professor of English at the University of Houston, teaches Mexican American literature, American literature, women writers, and feminist theory and criticism. She is presently conducting research on Chicana queer theory. Her publications include *Contemporary Mexican-American Women Novelists: Toward a Feminist Identity* and essays on Chicana literature and sexuality.

Julia De Foor Jay teaches literature and composition at San Jacinto College Central. She recently received a Ph.D. in English, with a specialty in American drama, from the University of Houston. The author of articles on Ntozake Shange, Beth Henley, and Cherrié Moraga, she is focusing her research on language and self-definition in the works of American women playwrights. She also acts in Houston area theaters.

Radhika Mohanram is a Lecturer in the Department of Women and Gender Studies at the University of Waikato in Hamilton, New Zealand, where she teaches gender and postcolonial theory. She has published articles and chapters on women in the nation and coedited *Postcolonial Discourse and Changing Cultural Contexts* and *English Postcoloniality: Literatures from around the World.* She is also coeditor of *SPAN,* the journal of the South Pacific Association for Commonwealth Literatures and Language Studies.

Sheryl A. Mylan is Associate Professor of English and Director of Lower Division Studies at Stephen F. Austin State University. She has written articles on the fiction of William Carlos Williams, on the war novels of Crane, Hemingway, and Mailer, and on F. Scott Fitzgerald. She is coauthor of the composition textbook *Voices and Visions: An Integrated Approach to Reading and Writing.*

Kimberly Pollock was educated at Shimer College and at the University of Southwestern Louisiana. She lives in Washington State, where she is

Chairperson of the American Studies program and teaches in the English and Interdisciplinary Studies programs at Bellevue Community College.

Fabian Clements Worsham, who died in 1994, was a poet and Associate Professor of English at the University of Houston—Downtown. Her poetry books include *The Green Kanagroo, Aunt Erma's Country Kitchen & Bordello* (winner of the Signpost Press Award), *Vulture Woman*, and *The Harlot's Child*. She reviewed many books of poetry and wrote critical essays on such topics as contemporary children's films, creative writing pedagogy, and contemporary African American women's poetry.

Patricia Lee Yongue is an Associate Professor of English and Women's Studies at the University of Houston. Her research and publications concentrate on women writers, especially Willa Cather. She currently devotes her free time to the education of academic, professional, and community groups on such women's issues as sexual abuse, domestic violence, and environmentalism (eco-feminism).

Joyce Zonana is Associate Professor of English at the University of New Orleans. She has published essays in *Victorian Poetry, Journal of Narrative Technique*, and *Tulsa Studies in Women's Literature*. Her essay "The Sultan and the Slave: Feminist Orientalism and the Structure of *Jane Eyre*," which appeared in *Signs*, won the Florence Howe Award. Born in Cairo to a Jewish family, she is now working on her "family autobiography."

Introduction

ELIZABETH BROWN-GUILLORY

Since the mid-1980s, the interest in mother-daughter relationships has become increasingly strong. National and international symposia have centered around the construction of motherhood, examining women as they relate both as mothers of daughters and as daughters of mothers. The leadership of the South Central Modern Language Association (SCMLA) was aware of the strong interest in mother-daughter relationships when it decided in 1986 to approve "Women of Color: Mother-Daughter Relationships in Twentieth-Century Literature" as a special session for its annual convention.[1] The "Women of Color" sessions quickly became very popular, particularly among feminists who had a strong interest in reshaping their course syllabi. Feminist scholars were especially interested in exploring critical approaches to the literature of diasporic women. After six years of drawing capacity crowds to the special session, the SCMLA leadership in 1993 approved permanent session status for "Women of Color" with a name change to "Race and Gender Issues in Twentieth-Century Literature." The papers presented in the session over the six-year period have insightfully explored numerous ways in which the mother-daughter dyad interacts and impacts their families, their communities, and the world. Such potent and poignant presentations needed a larger audience, a more permanent and accessible playing field—hence the idea of bringing together representative selections in *Women of Color: Mother-Daughter Relationships in Twentieth-Century Literature*. The original session had, indeed, given birth to something broader and perhaps even more inclusive. It seemed an appropriate time to commemorate the "Women of Color" session while at the same time allowing the newly named session to continue the dialogue.

The essays in this volume were presented at SCMLA or were submitted for consideration as a result of a national call for papers in several feminist journals. The support for this project was overwhelming, making it clear that there was a need and an audience for a volume that would explore mother-daughter relationships in the literature of women of color. There are several existing excellent volumes on mothers and daughters (namely, critiques of Euro-American, middle-class mother-daughter relationships), but this is the first work to study mother-daughter relationships in so many diverse cultures.

This project is an exciting and vital one because it brings together a multiplicity of critical approaches to literature written by and about diasporic women, including Native Americans, African Americans, Mexican Americans, Asian Americans, Africans, Indians, and Australian Aboriginals. This collection examines the myth and reality surrounding mother-daughter relationships, underscoring the tensions and conflicts which naturally occur as mothers and daughters attempt to communicate with each other. Research suggests that this mother-daughter dyad experiences a love/hate relationship, often because the mother tries painstakingly to convey knowledge about how to survive in a racist, sexist, and classist world while the daughter rejects her mother's experiences as invalid in changing social times. These biases coupled with the harm caused by societal homophobia test and stretch the relationships of mothers and daughters. Studies also suggest that when a mother looks at her daughter, she sees herself. She is constantly reminded of her mistakes, yearnings, dreams, successes, and failures. When the daughter looks at her mother, she often sees herself and rejects the image in the mirror. Sometimes the daughter rejects her mother's values as inappropriate to her reality. Yet a daughter often fears separation from her mother because it is to her mother that she most often turns for validation. It is the friction, inextricably linked to fear and frustration, which challenges both mothers and daughters to create a space in which the experiences of both members of the dyad can be valorized.

Several common threads run through each of the twelve essays in this volume. One of the most important issues addressed is the emotional and psychological condition of the mother as she transfers her values to her children. Martin Delany, a brilliant black nineteenth-century philosopher, astutely sums up the role women play in rearing children in his famous 1852 political treatise, "The Condition, Elevation, and Destiny of the Colored People of the United States, Politically Considered":

> Our females must be qualified, because they are to be the mothers of our children. As mothers they are the first nurses and instructors of children; from them children, consequently, get their first impressions, which being always the most lasting, should be the most correct. Raise the mothers above the level of degradation, and the offspring is elevated with them. . . . No people are elevated above the condition of their females; hence, the condition of the mother determines the condition of the child. To know the position of a people, it is only necessary to know the condition of their females; and despite themselves, they cannot rise above their level. (204–205)

Brenda O. Daly and Maureen Reddy reiterate Delany's view of motherhood in *Narrating Mothers*, where they note, "We should take care to remember that what happens to mothers happens to us all" (18). Another thread linking the essays is the notion that before a woman can be a good mother, she first has to be a good daughter, one who loves herself and who nurtures others. Essentially, daughters learn mothering skills from their mothers, biological or surrogate, a concept which is confirmed by Marianne Hirsch in "Mothers and Daughters":

> There can be no systematic and theoretical study of women in patriarchal culture, there can be no theory of women's oppression, that does not take into account woman's role as a mother of daughters and as a daughter of mothers, that does not study female identity in relation to previous and subsequent generations of women, and that does not study that relationship in the wider context in which it takes place: the emotional, political, economic, and symbolic structures of family and society. (202)

A third thread is the struggle at the core of the lives of these women of color, a struggle that usually is connected to race and ethnicity as well as gender and sexual orientation. A fourth thread is that the mothers insist that they can never be whole until they teach their daughters not to repeat their mistakes. Another commonality found in the essays is the degree of internal turmoil that the women experience as they prepare to send their daughters into a hostile world. Concomitantly, daughters often feel that they cannot live up to their mothers' ideals and dreams for them. They are torn between wishing to be an extension of their mothers and yearning for their own autonomy. Mickey Pearlman in *Mother Puzzles* posits that every mother-daughter story involves "how we find ourselves leaving, or in being left, in excoriating the past or beatifying it, about finding the missing connections or losing the infantilizing ones, and most certainly about being loved, being loved, and about what daughters do in solving mother puzzles" (8).

The essays in the volume are so valuable because each one explores, at some level, the confrontation and engagement of mothers and daughters. The mother-daughter relationships explored in the essays illuminate, in Marianne Hirsch's terms, "this complex process of identification and dis-identification, this slow emergence of maternal speech from silence . . ." (*The Mother/Daughter Plot*, 16–17). The mothers and daughters always seem to be struggling to get beyond the silences. Sometimes the texts point to consequences of continued silence and sometimes to the absolute joy of breaking silence and moving toward reconciliation and growth between mothers and daughters. The literary texts examined in this volume propel readers to look closely at the many constructions of femininity, particularly in terms of discourses of motherhood and daughterhood. Johnetta B. Cole's words in *Double Stitch: Black Women Write about Mothers and Daughters* accurately describe the women writers of color treated in this volume: "each writer speaks out of her own daughterhood, motherhood, or an analysis of another's particular encounters with this universal experience of femaleness" (xiii). The following brief summaries of the essays give a sense of the breadth of this volume.

Radhika Mohanram's "The Problems of Reading: Mother-Daughter Relationships and Indian Postcoloniality" is an examination of two Indian short stories, "Girls" by Mrinal Pande and "Her Mother" by Anjana Appachana. Mohanram concludes that mother-daughter relationships are inhibited from strong bonding largely because of the devaluation of females in Indian culture. In her analysis of "Girls," Mohanram argues that the misogyny and devaluation of daughters lead mothers in India to hope for a boy when they are pregnant because girl babies do not strengthen or enhance their lineage; they merely function as objects of patronymic exchange. A female child does not contribute to securing power for the maternal position and, in fact, is perceived as being temporarily on loan to the birth parents until she assumes her role in her husband's family. The mother in "Girls" announces to other adult women that if she has a boy it will relieve her of the aggravation of enduring another pregnancy. Because the value of a son is underscored in Indian culture, a woman brings honor and power to her family when she gives birth to a boy. She also displays fierce devotion to her son because he anchors her with a name and a family affiliation. This preferential treatment of the sons alienates and angers the daughters. It then becomes the role of the Indian mother to teach her daughters how to bend properly in order to serve their men and be content with a woman's fate. Mohanram notes that a daughter's difficulties with her mother's preferential treatment of her sons extend to other women in the community: daughters very often dislike other women and adopt a preference for men.

The second segment of the essay centers on "Her Mother," where the value of maternity and mother-daughter relationships is examined within the context of a father's relationship with the daughter. The mother passively reacts to her daughter's defiance, while privately contemplating, even protesting, the unfairness of the daughter's closeness to the father. Mohanram argues cogently that a mother in India often gives way to the father and the father gives way to his successor, the daughter's husband. The grief that the mother feels underscores the loss that all Indian mothers experience in a culture where women are the objects of patronymic exchange. Mohanram's interpretation of "Her Mother" is in keeping with Alice Jardine's critique that some women writers portray female characters who depend upon their fathers for nurturance. Jardine posits that turning to a man for nurturance often involves revalorizing the fantasy of the all-powerful phallic mother, which, in turn, often means dismembering the female body or killing the mother in the name of epistemological purity (130). Mohanram concludes her study of two Indian women writers by asserting that mothers and daughters can only sustain a tenable relationship if they live on different soils, which will afford them the distance to become close, particularly since mother-daughter relationships are not valorized in India.

Kimberly Joyce Pollock's "A Continuum of Pain: A Woman's Legacy in Alice Walker's *Possessing the Secret of Joy*" examines the novel as a vehicle which expresses the pain, madness, and healing transmitted from mothers to daughters not only in Africa but around the world. Walker tells the story of women who are stripped of their souls by other women at the insistence of men. The secret that she refers to in *Possessing the Secret of Joy* is resistance: women can only break the continuum of pain resulting from sexist cultural patterns by refusing to acquiesce and by creating new cultural patterns that allow women to trust, love, and celebrate themselves. In Walker's novel, genital mutilation is imposed upon Olinkan women, a cultural practice originated by the fathers, to ensure that women remained faithful and gave pleasure, at a terrible cost to the women. The tsunga, whose task includes sewing up each young woman's vaginal opening so tightly that sometimes only small droplets of urine can escape, ensures for the patriarchy that women will remain physically and psychologically mutilated. For these services, the fathers look upon her as a national monument and refer to her as mother of the country. Pollock argues that if the tsunga, M'Lissa, is the mother, the legacy she leaves is excruciating and lingering pain: she carves flesh from Olinkan women and leaves them maimed.

Pollock notes that one of the things an Olinkan mother teaches her daughter is silence, the first step on the path to becoming a woman in their culture. They are taught that pain is not to be given a voice, which often results in insanity. Those who can withstand the pain go on to teach their daughters to work hard, produce children, and endure pain. Tashi, Walker's heroine, is unable to confront her own biological mother about the mutilation because, as Pollock points out, daughters cannot challenge mothers about the devastation to which the mothers themselves have been subjected. However, Tashi does challenge the patriarchically sanctioned mother, the tsunga M'Lissa. Pollock argues that, by killing the tsunga, Tashi breaks the cycle of pain and gives life to all the Olinkan women. Essentially, in murdering the tsunga, Tashi symbolically destroys partriarchy's tyranny over women's bodies. Murdering her biological mother would merely have victimized the victim. Tashi's murder is not in vain. At the end of the novel the Olinkan women appear at her execution, allowing their little naked girls to give themselves pleasure and holding signs announcing that resistance is the secret of joy. Pollock argues that Walker's message is that without resistance self-love is impossible. If the continuum of pain is not broken, and if there is no new legacy for mothers to leave their daughters, then humans will cease to be.

Joyce Zonana's " 'I was cryin', all the people were cryin', my mother was cryin'': Aboriginality and Maternity in Sally Morgan's *My Place*" speaks to the spiritual maternity that overcomes patriarchal and racist violence to heal the wounds of separation and to foster a community in which people feel connected to each other. Zonana argues that *My Place* is a quest story in which the narrator chooses Aboriginality in order to reclaim the part of her that has been repressed by Australian patriarchy, which dictated that no half-caste (i.e., nearly white looking child) could be raised by its native / black mother. This disenfranchisement had devastating consequences and served to damage the self-esteem of Sally's mothers. Sally's grandmother tells her of the pain and humiliation she experienced every time her white son-in-law referred to her as a "bloody nigger." Zonana posits that this conjunction of racism, patriarchy, and colonialism in Australia severed the connection between Aboriginality and maternity. In order for Aboriginal women to be allowed to rear their half-caste children, they had to deny their Aboriginality, as do Sally's mother, grandmother, and great-grandmother. However, Sally chooses the stigmatized identity that comes to her through her mothers because Aboriginality is an expression of how she has been mothered and how she hopes to mother. Zonana argues that in choosing Aboriginality, Sally chooses maternity. In the text, Sally Morgan becomes a storytelling grandmother, keeping Aboriginality alive. Zonana notes that not only does the daughter define herself "to and through" her mother, grandmother, and great-grandmother, as opposed to through her white father, but the mother, grandmother, and great-grandmother define themselves to and through the daughter. This reciprocity is made possible because Sally's mothers fostered in her a strong Aboriginal spirit. Sally helps them embrace their own Aboriginality by her identification with Aboriginality. Zonana cogently argues that the pain of mother-child separation is the central issue in *My Place* and that this wound is opened and healed by Sally. Sally mothers her mothers in the spirit in which she has been mothered. Zonana asserts that in choosing Aboriginality, in both flesh and spirit, Sally heals not only herself but the wounds of her mothers, which were inflicted by a white Australian policy of genocide.

Patricia Lee Yongue's " 'My mother is here': Buchi Emecheta's Love Child" examines mother-daughter relationships as a target of sadistic patriarchal assault in *The Bride Price*, *The Joys of Motherhood*, and *The Family*. While Emecheta, a Nigerian novelist who lives in England, remains steadfastly loyal to the land, people, and traditions of West Africa, she refuses to overlook the tyranny that African and Western patriarchy has heaped upon mothers and daughters. Linking theories about women's bodies by Nancy Chodorow, Julia Kristeva, and Luce Irigaray, Yongue posits that Emecheta's three novels indict patriarchy for its systematic oppression of woman and the principle of the feminine. Yongue notes that Emecheta's novels suggest that dividing mother from daughter results in severing woman from herself. The daughter, then, becomes the object of attack as the fragmented mother emulates the discourse of the father.

Yongue calls attention to the commodification of woman's body in Nigerian culture, which reads very much like Mohanram's discussion of women's fate in Indian culture. A woman's body is the only value she retains, and that body is of value only as long as it enhances the economic and political interest of its owner, namely, the woman's father, his inheritor, or her husband. She is most valued when she produces sons, to whom she is fiercely loyal and attentive. When she bears sons, she maintains a preferred place among her husband's wives. Essentially she is a glorified object. However, in the words of Catharine MacKinnon, "objectification is alienation" (541), which inevitably occurs when a woman's body serves as an object of exchange. A daughter is a reflection of a mother's incompleteness, particularly since wholeness is defined in terms of how many sons she produces. While Emecheta is aware of the preference given to sons, she emphasizes the need for healing between mothers and daughters in her novels, argues Yongue. Emecheta clearly views healthy bonding between mothers and daughters as necessary for the health of the community. The breach is a serious one, however, particularly since mothers are expected to train their daughters to serve men and find joy only in the accomplishments of men. Yongue notes that in Emecheta's novels mothers are complicitous in their daughters' subjugation. They often look on passively as their daughters are beaten, sexually assaulted, and molested, all in the name of pleasing or pacifying patriarchy. Daughters painfully learn that their mothers are powerless and that patriarchy has manipulated the maternal body into the enemy of the daughter.

Yongue's view of the powerlessness of mothers is shared by Sara Ruddick, who notes in "Maternal Thinking" that "in any society a mother is unavoidably powerless. . . . Children confront and rely upon a powerful maternal presence only to watch her become powerless in front of the father, the teacher, the doctor, the judge, the landlord, the world" (343). Yongue argues that the resentment between mothers and daughters makes bonding difficult; daughters often feel that they cannot count on their mothers to protect them or even befriend them. She asserts that the major lesson to be learned from Emecheta is that mothers must resist patriarchal tradition and encourage their daughters to pursue education. Only through education will mothers and daughters be able to connect and heal the wounds inflicted upon them by sexist cultural practices.

Julia De Foor Jay's "(Re)claiming the Race of the Mother: Cherríe Moraga's *Shadow of a Man, Giving Up the Ghost,* and *Heroes and Saints*" examines mother-daughter relationships within a Chicana, feminist, and lesbian context. Jay asserts that Moraga is outspoken about the theme of betrayal, suggesting that women have been socialized by male-centered, heterosexual-centered ideologies into betraying their own daughters and preparing them for docility and servitude. Moraga claims that mothers often betray daughters because they are socialized to put men first. While several of Moraga's characters are autonomous and have embraced their racial and sexual identity, many of them continue to sell their daughters into patriarchal slavery. The predicament for some women in Moraga's plays resembles the status of women in India, Africa, and Australia as outlined earlier in essays by Mohanram, Pollock, Zonana, and Yongue. Moraga portrays women who are expected to serve the males, take care of the home, mother the children, give priority to sons, and give allegiance to the Catholic Church, which she views as an oppressive male-dominated institution. Jay argues that Moraga portrays mothers who have internalized feelings of inferiority and who transfer those feelings to their daughters, a view in keeping with Nancy Chodorow's argument in *The Reproduction of Mother* that mothers treat sons as differentiated beings but daughters as extensions of themselves (82–83).

Jay insightfully interprets Moraga's treatment of female myths and legends in Mexican American culture, such as La Malinche, La Virgen de Guadalupe, and La Llorona. She elucidates how these myths function in the socialization of Mexican American women and notes that these traditional images of motherhood—the violated one, the virgin or saint, and the weeping/sorrowful/suffering one—serve as stumbling blocks to women in their quest for self-determination. Jay claims that, by reinventing or reinterpreting these myths, Moraga creates revolutionary women, usually daughters, who are not easily controlled or manipulated by patriarchy and who are in the process of reclaiming their race and their sexuality. Moraga suggests in *Giving Up the Ghost* that lesbians must refuse to remain behind walls that define their sexual roles and force them into hurtful heterosexual relationships. Jay notes that Moraga is on a quest to dismantle limiting concepts of Chicana identity.

Fabian Clements Worsham's "The Poetics of Matrilineage: Mothers and Daughters in the Poetry of African American Women, 1965–1985" explores the relationships of mothers and daughters in poems by Alice Walker, Lucille Clifton, Carolyn Rodgers, Audre Lorde, and Colleen McElroy. Worsham's research suggests that black mothers and daughters prosper through relationships that are mutually loving and supportive. These interdependent relationships are made stronger as black mothers and daughters struggle to free themselves from thwarting influences of patriarchal culture. But Worsham claims that these relationships involve ambivalence and conflict. She posits that these loving relationships are not devoid of anger, guilt, and difficulties in communication. Worsham notes that the mother is a figure of such mythic proportions that her life haunts her daughters throughout their own lives. Very often the daughters feel that they cannot live up to their mothers' physical or emotional strength and express feelings of inadequacy. At other times daughters resent their mothers' complacency and lack of political awareness. There are instances in the poetry where daughters resent the manipulation and control that their mothers exercise over them. Sometimes the conflicts are magnified and are not readily resolved. Worsham seems to agree with Gloria Joseph in "Black Mothers and Daughters: Traditional and New Populations," who claims that while black daughters witness the racism directed at their mothers and are bolstered by their mothers' resiliency, they do not view their mothers as all powerful and therefore all responsible (17–21). Worsham concludes that, regardless of the differences between mothers and daughters, the daughters recognize that they are united by their love and fortified by the struggle they have experienced as black women.

Sheryl A. Mylan's "The Mother as Other: Orientalism in Maxine Hong Kingston's *The Woman Warrior*" explores Edward Said's concept of Orientalism as it relates to the heroine in the novel. Mylan argues that Maxine, the fictional narrator, is not to be confused with the author of the same first name. If Maxine is viewed as a fictional character, and not as an autobiographical figure, Hong Kingston should not be held accountable for authentic accounts of Asian cultural experiences. With this key point in mind, Mylan asserts that Maxine, the Westernized daughter, is guilty of

Othering her Chinese mother in the novel in an attempt to gain power over her. She suggests that in devaluing her mother's non-Western experiences, Maxine is guilty of Orientalism—holding up Western experiences as superior. Maxine's mother represents all that is mysterious and repulsive about Chinese culture to her daughter. Mylan's views about mothers and daughters in Hong Kingston's work parallel ideas expressed by Judith Arcana in *Our Mothers' Daughters*: "The oppression of women has created a break among us, especially between mothers and daughters. Women cannot respect their mothers in a society which degrades them; women cannot respect themselves" (1). Mylan argues that out of ignorance and misunderstanding of her mother's life in China Maxine imposes standards by which to judge her mother as inferior. Maxine, a Chinese American, sees her mother and Chinese culture as Other. Mylan claims that Maxine should be seen as a Eurocentric American who views Asian culture exotically. Her essay focuses on the fact that Maxine as daughter is obsessed with subduing her mother's power over her. In re-presenting her mother, Maxine creates her own self, a separate identity from her mother's. Mylan also cogently argues that it is a mistake to view Hong Kingston primarily as a Chinese writer who willfully misrepresents and betrays her cultural legacy: she should be seen as a writer struggling to understand her own biculturalism.

Maria Gonzalez's "Love and Conflict: Mexican American Women Writers as Daughters" explores mother-daughter relationships in the works of Helena María Viramontes, Lucha Corpi, Ana Castillo, Sandra Cisneros, and Denise Chávez. Like Julia Jay, Gonzalez examines three Mexican icons of mothers: La Virgen, La Malinche, and La Llorona. She theorizes that these traditionally male-defined images of motherhood are being remythologized by Chicana writers. Gonzalez's essay first examines the images of motherhood posited by Mexican American males and then illustrates that Chicana writers are recreating or reinterpreting those same myths to allow for less limiting images of mother-daughter relationships. One case in point is that Chicana writers revise the mother-child relationship by substituting son for daughter. Gonzalez notes that in texts by women the image of La Virgen is displaced by La Malinche, who often takes the form of the negligent mother, the failed mother, the wicked or promiscuous mother, a direct response to images in male narratives. Unlike the Chicano writers who offer "Americanization" as a reason for the failure of women to nurture, Chicana writers suggest that it is patriarchal vampirism in its many forms, particularly mass media. Chicana writers portray daughters who, because they are not nurtured properly, suffer from low self-esteem and who repeat their mothers' experiences of ignorance and poverty. La Llorona appears in their works as the suffocatingly nurturing mother who is capable of enormous passion and destruction. Another version of La Llorona is La Gritona, the image of the woman who rejects spousal abuse and learns to love herself. Gonzalez notes that Mexican American mothers and daughters have strong bonds and would argue, as does Jean Baker Miller in *Toward a New Psychology of Women*, that "the best conflicts are those that lead to more and better connection rather than disconnections" (140).

Charlene Taylor Evans's "Mother-Daughter Relationships as Epistemological Structures: Leslie Marmon Silko's *Almanac of the Dead* and *Storyteller*" explores the grandmother-granddaughter relationships which often supplant the mother-daughter dyad in Native American literature. Evans notes that while some Native American women writers focus on the mother/aunt/sister/neighbor and daughter relationships, many explore the grandmother-granddaughter relationships, particularly because grandmothers traditionally are the revered storytellers and primary spiritual nurturers. Evans posits that Native American women, particularly the grandmothers, carry the ontologies to their offspring, transmitting culture through songs, stories, ceremonies, legends, and myths. Mothers and daughters function as repositories and purveyors of knowledge about how to survive cultural disintegration threatened by Euro-American invasiveness. Evans apparently concurs with Dexter Fisher, who notes in *The Third Woman* that "as preservers of the culture, Indian women have continued in their traditional role as teachers" (12). Evans illustrates that the sacred and important history of Native Americans passed down from mother to daughter helps to preserve the individual and collective identities of these indigenous people and to minimize assimilation into Euro-American culture. Fisher claims that Native American women writers "examine the dilemma of the individual caught between two worlds and seek to resolve conflict through storytelling and a revitalization of the traditions and rituals of their inherited past" (9). Evans argues that daughters are told the stories of their past with fierce accuracy and are bound to retell these stories which will sustain the lives of future generations of Native Americans. The mother-daughter dyad, then, serves as a pipeline—an epistemological unit—a vehicle for intergenerational continuity. Evans incisively notes that the mother-daughter pairing symbolizes the merging of the Native American past and present and undermines blatant and subtle attacks on Native American cultural sensibilities.

Elizabeth Brown-Guillory's "Disrupted Motherlines: Mothers and Daughters in a Genderized, Sexualized, and Racialized World" examines the difficulties that mothers and daughters experience as a result of a disrupted mothering process. While racist cultural practices are recognized as destructive to the African American psyche, this study focuses on plays by black women which examine mother-daughter relationships that are thwarted because of internal as well as external forces that prevent mothers from adequately preparing their daughters to cope in a callous world. Angelina Grimke, Georgia Douglas Johnson, Shirley Graham, Lorraine Hansberry, and Alice Childress are playwrights who deserve serious critical treatment because their works poignantly and insightfully explore the lives of struggling black women from 1916 to 1971. Brown-Guillory notes in *Their Place on the Stage: Black Women Playwrights in America*:

> They looked at the world with feminine hearts and saw much that disappointed them in the American society. . . . Each of these women speaks to and for African Americans then and now. Becoming increasingly socially aware of the problems facing African Americans, these women move from the concerns of women to the concerns of colored women and their families. . . . With feeling hearts, they present a slice of United States history from the unique perspective of women who have been both midwives and pallbearers of African American dreamers. (20)

Brown-Guillory's essay explores the concept of mothers who commit horrific acts of reclamation in order to keep their children safe in a racist, sexist, classist world. The theme of women making sacrifices in an attempt to usher their daughters into womanhood dominates the plays of twentieth-century black women. In plays discussed in this study, mothers shelter their children, murder them, put them up for adoption, or consider abortion when they feel that they cannot protect them in a hostile world. While their acts of reclamation often are desperate and destructive, black women in these plays search for wholeness, as Brown-Guillory asserts in *Wines in the Wilderness: Plays by African American Women from the Harlem Renaissance to the Present*. Black mothers struggle "to empower their children to cope with and even triumph over the racism in society" (xv). What dominates black women's theater is the sense that, regardless of the obstacles, black women must find a way to teach their children how to carve a satisfactory place for themselves in a society that often looks upon them with hostile or apathetic eyes.

M. Marie Booth Foster's "Voice, Mind, Self: Mother-Daughter Relationships in Amy Tan's *The Joy Luck Club* and *The Kitchen God's Wife*" explores mother-daughter pairings in which the daughters' sense of self is intricately linked to an ability to speak and be heard by their mothers. Similarly, mothers experience growth only if they are able to broaden communication lines with their daughters. Foster's comments about the conditions of growth for mothers and daughters are reiterated by Bell Gale Chevigny, who writes, "Our difficulty in knowing our mothers dominates us as daughters and to some extent, blocks our growth and self knowledge" (95). The quest for voice by mother and daughter involves self-exploration, recognition and appreciation of their cultures, both Chinese and American. Foster's insights are in line with assessments made about Asian American mother-daughter relationships by Amy Ling in *Between Worlds: Women Writers of Chinese Ancestry*. Foster's essay illustrates that Chinese mothers and daughters experience conflict as the mothers try to convey their individual and collective suffering in China, the devaluation of women manifested through the practice of arranged marriage, concubinage, bound feet, adoption, and pawning. Sometimes the mothers feel that their daughters don't value their views and experiences. Concomitantly, daughters sometimes view their mothers' stories as a means of manipulation, an attempt to control every aspect of their existence. Foster's arguments parallel Nancy Friday's in *My Mother/My Self*, which posit that "what makes the mother-daughter relationship so poignant is its bewildering reciprocity. What one person does, feels, inevitably affects the other" (207). Foster argues that when American daughters begin to know their mothers' importance, they ultimately begin to recognize their own importance. These hyphenated women achieve voice, a key step toward wholeness. Foster's conclusions about achieving voice are echoed by Marina Heung in "Daughter-Text/Mother-Text: Matrilineage in Amy Tan's *Joy Luck Club*," where she suggests that "storytelling heals past experiences of loss and separation; it is also a medium for rewriting stories of oppression and victimization into parables of self-affirmation and individual empowerment" (607).

Lucille P. Fultz's "To Make Herself: Mother-Daughter Conflicts in Toni Morrison's *Sula* and *Tar Baby*" addresses the tension produced by the emotional and psychological distance between African American mothers and daughters. Fultz argues that distance results when daughters recognize that their mothers cannot provide them with tenderness and affection due to economic factors related to race, class, and gender biases. These material barriers to expressions of love force daughters to rebel against mothers who view their sacrifices as sufficient or substitutable for closeness. Fultz's insights are similar to Adrienne Rich's observations in *Of Woman Born* about the need for a mother's tenderness. Rich asserts that "the first knowledge any woman has of warmth, nourishment, tenderness, sensuality, mutuality, comes from her mother" (218). Fultz points out that when this tenderness is denied, daughters don't learn to transfer tenderness to their daughters. Confrontations erupt when mothers crave for their daughters' independence yet hope for acknowledgment of their influence. Fultz's arguments make clear that Alicia Suskin Ostriker's cynical indictment of American culture is accurate. Ostriker claims: "Good motherhood, in our culture, is selfless, cheerful, and deodorized. It does not include resentment, anger, violence, alienation, disappointment, grief, fear, exhaustion—or erotic pleasure. . . . Our culture does not give us images of the daughter desperate for the mother's love, or desperate to escape it, or contemptuous of the mother . . ." (179–180).

Fultz demonstrates that mothers and daughters are not "good mothers" in *Sula* because they do experience this gamut of emotions. She suggests that Sula and Eva spar because Sula rejects her grandmother's choices for her—the push for marriage and children—in place of freedom to live as she pleases. Fultz's assessment of Sula's need for independence is echoed by Jane Flax in "The Conflict between Nurturance and Autonomy in Mother-Daughter Relationships and within Feminism," where she posits that "nurturance means the expression of love that carries with it a deep concern for the well being of the person receiving it, without demanding that the person prove her worthiness of it" (187). The mother-daughter relationship in *Tar Baby* centers on a mother who feels guilty for isolating her daughter in a white world and not exposing her to the

African American community. In both novels, mothers and daughters break the silence and challenge each other to unite in the face of a hostile world that places African American women in multiple jeopardy.

Women of Color: Mother-Daughter Relationships in Twentieth-Century Literature pulls together a wealth of research about women of color whose roots spread throughout five of the seven continents. Were there to be a second volume, one might expect explorations of mother-daughter relationships in Caribbean texts by such writers as Jeanine Tavernier, Louise Bennett, Maryse Condé, Lorna Goodison, Michelle Cliff, Simone Schwarz-Bart, Marlene Nourbese Philip, Marie-Thérèse Colimon, Marie Chauvet, Liliane Dévieux, Zee Edgell, and Merle Hodge. Such a volume might include a study of two writers of West Indian origin who now live in the United States, Jamaica Kincaid and Paule Marshall. There are numerous African women writers whose work deserves serious critical attention, including Efua Sutherland, Zaynab Alkali, Nafissatou Diallo, Miriama Bâ, Aminata Maiga Ka, Daisy Kabagarama, Bessie Head, Farida Karodia, and Tsitsi Dangarembga. All of these women of color are linked by their texts which explore the psychic distress which occurs when a daughter matures without a positive mother image to teach her how to survive in a world fraught with obstacles. Natalie Rosinsky in "Mothers and Daughters: Another Minority Group" insightfully remarks: "An analysis of mother-daughter relationships in woman's minority group literature is both disheartening and encouraging. It is disheartening to see the pain inflicted upon so many women; it is encouraging to realize that individual women can transcend this mutilation to discover the deeper rapport that—along with suffering—unites them to their mothers" (290).

The thought-provoking unrecovered works of women of color call attention to the need for a total integration of these texts into the twentieth-century literary canon. Future studies, no doubt, will include an examination of the works of these and other women of color. This volume, then, will have served as an impetus for opening up the canon to include a plethora of writings by twentieth-century women of color from around the world.

Note

1. In 1986 Dr. Violet Harrington Bryan of Xavier University of New Orleans and I organized the "Women of Color: Mother-Daughter Relationships in Twentieth-Century Literature" special session. Six years later, I was successful in persuading the South Central Modern Language Association to approve permanent status for "Women of Color" with a name change to "Race and Gender Issues in Twentieth-Century Literature."

Works Cited

Arcana, Judith. *Our Mothers' Daughters*. Berkeley, Calif.: Shameless Hussy Press, 1979.

Brown-Guillory, Elizabeth. *Their Place on the Stage: Black Women Playwrights in America*. Westport, Conn.: Greenwood Press, 1988.

———. *Wines in the Wilderness: Plays by African American Women from the Harlem Renaissance to the Present*. Westport, Conn.: Greenwood Press, 1990.

Chevigny, Bell Gale. "Daughters Writing: Toward a Theory of Women's Biography." *Feminist Studies* 9, no. 1 (1983): 79–102.

Chodorow, Nancy. *The Reproduction of Mother: Psychoanalysis and the Sociology of Gender*. Berkeley: University of California Press, 1978.

Cole, Johnetta B. "Preface." In *Double-Stitch: Black Women Write about Mothers and Daughters*, ed. Patricia Bell Scott et al., xiii–xv. New York: HarperPerennial, 1993.

Collins, Patricia Hill. *Black Feminist Thought*. New York: Routledge, 1990.

———. "The Meaning of Motherhood in Black Culture and Black Mother-Daughter Relationships." *Sage* 4, no. 2 (1987): 3–10.

Daly, Brenda O., and Maureen T. Reddy, eds. *Narrating Mothers*. Knoxville: University of Tennessee Press, 1991.

Delany, Martin. Excerpts from "The Condition, Elevation, and Destiny of the Colored People of the United States, Politically Considered." In *Black Writers of America: A Comprehensive Anthology*, ed. Richard Barksdale and Keneth Kinnamon, 194–208. New York: Macmillan, 1972.

Fisher, Dexter, ed. *The Third Woman: Minority Women Writers of the United States*. Boston: Houghton Mifflin, 1980.

Flax, Jane. "The Conflict between Nurturance and Autonomy in Mother-Daughter Relationships and within Feminism." *Feminist Studies* 4, no. 1 (1978): 171–189.

Friday, Nancy. *My Mother/My Self*. New York: Delacorte Press, 1977.

Heung, Marina. "Daughter-Text / Mother-Text: Matrilineage in Amy Tan's *Joy Luck Club*." *Feminist Studies* 19 (Fall 1993): 597–616.

Hirsch, Marianne. *The Mother/Daughter Plot: Narrative, Psychoanalysis, Feminism*. Bloomington and Indianapolis: Indiana University Press, 1989.

———. "Mothers and Daughters: A Review Essay." *Signs* 7, no. 1 (Autumn 1981): 200–222.

Jardine, Alice. "Death Sentences: Writing Couples and Ideology." *Poetics Today* 6, no. 2 (1985): 119–131.

Joseph, Gloria I. "Black Mothers and Daughters: Traditional and New Populations." *Sage* 1, no. 2 (1984): 17–21.

Ling, Amy. *Between Worlds: Women Writers of Chinese Ancestry*. New York: Pergamon Press, 1990.

MacKinnon, Catharine. "Feminism, Marxism, Method, and the State: An Agenda for Theory." *Signs* 7, no. 3 (1982): 515–544.

Miller, Jean Baker. *Toward a New Psychology of Women*. Boston: Beacon Press, 1986.

Ostriker, Alicia Suskin. "The Imperative of Intimacy: Female Erotics, Female Poetics." In *Stealing the Language: The Emergence of Women's Poetry in America*, 164–209. Boston: Beacon Press, 1986.

Pearlman, Mickey, ed. *Mother Puzzles: Daughters and Mothers in Contemporary American Literature*. New York: Greenwood Press, 1989.

Rich, Adrienne. *Of Woman Born: Motherhood as Experience and Institution*. New York: W. W. Norton, 1976.

Rosinsky, Natalie M. "Mothers and Daughters: Another Minority Group." In *The Lost Tradition: Mothers and Daughters in Literature*, ed. Cathy N. Davidson and E. M. Broner, 280–290. New York: Frederick Ungar, 1980.

Ruddick, Sara. "Maternal Thinking." *Feminist Studies* 6, no. 2 (1980): 342–367.

———. *Maternal Thinking: Toward a Politics of Peace*. Boston: Beacon Press, 1989.

The Problems of Reading

Mother-Daughter Relationships and Indian Postcoloniality

RADHIKA MOHANRAM

The process of writing a paper on mother-daughter relationships in India is beset with a rather peculiar series of problems. The most significant difficulty is not interpretation of texts but location of materials. Stories of mother-son and father-daughter relationships abound in Indian mythic as well as modern literature, but there is a curious silence on the thematic of mother-daughter relationships. This fact in itself underscores the overwhelming investment in heterosexuality within Indian culture. As Western theorists such as Julia Kristeva have indicated in a number of texts, mother-daughter relationships fall within a homoerotic matrix.[1] The literary critic of this particular material is furthermore halted by the notion put forth by Ian Hacking in "Making Up People," in which he posits that only those categories that exist within discourse can shape experience. To illustrate his point, Hacking suggests that there was a curious lack of "perverts" until the second half of the nineteenth century because the comprehension of perversion as an abnormality was not yet in place. In other words, only the existence of the category of perversion will ensure the visibility of the pervert. To a large extent, this fact can explain the silence about mother-daughter relationships in Indian literature: if no such categories exist, or are valorized, or are articulated around Indian familial relationships, the literary critic will not be able to locate the necessary material. Not even a skeletal blueprint exists for the narrative of mother-daughter relationships within the master-discourse of Indian fiction. This is not to say that there are no significant female characters in Indian mythology—rather, this particular relationship is just not valorized. As Susie Tharu has pointed out in "Tracing Savitri's Pedigree," it becomes very difficult to read as woman or the woman in any Indian text because these texts "arose out of an encounter which sought to render feminine an entire nation" (254). Any discussion of the maternal figure has to include a discussion of Mother India. From individual biological body she becomes the maternal body of independent India. The trauma wrought by colonialism upon this maternal body can be revisited only in the nationalistic narrative of Mother India nurturing her brave sons who have rescued her from the rapacious hold of Britain. Every Indian woman thus gets conflated with the swollen maternal body of India. In a sense, then, there are only mothers and sons.

The problem of locating material is complicated in this instance by the peculiar structural position of the postcolonial (Indian) critic situated in the West. The Indian literary critic functions as the problematic native informant: by speaking in Western academies from within the discourse of Orientalism she shares complicity with her audiences in the Othering of India. Within the Western academy, she becomes the representative of India, an embodiment of the Indian subcontinent, fulfilling two simultaneous functions—to be an authentic metaphorical substitute for India while being contained within the hallways of Western universities. Thus, India is first transfixed and then made known to the gaze of the West, and the project of Orientalism is fulfilled. It is necessary to point out this obvious fact because the Indian academic in the West is thus marginalized not only in the West, but by her colleagues in India as well. What renders her palatable and authentic—her Indian presence in the Western academy—to her First World colleagues renders her inauthentic in India. After all, she has been co-opted by the Orientalist project by living in the West.

The native informant in the West must also avoid toppling over the precipice of the born-again nativist constructing a hegemonic counter-narrative which will capture the essence, the Indianness of India. This particular theoretical position is fraught with its own repugnant implications. It not only confirms her position as Other within Western academies but also simultaneously becomes a denial of the colonial history which properly belongs to India. It is a critical commonplace to point out that pure Indianness in this context is a retroactive construct, blind to the passage of history. As Gayatri Chakravorty Spivak comments on such an approach in "Who Claims Alterity?": "The new culturalist alibi, working within a basically elitist culture industry, insisting on the continuity of native tradition untouched by Westernization whose failures it can help to cover, legitimizes the very thing it claims to combat" (281). Though it is British postcoloniality that has interpellated the Indian national subject and India as a subject, there is an underlying premise of the denial of the colonial moment, of ahistoricity and essentialism in the nativist position. This position also presumes the construction of India as one willed by a sovereign Indian national ego. While such a move is absolutely necessary for a decolonizing nation attempting to discard the shackles of colonial rule, it also denies that meanings are dialectically and dialogically produced and that India can no more deny its postcolonial status than it can deny its communal problems. The influence of Britain and the West will forever be a part of the production and circulation of meanings of India.

The postcolonial critic situated in the West has to be aware of one last pitfall—the accusation of Eurocentricity in her analysis, leveled at her, surprisingly, by Western theorists. Such an accusation is based on a notion of Western liberalism which presumes that despite the epistemic violence as well as the occlusion of reverse discourses of the marginalized group by the British colonial fathers, somehow the native has maintained intact an-Other knowledge, an-Other tradition which not only runs counter to the structures of the master discourse but, in fact, does not even engage with it. The preference of critics such as Benita Parry to listen to uncontaminated native voices reveals a penchant for the exoticization of the native. It is exactly within this context that one must consider the point made by Gilles Deleuze and Felix Guattari, who in *Anti-Oedipus* insist on the significance of Western theoretical paradigms such as those within psychoanalysis not because such paradigms are universal but rather because the colonial enterprise of eighteenth- and nineteenth-century Europe was so entirely successful. Such theoretical paradigms are therefore pertinent not only to the critic in the West but also to the Indian critic in India writing about India. Deleuze and Guattari admit that the analysis of non-Western contexts via the Oedipal paradigm is another manifestation and continuance of the colonizing process: "Oedipus is always colonization pursued by other means, it is the interior colony, and we shall see that even here at home, where we Europeans are concerned, it is our intimate colonial education" (170). The Indian theorist Ashis Nandy has pointed out in *The Intimate Enemy* that waiting to hear uncontaminated voices will be a wait in vain because "the west is now everywhere, within the west and outside; in structures and in minds. . . . The west has not merely produced modern colonialism, it informs most interpretations of colonialism" (xi–xii).

So what is the Third World (Indian) critic who is situated in the West to do? Every position that she takes is either politically or intellectually incorrect. Only one position is viable for her—she has to locate herself as oppositional, balancing herself on a tightrope of spiraling identities or shuttling back and forth between anthropologist and native informant.[2] Penelope-like, she must constantly undo as she consolidates, constantly teasing out her complicity in all the layers of social, political, cultural, nationalistic, and internationalistic discourses of India.

Despite all these qualifying statements on the difficulty of locating materials on mother-daughter relationships, I did find two Indian short stories, "Girls" by Mrinal Pande and "Her Mother" by Anjana Appachana. Pande's story was originally written in Hindi and appeared in 1983 in *Dharmayug*, a magazine with a fairly large readership in Northern India. The English translation of this story appeared the same year. This story is a first-person narrative about an eight-year-old girl's relationship with her mother, who is reluctantly pregnant for the fourth time in her attempt to give birth to a son. The young protagonist attempts to reconcile the binary opposites of the negative value placed upon her and her sisters by her mother and her (female) relatives and the culture's positive value placed upon her on one day of the year, Chaitya Shukla Ashtami day, when young girls are worshiped as the incarnation of the divine feminine principle. The coterminous nature of the veneration and devaluation of girls and women is underscored in this story.

Appachana's short story "Her Mother" does not make any explicit social commentary on the condition of women or their economic or social value within Indian culture. In contrast to the Pande story, this story is from the narrative consciousness of a mother writing a letter to her daughter who has just left for graduate school in the United States. Although the entire narrative alternates between the mother's attempt to express her sense of physical loss at their separation and her growing discovery and comprehension of her daughter's sexual secrets, what this story underscores is the girl's relationship with her father, who is *not* writing a letter to her.

The juxtaposition of "Girls" and "Her Mother" is not coincidental. Only in their conjunction can these two stories attempt to articulate a discourse which has no category within the narrative economy of Indian fiction. The two short stories fit together seamlessly. The daughter's narrative consciousness in "Girls" articulates the function of daughters within the Indian economy. The mother's perspective on the relationship between mother and daughter is dealt with in "Her Mother." In this juxtaposition, not only are both the young and the adult points of view represented, but the faint smudges of the functioning of Indian women's sexuality finally become partially visible. Accordingly, the first part of this critique explores the social and economic value of women through an analysis of "Girls." The sheer transparency of the story is due to two reasons. First, the connotations of the feminine social and economic position set in motion by the text far exceed the biological aspects of women. However, and this is the second reason, it is the biological fact of womanhood that is used to make women's social position an irrefutable fact. The second part of the paper focuses on "Her Mother," where the value of maternity and mother-daughter relationships is examined. Within this context, a father's relationship with the daughter dominates this reading of the story.

Femininity and Identity

In his essay on "Femininity," Sigmund Freud insists on the young girl's hostility toward her mother, who makes her imperfect by creating her as always castrated. In fact, a young girl needs to develop hostility toward her mother if she is to accede properly to heterosexuality. Toward the end of this essay, Freud discusses the implications of this theme when the young girl becomes a mother herself:

> Under the influence of a woman's becoming a mother herself, an identification with her own mother may be revived, against which she has striven up till the

time of her marriage. . . . The difference in a mother's reaction to the birth of a son or a daughter shows that the old factor or lack of a penis has even now not lost its strength. A mother is only brought unlimited satisfaction by her relation to a son; this is altogether the most perfect, the most free from ambivalence of all human relationships. A mother can transfer to her son the ambition which she has been obliged to suppress in herself, and she can expect from him the satisfaction of all that has been left over in her of her masculinity complex. (*New Introductory Lectures*, 118)

In Freud's mapping of a woman's femininity, its very construction is dependent on her idyllic relationship with her son. While Freudian discourse emphasizes the psychical and not the physical, the old childhood trauma or factor of her lack is still powerful and metaphorically substitutes her son's anatomy for her lack. Only through her relationship with her son does a woman feel emotionally and physically complete; the psychical and the physical are mutually interdependent.

While Freud's development of the Oedipal paradigm has seemed pertinent only to the Western (Eurocentric) psyche, its pertinence to the Indian context is evident: the Indian nuclear family portrayed in "Girls" is modeled on a Western one—the protagonist, her parents, and her siblings live together, separate from the Hindu joint family. Moreover, though Freud pieces together the psyche and interaction of individual members of the Western nuclear family and mother-son attachment, the fierce love between mother and son is especially valid in the Indian context. The birth of a son validates an Indian Hindu mother far more than the birth of a daughter. He makes her position within her husband's family more secure. He grants her an identity that her daughter cannot.

It is precisely the misogyny and devaluation of daughters evident in this familial attachment that the protagonist of "Girls" protests against. The cultural discrimination against female children becomes evident not only in the statements that her mother makes but also in those made by other adult women relatives. For instance, her mother comments on her pregnancy at the beginning of the story: "I hope it's a boy. It will relieve me of the nuisance of going through another pregnancy" (57). At another moment, the servant massaging the pregnant mother's feet says, "If it's a boy this time, I will demand a sari with stainless steel zari" (60). In other words, since the household would celebrate the birth of a son, gifts would be distributed to the servants. The maternal grandmother prays, "Oh goddess, protect my honour. At least this time let her take a son back from her parents' home" (59). In these instances, the value of a son is underscored, implying the contrast in the devaluation of a daughter. Overtly, the mother's desire not to be perpetually pregnant is understandable, but the term "nuisance" associated with another pregnancy metonymically extends her comprehension of giving birth merely to daughters. Only a son can possibly save her from endless pregnancies. Similarly, the grandmother to whose home a daughter traditionally returns to have her baby feels that her honor is at stake if her granddaughter does not give birth to a son. Even the servant feels that a son's birth is an occasion to ask for a more expensive gift. The cultural lack of worth of a daughter is also emphasized by their preference for the protagonist's five-year-old cousin. Comparisons are constantly made between them: she is short for her age and he is tall for his; in the narrator's words, he is "supposed to be cute" (59), and, by implication, she is not. He is also given preferential treatment: their grandmother allows him to sleep beside her but will not allow the narrator to do so. The higher status accorded to boys ultimately becomes so explicit that the narrator watching birds fly wonders, "Do mother birds too think their girl birds are inferior?" (62). The story concludes with the family honoring the young girls who on Chaitya Shukla Ashtami day represent the *kanyakumaris* or virgin goddesses who are to be worshiped. The narrator protests: "When you people don't love girls, why do you pretend to worship them? . . . I don't want to be a goddess" (63–64). Instead of feeling ashamed, the adult women respond: "Ma-ri-ma, just listen to her. What a temper for a girl to show!" (64).

The girl's final statements are inevitable and relegate the critique of the cultural positioning of women in the whole text to a transparency—it becomes a discourse of the obvious. The text constantly points to the social positioning of girls rather than their biological positioning as evidenced in their honoring of *kanyakumaris*, but it is the biological difference of women and girls that grants them any meaning and anchors their social positioning. The adult women sigh, "Ah, a woman's fate" (60). When the protagonist bends to touch her grandmother's feet to show her respect, she is urged: "Not like that . . . bend properly. You are born a girl and you will have to bend for the rest of your life, so you might as well learn" (59). This underscoring of biological difference saturates this text in the realm of the obvious. As Mary Ann Doane has pointed out in *The Desire to*

Desire, within the context of the maternal melodrama, this very readability "then lend[s] credibility to another level, a different order of interpretation of sexual difference which assigns fixed positions to mother, father, and child—positions authorized by the weight of the primal configuration" (71). Within this context, then, the traditional cultural positioning of women—sharing equal power with men and honored as the divine feminine principle—is at variance with cultural practices which are anchored in biological difference. In this primal configuration, authority or power is obviously invested in the male and, by extension, boys. In contrast, even the mother lacks authority. If the various familial positions in India are preassigned and fixed—and they are—the only way the mother can negotiate any power is via the male child. A female child has no particular value because she does not contribute to securing power for the maternal position. Traditionally, an Indian daughter is perceived as being temporarily on loan in her birth parents' home, for she rightfully belongs only to her husband's family. In effect, she is valueless to her mother because she does not help her aggrandize her position.

To understand the (lack of) women's position better, Freud's thesis on a woman's preference for her son has to be read via Claude Lévi-Strauss's contention that a universal structure regulates exchange, a characteristic of all systems of kinship. In *The Elementary Structures of Kinship,* Lévi-Strauss argues that woman as an object of exchange (through marriage) from one patrilineal clan to another consolidates as well as differentiates kinship relations between the two clans. As Judith Butler points out in *Gender Trouble,* "The bride functions as a relational term between groups of men; she does not *have* an identity, and neither does she exchange one identity for another. She *reflects* masculine identity precisely by being the site of its absence" (39). Within the Indian context, if the woman in marriage even lacks family identity of her own, only the birth of her son—or meaningful contribution to the family—can make her belong to the family. In other words, it is not her husband's name, but that of her son which grants her a name. Hence her fierce devotion to her son. He anchors her with a name and a family affiliation.

It is precisely her lack of an identity (in contrast to a fully assigned identity for her yet unborn brother) that the protagonist decries. At one point in the text, the young girl muses: "Baabu [her father] used to say that if I worked hard I could be anything I wanted. . . . But I can't become a boy, can I?" (60).

Dissolving Identity

The young girl wants to become a boy, but does she really? This final section of the analysis of this text argues that the semiosis of the story undercuts the lament of the young girl to reveal that the social and cultural machinery is already at work in the consolidation of preferred and acceptable femininity for the protagonist.

The text opens with a curious gesture drawing attention to its own temporality and narrative progression. The protagonist begins the story: "Baabu broke a *surahi* [jug]. I don't know whether he did it on purpose or by accident, but anyway the floor was flooded with water" (57). Her mother reacts by wordlessly mopping it up. This image of spilling water from the *surahi* is repeated later in the story, reminding the protagonist of her father. In this instance, the mother hisses at the girl, "You are the cause of all my problems" (58). The repetition of images is again seen in the description of her father: "how good he smelt and the softness of his lap." This description is juxtaposed with her mother's refusal to allow her to lie in her lap: "My bones are aching, my sari is all crushed. Get up now" (59). This image is, furthermore, placed beside the description of the jeep driver who comes to pick them up at the railway station: "He had a big moustache, smelt of tea and bidis, and wore a uniform made of coarse wool which tickled me and made me sleepy" (58). The jeep driver who smells like her father and the mother whose lap is *not* like her father's are metonymically linked to Baabu. However, the girl prefers the jeep driver and Baabu. In her assessment, the men are nicer to her than the one significant woman in her life. The repetition in the story also draws attention to a cyclical pattern in the narration.

The significance of the girl's preference for men should also be read within the context of her description of her older sister, the only one "who really loves [her]" (58). The older sister, like the narrator, distrusts adult women (60). Yet it is the older sister who warns her of the terrible fate that awaits her if she does not stop misbehaving: "If you keep on like this, one day these people will beat you so hard that you will die" (61). The older sister has learned her lesson on the demeanor of proper femininity well. She helps her grandmother, who praises her loudly so that the recalcitrant narrator can hear and learn (61). The lesson to be learned here is that acquiescing to femininity is praiseworthy.

The narrator's difficult relationship with her mother quickly extends to all the other women in the text. The girl refers to her mother moaning "just like the cow does" (60). At another moment, when all the women are relaxing with their feet stretched out, the girl tells them, "You all look like cows" (61). The descriptions of women resembling animals continue. Her aunt's nose is "like a frog's" and her "cheeks hang loose like dead bats" (62). It becomes evident that, just as the adult women "don't love girls" (63), this young girl doesn't like adult women either. Her description of the two men in the text is in marked contrast: they smell nice and their laps feel good.

If these elements of the story—the older sister's acceptance of her reconfigured femininity and her acceptance of a woman's fate, the narrator's own dislike of women and preference for men—are placed against a rhetorical structure of repetition, a differential meaning emerges that destabilizes the sheer readability of the manifest text. If the overt text emphasizes the rebellious nature of the protagonist, who questions gender inequity and lack of a relationship with her mother, the semiotics of the text, saturated with repetitive moments, suggests that the narrator's loving sister who distrusts adults had at one time gone through all the same emotions. The repetition, therefore, suggests a dissolving identity: the narrator is at the cusp between rebellion and acquiescence, between desiring male privileges and accepting her woman's fate. Like the narrator, her sister, her mother, and her grandmother, then, must have all been angry once.

The Construction of Maternity

If "Girls" deals with a young girl's lament for her loss of her mother and self-worth, "Her Mother" is the converse. It is the ritualized mourning of maternal losses in patriarchal society. This story is the plaintive lament of a mother for her daughter, who even prior to her departure to graduate school in the United States did not quite belong to her. While the previous section examines the reasons a mother cannot love her daughter, this section discusses the only possible way in which a mother's love for a daughter can be encoded in an Indian text and attempts to unravel a father's loving relationship with his daughter.

In his 1925 essay "Some Psychical Consequences of the Anatomical Distinction between the Sexes," Freud suggests that it is the mother who draws attention to the girl's lack by not loving her in return. Instead, she indicates her preference for the superiority of the phallic father. This event leads to penis envy in the girl; eventually, she substitutes "a wish for a child . . . and *with this purpose in view* she takes her father as a love object" ("Some Psychical Consequences," 191). In "Femininity," Freud revises this statement and adds a new twist to the little girl's switching of affection and desire from mother to father. He suggests that this movement is signaled by the girl's attaining of passivity: "Passivity now has the upper hand, and the girl's turning to her father is accomplished principally with the help of the passive instinctual impulses" ("Femininity," 113). In other words, the girl's attachment to her father is already a substitute for her originary love for her mother. She enters into a heterosexual attachment, as Naomi Scheman states in "Missing Mothers / Desiring Daughters: Framing the Sight of Women," "through learning what it is to transfer love and desire from one object to another: it is the model of fungibility" (replaceability by a substitute) (68).

Moreover, the investment in heterosexuality is great, especially if a woman is to function as a relational term who will allow different groups / clans of men to make kinship bonds. As Butler puts it, "As the site of a patronymic exchange, women are and are not the patronymic sign, excluded from the signifier the very patronym she bears" (39). This intersection of Freud and Lévi-Strauss's theories suggests, first, that the construction of femininity is contingent upon the girl's fungibility of desire and, second, that this fungibility of desire is a *structural necessity for the heterosexual exchange of women by men*.

Since the organization of kinship systems is as much about incest taboos as it is about the extension of one's kin network, an example of kinship alliance and incest taboo from Indian culture proves that here, too, women function as objects of patronymic exchange. Members of South Indian brahmin families organize themselves, among other categories, according to *gothram* or lineage, taking on the name of the originator of the lineage. This line of descent and lineage is ancient. A child normally assumes the paternal lineage. *Gothram* functions to prevent incest: a man cannot marry within his *gothram* even if the woman is not a blood relative. Similarly, a daughter who bears her father's *gothram* cannot marry her paternal cousin (same *gothram*, therefore, incestuous); however, she can marry her maternal cousin (different *gothram*, therefore not incestuous). While the mother does not change her *gothram* at her marriage, her very retention of *her* paternal lineage excludes her from her husband's family. This particular example is used not only to reiterate the reason for a mother's fierce devotion to her firstborn son—he literally marks her with the signifier of his paternal lineage and allows entry into her husband's family—but also to suggest that the father-daughter bond is based on the same reason. She is the daughter of her father, not her mother, who is, literally, a stranger to the family because she belongs to a different family.

So what is the mother to do if she has no familial claims on her daughter? Appachana's short story "Her Mother" deals precisely with this dilemma. It is a record of a mother's grief at the fungibility of a daughter's desire as well as her anger at her exclusion from the signification system which is shared between father and daughter.

In a very telling moment of the text, the daughter returns home after having her long hair cut off without having discussed it with her parents first. For an Indian girl, this would constitute an act of defiance:

> That evening when she opened the door for her daughter, her hair reached just below her ears. The daughter stood there, not looking at either her mother or father, but almost, it seemed beyond them, her face a strange mixture of relief and defiance and anger, as her father, his face twisted, said, why, why. I like it short, she said. Fifteen years of growing it below her knees, of oiling it every week, and washing it so lovingly, the mother thought as she touched her daughter's cheek and said, you are angry with us . . . is this your revenge? Her daughter had removed her hand and moved past her parents, past her brother-in-law who was behind them, and into her room. For the father it was as though a limb had been amputated. For days he brooded in his chair in the corner of the sitting room, almost in mourning, avoiding even looking at her, while the mother murmured, you have perfected the art of hurting us. (182)

While this scene records a dramatic act of defiance on the daughter's part, it is not out of the ordinary for her to be defiant within the context of the rest of the narrative. The daughter has been behaving strangely for a while. The parents have been reacting to her as they normally have—accepting her strange behavior. Her haircut is really of no concern to her brother-in-law. Nothing significant happens to move the plot forward; it is a moment of stasis in the text.

Rather, this scene ought to be seen as a *mise-en-abîme*, a blueprint, for the reading of this story. Why are the characters positioned in the way that they are? The mother faces her door with her husband standing behind her, and their son-in-law who is staying with them stands behind them. Moreover, the father appears to overreact to this act of defiance on his daughter's part. He is not just upset because of the erosion of his authority. Words fail him. His twisted face expresses his anger. Her hair is metaphorically linked to his member, and her haircut sends him into days of mourning. His twisted face, his amputated limb, and his mourning express the severity of his loss. Love can be expressed only via facial expressions, body language, and the positionings of individuals in the hallway of the house. Three pairs of eyes look at the girl standing in the doorway. The girl looks beyond her parents at her brother-in-law, who is in a long-distance commuter marriage with her sister. The positioning of bodies and the melancholia of the parents express not only mother-daughter but also father-daughter relationships.

The mother's epistolary structuring of the story itself becomes a search for meaning and an expression of the unfairness of the fungible nature of a girl's desire. The mother attempts to search for clues about her daughter's life. She slowly realizes that more than fraternal feelings exist between her second daughter and her son-in-law. The clues lie not in anything spoken but in the unspoken, the semiosis of the text, in their body language, in their gestures. However, it is the father's grief rather than the mother's that gets recorded. The mother merely writes a letter in passive resignation.

The mother-daughter bond which has been displaced into a closeness between father and daughter is recorded in a number of moments in the story. For instance, the mother realizes that the daughter loved solitude like her father, demanded it, and got it, unlike the mother, who never had the solitude to think (183). The younger girl is considered unfeminine because she is inept at doing housework (183–184). The father reprimands the mother for this. However, the mother states that "her own husband fell to pieces everytime she visited her parents without him . . . [he] could never find his clothes, slept on the bedcover, constantly misplaced his spectacles, didn't know how to get himself a glass of water . . ." (186). The mother finally writes to her daughter: "You talk like [your father], look like him, are as obstinate and as stupidly honest. It is as though he conceived you and gave birth to you entirely on his own" (184). In all these instances, it is apparent that the mother protests the cooptation of the girl from the maternal body by the paternal signifier. The girl shows her complete allegiance to her father by the time she is six years old by responding to her mother's question, "Isn't your mother a good woman?" with the response, "Daddy is gooder" (184). The daughter's replacement of her mother with her father is obviously complete by the age of six, an essential component in eventually transferring her affection to her brother-in-law.

The text seems to indicate perversion and incest in the doomed affair between the girl and her brother-in-law. However, the text primarily reveals that any kind of licit (heterosexual) sexuality is always already illicit (incest) in that it is modeled after the father-daughter bond, which in itself is a replacement for the originary mother-daughter (illicit) love. This revelation is the focus of the text—to expose the mechanisms and deployment of sexuality. The mother has to give way to the father; the father has to give way to his successor. The paternal grief at the loss of his daughter's hair reveals the undercurrent of the loss of his daughter. The economics of heterosexual exchange prevails, but it is the m/paternal body that portrays the loss.

Conclusion: Nation and Maternal Loss

Finally, the question of the connections among mother-daughter relationships, femininity, and nation state must be raised. This issue is directly posited by the mother in the second story when she juxtaposes India with America, the new temporary home of her daughter. She vehemently declares:

> In America fathers molested their own children. Wives were abused and beaten up, just like the servant classes in India. Friends raped other friends. No one looked after the old. In India every woman got equal pay for equal work. In America they were still fighting for it. Could America ever have a woman President? Never. Could it ever have a black President? Never . . . As for discriminations against the untouchables in India—it only happened among the uneducated, whereas discriminations against blacks were rampant even among educated Americans. Blacks were the American untouchables. . . . (189–190)

This deliberate introduction of the anti-American theme is interesting in that it reveals the interconnection between the notions of nation and gender / sexuality, which are normally constructed as unrelated and separate. The mother's remarks indicate that India is identified with the ideal wife, the ideal mother, ideal relationships—the ideal, in short. Her politically correct discourse expropriates an entire cluster of connotations which are then associated with the maternal / India—civility, unity among people, respect for elders, equality.

Benedict Anderson points out in *Imagined Communities* that "in the modern world everyone can, should, will 'have' a nationality as he or she 'has' a gender" (16). Nationality, then, like gender is a relational term "whose identity derives from its inherence in a system of differences" (Parker et al., *Nationalisms and Sexualities*, 5). Within this context, the mother's anti-American sentiments reflect a search for her (non)identity in India. As George Mosse has indicated in *Nationalism and Sexuality*, the definition of any nation is predicated on the valorization of manliness and heterosexuality, with a robust, firm, male body signifying perfection. That is to say, any form of effeteness such as femininity and homosexuality can weaken the fabric of a nation. In such a definition of the nation the woman does not have a comfortable place. Her very presence renders the nation weak. Within such a rationale, one can see the relegation of woman to a role only as mother, who is *beyond* femininity and sexuality. The anti-American theme, then, is not insignificant. Only through a reviling of the United States can an Indian woman derive any identity. Anti-American sentiments negatively grant an Indian woman some positive Indianness, which her country, her husband, and her daughter cannot grant her. Similarly, mothers and daughters cannot have a relationship while in India. They can only have a relationship if they live on separate (Indian and American) soils. The category of mother-daughter relationships can be formed only on the condition of distance and separation. Distance grants them closeness and a relationship.

Thus, an examination of two Indian texts reveals that mothers and daughters are inhibited from strong bonding largely because of the devaluation of females in Indian culture. Females do not strengthen or enhance their lineage and, therefore, are undervalued. Women are taught early to know their place and to accept their fate as Other within culture. Both Pande and Appachana suggest that the female as agent in Indian society can inscribe herself only through anger or subversion.

Notes

1. For example, see Julia Kristeva's "Motherhood according to Giovanni Bellini," "Place Names," and "Stabat Mater" in *Desire in Language,* in which she refers to the homosexual-maternal facet.
2. See Mary John's fine piece "Postcolonial Feminists in the Western Field: Anthropologists and Native Informants" (in *Traveling Theories, Traveling Theorists,* ed. James Clifford and Vivek Dhareshwar, *Inscriptions* 5 [1989]: 49–74), in which she analyzes the predicaments which face a Third World scholar who works within First World academies.

Works Cited

Anderson, Benedict. *Imagined Communities: Reflections on the Origin and Spread of Nationalism*. London: Verso, 1983.

Appachana, Anjana. "Her Mother." In *The Inner Courtyard: Stories by Indian Women*, ed. Lakshmi Holmstrom, 180–194. Calcutta: Rupa, 1991.

Butler, Judith. *Gender Trouble: Feminism and the Subversion of Identity*. New York and London: Routledge, 1990.

Deleuze, Gilles, and Felix Guattari. *Anti-Oedipus: Capitalism and Schizophrenia*. Trans. Robert Hurley, Mark Seem, and Helen Lane. New York: Viking Press, 1977.

Doane, Mary Ann. *The Desire to Desire: The Woman's Film of the 1940s*. Bloomington: Indiana University Press, 1987.

Freud, Sigmund. "Femininity." In *New Introductory Lectures on Psychoanalysis*, trans. James Strachey, 99–119. New York and London: W. W. Norton, 1965.

———. "Some Psychical Consequences of the Anatomical Distinction between the Sexes." In *Sexuality and the Psychology of Love*, ed. Phillip Rieff, 183–193. New York: Collier, 1963.

Hacking, Ian. "Making Up People." In *Reconstructing Individualism: Autonomy, Individuality and the Self in Western Thought*, ed. Thomas C. Helle, Morton Sosna, and David Wellbury, 222–236. Stanford: Stanford University Press, 1986.

Kristeva, Julia. *Desire in Language*. Trans. Thomas Gora, Alice Jardine, and Leon S. Roudiez. New York: Columbia University Press, 1980.

Lévi-Strauss, Claude. *The Elementary Structures of Kinship*. Boston: Beacon Press, 1969.

Mosse, George. *Nationalism and Sexuality: Respectability and Abnormal Sexuality in Modern Europe*. New York: Howard Fertig, 1985.

Nandy, Ashis. *The Intimate Enemy: Loss and Recovery of Self under Colonialism*, New Delhi: Oxford University Press, 1983.

Pande, Mrinal. "Girls." In *The Inner Courtyard: Stories by Indian Women*, ed. Lakshmi Holmstrom, 56–64. Calcutta: Rupa, 1991.

Parker, Andrew, Mary Russo, Doris Sommer, and Patricia Yaeger, eds. *Nationalisms and Sexualities*. New York and London: Routledge, 1992.

Parry, Benita. *Delusions and Discoveries: Studies on India in the British Imagination, 1830–1930*. Berkeley: University of California Press, 1972.

Scheman, Naomi. "Missing Mothers/Desiring Daughters: Framing the Sight of Women." *Critical Inquiry* 15 (Autumn 1988): 62–89.

Spivak, Gayatri Chakravorty. "Who Claims Alterity?" In *Remaking History*, ed. Barbara Kruger and Phil Mariani, 269–293. Seattle: Bay Press, 1989.

Tharu, Susie. "Tracing Savithri's Pedigree." In *Recasting Women: Essays in Colonial History*, ed. Kumkum Sangari and Sudesh Vaid, 254–268. New Delhi: Kali for Women Press, 1989.

A Continuum of Pain

A Woman's Legacy in Alice Walker's *Possessing the Secret of Joy*

KIMBERLY JOYCE POLLOCK

Alice Walker's novel *Possessing the Secret of Joy* applies concepts from religion, anthropology, and psychology to the study of one woman, Tashi. Through this journey into her character, Walker opens up new possibilities for the relationships between all mothers and daughters. In an epigraph to the novel, Walker delves into popular wisdom, quoting a bumper sticker: "When the axe came into the forest, the trees said the handle is one of us." This unlikely jewel expresses the legacy that mother gives to daughter in this novel of pain, madness, and, ultimately, healing. Here myriad mother-daughter relationships are seen, all cast on a continuum of pain. Pain is the only reality, yet the actuality of this pain must be constantly hidden, thus denying reality.

By completely controlling the sexuality of women, the traditional practices of religion and nationalism inflict immeasurable pain on all of humanity and, if left unchecked, will lead to its total annihilation. In "From an Interview," published in *In Search of Our Mothers' Gardens*, Alice Walker states, "I am preoccupied with the spiritual survival, the survival whole of my people" (250). Always associated with both African Americans and women, in *Possessing the Secret of Joy* Walker broadens her focus to include all of humanity. By telling this story, she reveals a truth long concealed, and at last the healing process can begin.

Because of *Possessing the Secret of Joy*, women are able to speak the unspeakable. This becomes true not only for the women in the novel, but for the women who read the novel as well. Through Walker's reading/telling of Tashi's story, women are able to undo the "immasculation of women by men" suggested by Judith Fetterly.[1] In the introduction to *The Resisting Reader*, Fetterly states that "women are taught to think as men, to identify with a male point of view, and to accept as normal and legitimate a male system of values, one of whose central principle is misogyny" (xx). The effects of this value system have no clearer example than the circumcised woman, Tashi. Fetterly posits that by resisting, not allowing ourselves to submit to the immasculating effect of literature, women can gain a true sense of self. The secret to be possessed in *Possessing the Secret of Joy* is resistance. As novelist, Walker becomes the mother who breaks the continuum of pain by resisting sexist cultural patterns, thus leaving her daughters (readers) a legacy, not of pain, but of joy.

Walker first brought Tashi to life in *The Color Purple*, and she makes a brief reappearance in *The Temple of My Familiar*. This child of Africa would not rest until her story had been told. She was not content simply to be a part of other characters' stories. Here Walker has once again created characters that are so well drawn that it is hard for readers not to think of them as having a life of their own. Tashi represents all the women who have been forced to experience the brutalities of sexist cultural patterns. Walker's story of Tashi's coming to terms with the devastation of genital mutilation offers readers a balm for their wounds. Walker speaks of taboos more ancient than memory and has provided a language in which the unspoken can be spoken, thereby giving reality to women's pain, to women's existence.

Walker presents Tashi's story in a series of memoirs by the people who were most important in Tashi's life. Through the fragmented stories of these narrators, the reader pieces together Tashi's life as if sewing together a patchwork quilt. Each memory tells something different, not only about Tashi, but about the worlds in which she lived. As Tashi's story unfolds, so do many others, such as those of Tashi's mother, Nafa, and of her sister, Dura. Walker tells the story of M'Lissa, the tsunga (the word that Walker creates to name the women who are responsible for performing the rite of initiation and serving as midwives). Readers are told of the relationship between Tashi and Raye and Carl Jung, her psychoanalyst. Walker elaborates on the relationship between Tashi and Lizette, who in Africa would probably be considered her co-wife. And through Raye, the readers see the relationship between an American, Amy, and Amy's son.

Each narrator remembers Tashi differently. Only through becoming a quilter can the reader reap the benefits of this rich piece.

In an article titled "Mothers and Daughters: Another Minority Group," Natalie M. Rosinsky states, "Being a 'good' woman in a sexist society requires conformity to feminine stereotypes such as passivity, spirituality, or irrationality; being a 'good' mother entails indoctrinating one's daughter with these false ideals" (280). According to this definition, Nafa was a "good" mother. She taught both of her daughters the lessons which must be learned to be "good" women, "good" members of society. Yet this duty of motherhood was an extremely complex task for Nafa because of the changing society in which she produced her daughters.

Nafa's daughters were born at a time of unrest in the Olinkan village. An entire way of life was coming to an end. As white colonialists invaded Africa, there was increasingly little on the continent that was truly African. All of the traditions—religious, family, national—were in upheaval. Even in remote villages, changes were occurring. Missionaries had visited the Olinkan village and converted many to Christianity. Nafa herself had been converted and had taken a Christian name, Catherine. But the missionaries came and went rather frequently, and the Olinkan mothers were left unsure of which traditions were appropriate to pass on to their daughters.[2]

The tsunga M'Lissa is a fascinating character. The government of the society in which she lives privileges her. She is recognized as a national monument, a heroine, by every faction of the government, including the National Liberation Front (Walker, 150). As the mother of her country, it is M'Lissa who gives the history of her family and explains the origins of the practice of female genital mutilation. M'Lissa recalls that from the time of earliest memory the women in her family were always tsungas, charged with irrevocably destroying women's sexuality.

According to Luce Irigaray, in *This Sex Which Is Not One*, "Female sexuality has always been conceptualized on the basis of masculine parameters. Thus the opposition between 'masculine' clitoral activity and 'feminine' vaginal passivity, an opposition which Freud—and many others—saw as states or alternatives, in the development of a sexually 'normal' woman, seems rather too clearly required by the practice of male sexuality" (23). Olinkan society believed that there was only one alternative: there must be no blurring of the lines between the sexes. That which could possibly be construed as male must be removed from the female body. Therefore, women gave their daughters up to the gruesome rites of initiation, which involved circumcision. But this circumcision was much more radical than that which is experienced by males and much more individualized. According to Evelyn (Tashi's Christian name), "Some cultures demanded excision of only the clitorises, others insisted on a thorough scraping away of the entire genital area" (Walker, 118). This is radically different from the simple removal of a piece of skin. That is the tradition which Nafa was to pass on to her daughters, if she was to be a "good" Olinkan mother. For Catherine, there is a different set of traditions to be transferred.

Christian missionaries argue that the practice of the "bath," the rite of female initiation, is barbaric. They say that such things are not done in the civilized world. Yet they insist that the concepts of the virgin birth and the immaculate conception be accepted without question. For Nafa, Christianity presents a way to refuse to submit her daughters to the lifelong torture to which her own culture says all women must submit if they are to be true women. As a "good" Christian mother, Catherine does not have either of her daughters initiated at the proper time. M'Lissa remembers that she tried to convince Catherine to have the operation done for Tashi when she was at the proper age. However, Catherine refused M'Lissa's counsel because of her conversion to Christianity.

But Christianity tricks Catherine. For all of the Olinkans, Christianity is interchangeable with whiteness. Yet in the form of African Americans, a people who are culturally both black and white, new black missionaries come to lead Catherine's flock. When Nafa finds out that the new missionaries are black, she is sure that black traditions will be restored and that the uncircumcised girls will be chastised. M'Lissa tells Tashi: "She could not imagine a black person that was not Olinkan, and she thought all Olinkans demanded their daughters to be bathed. . . . She was the kind of woman who jumped even before the man says boo. Your mother helped hold your sister down" (253). In an act which is meant to protect her daughter from harm, in an attempt to be a "good" mother, Nafa brings about the death of her own daughter, Dura.

The experience that causes Tashi's initial pain is the death of this sister, brought on by Nafa's conformity to the dictates of her society. Through fear of authoritative retribution, Nafa has Dura initiated into womanhood, even though she knows that Dura is a hemophiliac. The pain that Nafa experiences as a result of her own "bath" has so completely crushed her spirit that only fear is left. Dura dies a slow and painful death, while dreaming of the promise of womanhood, because this is the only gift that Nafa is capable of leaving to her daughter. Through the death of her sister, Tashi learns the lesson of silence, the first step on the path to becoming a woman. Olivia, Tashi's sister-in-law, recalls her first memory of Tashi, who cried without making a sound. Her little body trembled from trying to control her emotions (7–8).

The silence of Tashi revealed in this quilt square is significant. Even a female child of six or seven is expected to control her emotions, to deny pain a voice. This is the beginning of the deadly silence that becomes too much for Tashi. Because of society's demand for silence, Tashi has great difficulty maintaining her sanity. Indeed, not only is her pain not recognized by her own people, but when the American missionaries ask about the crying girl, the elders reply, "What little girl, Pastor? There is no little crying girl here" (8). The elders are able to say this since Nafa has removed Tashi because of her inability to control her emotions, but this initial denial of her pain is in actuality a denial of the existence of the entire woman (girl). The reality is too awful to face, so a story, an alternative reality, is created, and the mother becomes a part of the conspiracy against the daughter. Nafa participates in, though she does not initiate, the silence that eventually drives Tashi mad. Nafa's denial of her daughter's pain is a behavior that she has learned from her own mother.

In another square of the quilt, this one sewn by Tashi, one sees a different view of the black missionaries' entrance into the village. Tashi feels betrayed by her own mother and by all of the other women (mother figures) in the village. She resents that the woman she respected and loved insisted that she hide her feelings and make the foreigners welcome. She is troubled that her elder mothers could silence their pain over Dura's death so quickly to greet the missionaries. The arrival of the missionaries brings Tashi a lesson of self-immolation. She begins to realize that she does not really know the women who have been a part of her daily life. Everything that Tashi thinks she understands about love and loyalty comes crashing down around her. There is a sudden void that she does not know how to fill. And so, being a "good" mother, Nafa teaches her daughter a third lesson in being a woman. She instructs her daughter that only hard work will fill the vast emptiness in her life. The woman becomes the beast of burden because of her own burdens of which she cannot speak. Her own silence forces her to produce for the society which does not even acknowledge her as a person. She is just a woman; she must produce children, work, and teach her daughters to do the same. Tashi finally comes to know her mother:

> I studied the white rinds of my mother's heels, and felt in my own heart the weight of Dura's death settling upon her spirit, like the groundnuts that bent her back. As she staggered under her load, I half expected her footprints, into which I was careful to step, to stain my own feet with tears and blood. But my mother never wept . . . when called upon to salute the power of the chief and his counselors she could let out a cry that assaulted the very heavens with its praising pain. (17)

Tashi takes the first step in becoming her own mother; she joins the continuum of pain.

The colonial invasion has a devastating effect on Tashi. War springs up all around. The Olinkans lose their village to the white colonialists' road. The black missionaries return to America and leave the remaining Olinkans to deal with what is left of their way of life. The Olinkans transfer the new traditional love for Christ to their own revolutionary leader, who says that the only way to remain Olinkan is to return to the Olinkan traditions. All of this happens when Tashi is little more than a confused adolescent. Walker sets up a paradoxical situation. The loss of a tribal or even a national identity that Tashi experiences when the white colonialists figuratively "bathe" Africa leads her to conclude that being initiated or genitally mutilated is the only act which will link her irrevocably to all the generations of the Olinkan women who have come before her and with her mother country. In order to live as a true African, she must die as a woman. In a show of love and solidarity with her people, even after she has experienced the joy of sexual freedom, Tashi, too, is bathed. She moves further along the continuum of pain; the practices of two cultures that seem at first to be antithetical to each other have the same destructive effect on women. The colonialism of the West "bathed" Africa as M'Lissa, the Olinkan tsunga, "bathes" Tashi. Her own sense of self, her pride, leads her to an act which she sees as at once defiant and empowering. She is happy that the initiation ceremony is not performed in Europe or America because that makes the "bathing" more valuable to her as an African woman. Before the operation Tashi believes that she will be "completely woman. Completely African. Completely Olinka" (63). Yet she finds that after the operation, when she has healed, "her own proud walk had become a shuffle" (64). Tashi, indeed, becomes her own mother.

Greer Litton Fox, in "'Nice Girl': Social Control of Women through a Value Construct," posits that "there are three basic strategies used to regulate the freedom of women and to exert control over their behavior in the world . . . *confinement* . . . *protection* . . . [and] *normative restriction*" (805). Not only are the normative restrictions of the "nice girl," "good mother" syndrome at work in this novel, but the circumcision also functions as a means of confinement, like the act of foot binding. As the wounds heal, movement becomes restricted, thus limiting the mobility and freedom of the woman.

The sexist cultural patterns of both the native religion of the Olinkans and Christianity contribute to the suffering of women. The women of the Olinka tribe submit their daughters to the tsungas because they believe that if this ritual is not performed the woman will never be able to have a husband, because her clitoris will become so elongated that it will be impossible for a man to have sexual intercourse with her: "Everyone knew that if a woman was not circumcised her unclean parts would grow so long they'd soon touch her thighs; she'd become masculine and arouse herself. No man could enter her because her own erection would be in his way. . . . Everyone believed it, even though no one has ever seen it" (119). This is the story that all children are told. The practice of female genital mutilation is so completely ingrained in Olinkan tradition because it came into existence at the same time that the Olinkans became a people. M'Lissa, the tsunga responsible for performing the rite of initiation on both Tashi and Dura, is also the midwife who is called to preside over their births. Through the practices of this native religion, birth and death are experienced through the same hands. The hands that help mothers give life to daughters take away the life that they have given in the name of making them truly women.

Contrary to Hélène Cixous's statement in "Castration or Decapitation?" that women do not have a relationship with culture because they are not driven by the male fear of castration, the Olinkan women know mutilation. There is no need to look to decapitation as the driving force for women because, quite clearly, these women have been castrated. Cixous also comments that "silence is the mark of hysteria" and that the hysteric is a divine spirit who "does not make herself but she does make the other" (484). Nafa, as mother, and M'Lissa, as mother, both play the father by becoming the creator of the daughter, who is created in her (their) own image(s). Walker makes little or no mention of Tashi's father in the novel.

The Christian concept of the virgin birth so completely controls the sexuality of women that it performs the same function as the Olinkan practice of genital mutilation. The only "good" mother never lives as a woman. If the precepts of Christianity are taken to heart, it follows that all women, not only those whose mates have been unfaithful, will be frigid. Through conversion to Christianity, Catherine and Tashi/Evelyn have been both physically and psychologically circumcised. The psychological circumcision happens when Tashi's husband is forced to seek his sexual satisfaction outside of their marriage because sexual intercourse with Tashi is too painful for both of them.

In "Stabat Mater," Julia Kristeva speaks of a masculine appropriation of the maternal which in actuality is masking a "primary narcissism." Kristeva also states that "a mother is always branded by pain, she yields to it. 'And a sword will pierce your own soul too' . . ." (190). Walker seems to echo Kristeva's sentiments when Pierre, Tashi's stepson, insists that man is jealous of woman's pleasure because she can achieve it without him. He explains that man wants to believe that, even after a woman's outer sex is excised, his penis can reach her inner parts and satisfy her desire. Pierre notes that it is only man's lust to conquer woman that drives him to try to force his penis into the tiny, inelastic opening which results from mutilation. The male is unable to bear not being the center of the universe and so mutilates woman physically to gain complete control over her.

The tsunga has always been the sword of the government—first the tribal government, later the national government. The entire initiation ritual was contrived by the male so that paternity could be certain, thus giving a father control of his children and control over their mothers. The tsunga used the needle, after the horrors of the knife, to make certain that a woman's husband is the only man who can enter her.[3] Before this ritual was practiced, there was no certainty about paternity (because any man could easily enter any woman) and the control that men had over women was limited; when a man can claim a woman's child as his own, then he controls not only the child, but the woman who produced the child. In her essay "Reproduction, Mothering, and the Origins of Patriarchy," Azizah Al-Hibri traces the male desire for immortality as one of the main factors which contributed to the rise of patriarchy: "There is an Arabic saying that 'he who reproduces does not die.' But we need to keep in mind that the desire for offspring is directly connected to the desire for *immortality*" (82). Only by being certain of his paternity could a man assure his own immortality. No longer were women having their own children; from that point on they were producing their husbands' offspring. And the woman herself was used as the instrument of control. The tsunga, the giver of life in the role of midwife, became the instrument of death for women, in the governmentally sanctioned role of the one who made girls become women and in so doing assured the immortality of the male. The axe entered the forest, and each tree recognized the handle as herself.

In the story of M'Lissa, the price that the tsungas must pay for holding such a status is made clear. M'Lissa's mother, because she was a tsunga, knew better than any other woman what each excised woman had lost. She was cognizant of the time before the ritual was practiced and secretly worshiped a doll, an idol of a woman with her genitals intact, giving herself pleasure. Yet she had been excised herself. In her role of tsunga, it was her duty to perform the ritual on her own daughter. How could a society ask a mother to mutilate her own daughter willingly? In her attempt to save her daughter, M'Lissa's mother left a piece of M'Lissa's clitoris intact. This act of a mother's love caused grave punishment to be inflicted upon the child. M'Lissa tells Tashi of the consequences of disobeying the cruel edicts of a sexist society: a witch doctor was called in to complete the job that her mother had left undone. She allows Tashi to touch the keloidal tissue on a gash which travels right through the tendon of her inner thigh.

While it took M'Lissa three months to heal from the physical wounds inflicted upon her, she never healed from the emotional wounds. Indeed, whatever was left of her emotions also became crusted over with keloidal tissue. In an act of self-preservation, M'Lissa cannot allow herself to feel anything. Her life becomes like that of her grandmother before her. She merely exists to perform the horrific act that society demands of her. The tsunga becomes the invisible hand of the government, controlling women through the infliction of pain and sexual violence. The total possession of women is accomplished by the dehumanization of the victims. The woman who was M'Lissa's grandmother is reduced to a body part; Africans are reduced to heathens, animals. And the role of mother, including Africa herself, becomes "She Who Prepares the Lambs for Slaughter" (273).

Tashi eventually marries Adam, the son of the African American missionary who came to the Olinkan village, and makes a home with him in America. But this change in venue does not produce the desired healing effect. Simply removing herself from a society that treats women as nonbeings does not heal the psychological wounds that she experienced by participating in the process of becoming a woman. In her anguish, Tashi begins a process of self-mutilation which will last until her freedom comes with her death. She starts to decorate her body with bracelets and anklets forged by razors digging into her own flesh. Eventually she travels to Europe to be treated by Carl Jung, father of his own branch of psychoanalysis.

The relationship that Tashi shares with Jung can also be seen as a mother-daughter relationship. Tashi sees an old man and is transported back to her homeland. She envisions an old African grandmother cooking over an open fire who somehow transforms into a pink-faced witch doctor on American soil (52). He even becomes associated not only with cooking, but with blood, a universal sign of womanhood: "A small bloodstain glowed maroon near his waist" (79). Thus Jung is both male and female, a bloody midsection and a witch doctor, a male version of a woman who has the power to heal. Jung is not afraid to deal with his entire self. Wearing clothing associated with women (he wears an apron and a skirt is suggested by the reference to a witch doctor) is not threatening to this man. He seems not to have the need to control women. And so, with this "grandmother," Tashi is able to examine her relationship with her own mother and her motherland. Tashi's mutilation at the hands of both of these mothers is locked inside of her, buried in the silence that accompanies all traditional taboos. To speak of a taboo strips it of its power. So daughters never confront their mothers about the devastation to which the mothers themselves have been subjected. They remain trapped in the silence that they have learned from their mothers, which is so essentially a part of womanhood. The purpose of psychoanalysis is, of course, to verbalize, to create a language in which the unspeakable can be spoken.

So while the character Tashi is psychoanalyzed, Walker's novel itself becomes the "break-through session," where the pain of mutilation, of psychological circumcision, is verbalized for all women.

"Negro women, the doctor says into my silence, can never be analyzed effectively because they can never bring themselves to blame their mothers" (18). But what would it mean for an African woman to blame her mother for what has been done to her? If it is true that the child becomes the parent, then it is also true, particularly in the case of Tashi, that she must ultimately hold herself responsible for what has happened to her. The mother is the daughter who is submitted to the tsunga's tortures. The tsunga is her own victim, a perfect illustration of Fetterly's "immasculation of women." "She is asked to identify with a selfhood that defines itself in opposition to her; she is required to identify against herself" (Fetterly, xii). M'Lissa says that she never again saw the child who was herself, after the torture of her mother and the witch doctor's retribution. But Tashi corrects her: ". . . you saw her over and over again, hundreds, thousands of times. It was she who screamed before your knife" (216). The pain that must come with this realization cannot be measured on any continuum.

In the face of all of this, how can a woman's, a mother's, worth be judged? M'Lissa explains to Tashi that "only the murder of the tsunga, the circumciser, by one of those whom she has circumcised . . . proves her (the circumciser's) value to her tribe. Her own death . . . had been ordained. It would elevate her to the position of saint" (204). Only the murder of the tsunga, of the mother, by the daughter can prove the worthiness of the mother. Only if the mother has so destroyed her daughter can she be certain that she has performed the duties of motherhood successfully. And through the martyrdom of the "good" mother, the state creates the role model of successful motherhood for all women to follow. The most saintly woman, the mother of the entire nation, is the tsunga who has mutilated the most girls.

Adrienne Rich, in *Of Woman Born*, examines the concept of violence in the institution of motherhood. In addressing the concept of mothers who have mutilated their children, she states, "The scapegoat is different from the martyr; she cannot teach resistance or revolt. She represents a terrible temptation: to suffer uniquely, to assume that I, the individual woman, am the *problem*" (277). The mother cannot teach the daughter resistance because the mother is only redeemed through the total destruction of the daughter. To teach the daughter to resist is to become a "bad" mother. The tsunga's suffering is unique; she is, indeed, the problem.

In the Christian counterpart, virginity is insisted upon. The only "good" mother is one who has suffered the pain of childbirth, yet has not experienced the joys of sexual satisfaction. "Good" women do not experience pleasure; they only suffer and sacrifice their children for the glory of God. Walker points out that genital mutilation was practiced on women during the time of Christ in the region of his birth. It is quite probable that Mary was able to give birth and yet remain a virgin because her own excision had made penetration impossible. Walker is postulating that the ideal woman in Christian culture is the woman who is excised. Once again, Christianity is seen as not being much different from the heathen religions which it has sought to make extinct.

Tashi, who becomes Evelyn when she converts to Christianity and whose husband is a Christian minister, has both M'Lissa and the Virgin Mary as her role models for successful womanhood, each leaving a legacy of pain and fragmentation. Neither of these is a whole, complete woman. Yet through the talks with the old man who is a woman, Carl Jung, the verbalization of the horrors that she has experienced helps Tashi to begin to deal with the reality of the pain, with the reality of her selfhood.

Through her relationship with Adam, Evelyn becomes an American. She adopts the land of opportunity and equality as her homeland. Evelyn / Tashi's identification of herself as American becomes vital in understanding the process of healing that she undertakes. America represents the chance to do things right; America becomes the new promised land. Evelyn believes that the definition of womanhood is different in America than in her Olinkan homeland. She believes that in America taboos that cannot be spoken of do not exist. Yet she finds that America does not offer her the freedom that she expected. Her position in America is that of the crazy foreign wife of an African American Christian minister. When Evelyn asks Adam to participate actively in her healing by speaking to his congregation about the devastation she has suffered, Adam says that he cannot because no one would understand. Taboos do exist in this land of the free. Tashi cannot be Evelyn, and her healing comes to a standstill. America does not fulfill its promise. She realizes that being American means continuing to be the same wounded African person. Seeking wholeness in America, Tashi finds instead a nation of people who are wounded, incomplete. Still, even this realization is an important square in the quilt of Tashi's journey to sanity. She begins to understand that she deserves love, even when incomplete.

Carl Jung sends Tashi to an African American woman to complete her analysis after his death. Raye is what Tashi wishes to be; she is both African and American, and she is complete. Through the guidance of this mother, Raye, Tashi begins the last leg of her journey to completion, to self-actualization. Through Raye, Evelyn/Tashi discovers that Africans are not the only people who practice circumcision on females. Raye introduces Tashi to Amy, a white American woman from New Orleans whose mother took her to a doctor for a clitorectomy as a "cure" for masturbation. Accepting the truth of Amy's story gives Tashi new insight; she is no longer a single woman struggling alone, but part of a much vaster system. Tashi always understood that she shared this pain with the women of her own people, but Amy makes Tashi connected with all women; Tashi begins to recognize the continuum of pain that is women's legacy.

Walker uses the story of Amy and her son to show the universality of the act of genital mutilation. Amy was circumcised in New Orleans as a young child; although she leads a "normal" life, her neurosis is passed on to her son, who is homosexual and who carries all of his mother's pain for her. Walker uses the story of Amy and her son to show that this destruction of women causes the entire human race pain. Through the use of genital mutilation to define sexual roles, human beings become locked into forms of sexuality that are not natural to any individual.[4] During slavery, the white American doctors studied circumcised women and began to use the same practice to control their own women. "They wrote in their medical journals that they'd finally found a cure for the white woman's hysteria" (186). The cure for hysteria is, in essence, the cure for womanhood. The doctors believed that they could finally make women not be women. And if women cannot be women, what becomes of men?

As Evelyn begins a discussion with Raye, she mentions her strange habit of drifting off into the world of fantasy and storytelling. It is because of this habit that Evelyn becomes aware that something out of the ordinary happened to her. Storytelling is essential: "the story is only the mask for the truth" (130), yet the truth always lies somewhere in the story. Only by discovering the story of how all women have come to be circumcised can Tashi become whole. And this story is told to her by a most unlikely mother figure. Tashi's husband, Adam, has had a life-long affair with the liberated Frenchwoman Lizette, and they have a son, Pierre. Pierre is a sensitive child, and his mother has given him the legacy of knowledge of the pain of women. Pierre is born as all children should be born; his birth is both a spiritual and sexual experience: "My vulva oiled and massaged to keep my hips open and my vagina fluid, I was orgasmic at the end. Petit Pierre practically slid into the world at the height of my amazement, smiling serenely even before he opened his eyes" (99). This serene being becomes an anthropologist and devotes his life to finding the story of Tashi's pain. Because Lizette chooses to give the legacy that women give to their daughters to her son instead, Pierre becomes an unusual man. He is bisexual; he is capable of loving all humans and does not try to force others into a form of sexuality that is unnatural for them. Through his studies, in the role of mother, he gives to Tashi the story of God and the termites, which is the key that opens the door to her life.

Through anthropological studies, Pierre discovers that the ancients who began the ritual of female circumcision believed that they had learned the ritual by watching God cut off the hill of a termite mound before having intercourse with the earth. From this, people learned that a woman's clitoris must be cut, the male part of the woman must first be removed, for the man to experience "God-like" pleasure. This idea is directly in line with those expressed by Kate Millett in *Sexual Politics*, where she states that "patriarchal religion, popular attitude . . . assumes these psycho-social distinctions to rest upon biological differences between the sexes, so that where culture is acknowledged as shaping behavior, it is said to do no more than cooperate with nature" (26–27). The Olinkans simply imitated nature. Armed with the knowledge of the source of her own pain, Tashi can take the final steps to reclaiming all that has been taken from her.

Tashi realizes that she must confront the mother who has allowed such pain to be inflicted upon her. She returns to Africa to murder M'Lissa. But when she finds M'Lissa, Tashi also unexpectedly becomes the mother of a daughter. Mbati is attending M'Lissa, and an immediate kinship is established between Tashi and Mbati. She informs Tashi that frightened women with daughters seek advice from M'Lissa, who reassures them. Mbati gives Tashi another reason for confronting her own mother. Tashi must confront M'Lissa so that her own daughter, Mbati, and the daughters of those frightened women who come seeking advice can be free. After talking with M'Lissa and listening to her stories for days, Tashi finally kills the tsunga, in an act which gives life to all women.

She breaks the cycle; she refuses to hold her own daughter down for the tsunga's knife. The legacy which Tashi leaves to Mbati is the story of God and the termites that Pierre has discovered; this is the story of her own pain, and thus the key to sanity. As a truly grateful daughter, Mbati gives her mother a gift in return.

Tashi is tried and convicted of M'Lissa's murder; in prison, for the first time in her life she shares the experience of a functional family. Adam, Olivia, Pierre, Benny (Adam and Tashi's son), Mbati, and Raye all study the concept of the genital mutilation of women and its effects on society as a whole. In a powerful move, Walker connects the rapid spread of AIDS in African society with the practice of female circumcision and thus shows that the devastation of women ultimately means the death of all human beings.

In an act of reconciliation of the mother and daughter forming a complete, healthy unit, Tashi and Mbati exchange truths. Tashi confides in Mbati, "I am miserably flawed." Mbati responds, "That is your greatest gift to me" (270). Then Mbati gives Tashi a figure of a woman giving herself pleasure, the symbol of ultimate freedom.

In the family's studies, Mbati uncovers the writings of a white colonialist who notes that black people possess the secret of joy. She sees black people as naturally exotic and able to survive tremendous suffering and humiliation, but, clearly, she has lived among Africans without perceiving them as human beings. Mbati, however, has a very different notion of what it means to possess the secret of joy. Mbati vows not to let Tashi, who has received the death sentence, die without knowing what this "secret" is. On the morning of Tashi's execution, women line the streets with their naked infant daughters on their heads, allowing these children to please themselves sexually. And just before the shots ring out that will mark the end of Tashi, her family holds up a banner:

> All of them—Adam, Olivia, Benny, Pierre, Raye, Mbati—hold it firmly and stretch it wide.
>
> *RESISTANCE* IS THE SECRET OF JOY! it says in huge block letters.
>
> There is a roar as if the world cracked open and I flew inside. I am no more. And satisfied. (279)

Daughter has given mother the gift of self; the legacy of pain has been broken; there is no continuum of women's pain from this time on; women can be complete. Through resistance to destructive, sexist actions, the human race can survive. Without resistance, there is a life without joy. Without resistance, self-love is impossible. The quilt of the mothers is now finished; women can hand their own daughters a legacy of joy.

Rudolph P. Byrd, in his article "Spirituality in the Novels of Alice Walker," says, "Since Walker's material is the stuff of human experience each situation is, in its essentials, universal" (363). This is true for the "stuff of human experience" that is *Possessing the Secret of Joy*. Through the language that Alice Walker has created, all people, male and female alike, can begin to talk about the taboos which, if left unchecked, will lead to the destruction of all. But learning the language is difficult; change is never easy. When speaking of her own death, Tashi tells Olivia that "maybe death is easier than life, as pregnancy is easier than birth" (249). Yet not to give birth means the death of both the mother and the child. Walker's message is clear: if the continuum of pain is not broken, if there is no new legacy for mothers to leave their daughters, then humans will cease to be. Resistance is the only hope for survival.

Notes

1. In the introduction to her *The Resisting Reader: A Feminist Approach to American Fiction* (Bloomington: Indiana University Press, 1978), Judith Fetterly discusses the process by which literature is used to immasculate women. Immasculation is the opposite of emasculation. In immasculation, the woman is given male sexual attributes. Women are taught to identify with the male view point on all issues, which leads to self-hatred. In the practices of the Olinkans, not only are women taught to think like males, but they are physically mutilated.

   Fetterly also talks about the process of reading as a method by which immasculation can be reversed. Walker's writing of Tashi's story is itself a resistant reading of sexual cultural patterns, by which she reverses the process of immasculation. See "Reading Ourselves: Toward a Feminist Theory of Reading," by Elizabeth A. Flynn and Patrocinio P. Schweikart, in *Gender and Reading: Essays on Readers, Texts and Contests* (Baltimore: Johns Hopkins University Press, 1986).
2. The decision of whether or not to have a female child circumcised is still a difficult one. According to the Papers of the Arab Women's Solidarity Association Conference, *Women of the Arab World: The Coming Challenge*, edited by Nahid Toubia and translated by Nahed El Gamal (London: Zed Books, 1988), "Most recent statistics reveal that 98% of females in the northern regions are circumcised, regardless of their level of education (or rather the level of the parents' education), social class or degree of health awareness, including the daughters of doctors, university professors, educationalists, and social workers. . . . In the majority of cases pharaonic circumcision (excision of the clitoris, labia minora and labia majora with stitching of the raw edges over the urethral meatus) or intermediate circumcision (excision of labia minora and clitoris with stitching) are performed" (101).
3. There are descriptions in the novel of a straw being placed in the vaginal opening and all of the skin being sewn up around the straw so that this is the only opening for intercourse, for menstrual flow, and for childbirth. Many women are apparently re-sewn after childbirth has stretched the skin. With an opening so small, intercourse is guaranteed to be so painful that a husband would know if his wife had been unfaithful. Each wife has been made to fit her husband as a custom-made glove fits the hand of its owner.

4. Genital mutilation of women is used to define such roles as "good mother" and "good wife." The only good women are those whose vaginas have been customized to service only their husbands, thus assuring paternity. The devastating effects of any exterior force defining sexual roles are best illustrated in Amy's son. Because Amy's practice of giving herself sexual pleasure was defined as sinful by her mother, the girl is circumcised and is therefore no longer capable of the sin. As an adult, she passes all of her own grief and pain to her son, whose own sexual habits are outside of societal norms. The torment that Amy's son experiences through outside forces defining sexuality are finally too much for him, and he commits suicide. Being locked into forms of sexuality that are not natural to an individual leads to insanity, as in the cases of Tashi and Amy, and death, as in the case of Amy's son. For more on the concept of societally imposed sex/gender roles, see Gayle Rubin, "The Traffic in Women: Notes on the 'Political Economy' of Sex," in *Toward an Anthropology of Women,* ed. Rayana R. Reiter (New York: Monthly Review Press, 1975).

Works Cited

Byrd, Rudolph P. "Spirituality in the Novels of Alice Walker: Models, Healing and Transformation, or When the Spirit Moves So Do We." In *Wild Women in the Whirlwind: Afro-American Culture and the Contemporary Literary Renaissance,* 363–378. New Brunswick, N.J.: Rutgers University Press, 1990.

Cixous, Hélène. "Castration or Decapitation?" In *Contemporary Literary Criticism: Literary and Cultural Studies,* 2nd ed., ed. Robert Con Davis and Ronald Schleifer, 479–491. White Plains, N.Y.: Longman, 1989.

Fox, Greer Litton. "'Nice Girl': Social Control of Women through a Value Construct." *Signs: Journal of Women in Culture and Society* 2, no. 4 (Summer 1977): 805–817.

Al-Hibri, Azizah. "Reproduction, Mothering, and the Origins of Patriarchy." In *Mothering: Essays in Feminist Theory,* ed. Joyce Trebilcot, 81–93. Totowa, N.J.: Rowman and Allanheld, 1983.

Irigaray, Luce. *This Sex Which Is Not One.* Trans. Catherine Porter and Carolyn Burn. Ithaca, N.Y.: Cornell University Press, 1977.

Kristeva, Julia. "Stabat Mater." In *The Kristeva Reader,* 160–186. New York: Columbia University Press, 1986.

Millett, Kate. *Sexual Politics.* New York: Avon Books, 1969.

Rich, Adrienne. *Of Woman Born: Motherhood as Experience and Institution.* New York: W. W. Norton, 1976.

Rosinsky, Natalie M. "Mothers and Daughters: Another Minority Group." In *The Lost Tradition: Mothers and Daughters in Literature,* ed. Cathy N. Davidson and E. M. Broner, 280–290. New York: Frederick Ungar, 1980.

Walker, Alice. "From an Interview." In *In Search of Our Mothers' Gardens,* 250. New York: Harcourt Brace Jovanovich, 1983.

———. *Possessing the Secret of Joy.* New York: Harcourt Brace Jovanovich, 1992.

"I was cryin', all the people were cryin', my mother was cryin'"

Aboriginality and Maternity in Sally Morgan's *My Place*

JOYCE ZONANA

Hailed as the "finest example of the reconnecting of the broken tissue of Aboriginal identity to date" (Healy, 81), Sally Morgan's *My Place* has been a bestseller in Australia since its publication in 1987, although it remains relatively unknown in the United States. A detective story, an autobiography, a family and cultural history, *My Place* richly repays even the most casual reading. Yet an examination of its portrayal of mother-daughter relations reveals the book's greatest power. Quietly yet emphatically, *My Place* articulates and celebrates a spiritual maternity that overcomes patriarchal and racist violence to heal the wounds of separation and to re-create a community in which people "belong" to one another.

Brought up in Western Australia believing herself to be white or East Indian, Sally Gilroy Morgan is fifteen before she discovers that the maternal grandmother with whom she has lived most of her life is black. She then begins what will become a seventeen-year quest, an "inner search" (106), to ascertain her Aboriginality and to understand why her mother and grandmother have kept their "history" a "secret" (163). Her book is the story both of her childhood and of her quest. In addition, and perhaps even more importantly, it is the story of the women and men who have gone before her, creating the conditions for her particular experience of Aboriginality.

Embedded within Sally's written narrative are three oral narratives, painstakingly elicited, tape-recorded, and transcribed: "Arthur Corunna's

Story," "Gladys Corunna's Story," and "Daisy Corunna's Story"—the stories of her great-uncle, her mother (Mum), and her grandmother (Nan). In its presentation of these narratives, *My Place* becomes what Trinh T. Minh-ha has called "Grandma's story," the story that "must be told," "the story of a people" (119). In telling such a tale, Sally Morgan herself becomes a storytelling "Grandma," keeping Aboriginality alive. Asked why she wrote her book, she explains, "I didn't want my own children to be deprived" of the "crucial knowledge" of Aboriginality: "I felt that it was a record for them and if no-one else read it, it kind of didn't matter" (Wright, 94).

Sally is one-eighth Aboriginal: her great-grandfather, grandfather, and father were white. She had only one Aboriginal great-grandparent—Annie Padewani, a petite and pretty woman who had lived at Corunna Downs Station in the north of Western Australia; as her friends insist, she could pass for anything (139). Yet Sally chooses Aboriginality, the stigmatized identity that comes to her through her mothers. For Sally, Aboriginality is not a matter of skin color; it is, rather, an expression of how she has been mothered and how she will herself mother. Aboriginality ultimately is equivalent in this text with maternity itself. And in choosing Aboriginality, Sally Morgan chooses maternity.

Traditional autobiography, as Sidonie Smith and others have argued, "serves as one of those generic contracts that reproduces the patrilineage and its ideologies of gender" (44). Patrilineal autobiography silences women, represses the maternal; yet in autobiographical writings of twentieth-century women, and particularly women of color, Smith observes that the writer "traces her origins to and through, rather than against, the mother" (57). *My Place* is such a "matrilineal" autobiography, though maternity in *My Place* is not simply a linear relationship: it resonates in multiple temporal dimensions. For in this "family autobiography" (Wright, 93), not only does the daughter define herself "to and through" her mother, grandmother, and great-grandmother, but the mother, grandmother, and great-grandmother define themselves to and through the daughter.

What Sally discovers and affirms in the course of her quest is the profound connection between Aboriginality and maternity—but not before she first learns the terrible ways in which the two have been severed. Because of Western Australia's policy of removing "half-caste" children from their native mothers, the specific conjunction of racism, patriarchy, and colonialism in Australia required either a break in Aboriginal identity or a break in maternity and love. Only if Sally's "mothers," Daisy and Gladys, pass as white can they be certain to mother Sally and her siblings. First Daisy and then Gladys had been taken away from their mothers; in their effort to keep that from happening to the next generation, they decide to hide their Aboriginal identity. They bring up Sally to identify with her white father and their white fathers so that they can mother her. Thus, when Sally seeks to uncover her Aboriginal heritage, she threatens her mothers with the loss of all they have struggled to maintain. Paradoxically, she also pays tribute to what they have achieved.

The older women sacrifice Aboriginal identity in order to preserve maternity; yet, in asserting maternity at the expense of Aboriginal identity, Nan and Mum simultaneously stand for and claim Aboriginality. They hide their skin color—their Aboriginal flesh—but they assert their values—their Aboriginal spirit. This spirit, *My Place* suggests, is in fact the essence of Aboriginality. As she concludes the narrative of her life, Gladys muses that in hundreds of years there will not be any black Aboriginals left. She fears that because of racial mixing the color will die out, yet hopes that generations after her will maintain their link with the land. The "unique qualities" of Aboriginality limned in *My Place* include not only what Gladys calls the "spiritual tie with the land" (306), but an intense commitment to family and community, a deep involvement with animals and plants, and, perhaps most importantly, an openness to alternative modes of knowing that include waking visions, dreams, and auditory "hallucinations." Nan comments that "blackfellas" know all about spirits because they were always a part of their upbringing. From an early age, Sally has revelatory dreams and visions; her grandmother and mother hear beautiful music coming from the swamp behind their house even when there is no one there; throughout her life, Nan engages in spiritual healing: Sally remembers being cured of rheumatic fever when Nan ran her hands slowly along her body, saying that everything would be fine.

Woven as a central thread in the luminous pattern of beliefs, practices, and values that constitutes spiritual Aboriginality in *My Place* is what, in another context, Carol Gilligan has called an "ethic of care" (173), a deep sense of being that places each individual in nurturing relation to others—including humans, plants, animals, and spirits. And while it has become a commonplace of contemporary feminist and anti-imperialist discourse to contrast an often romanticized sense of female and native communion with patriarchal and European imperialist exploitation and separation, such a contrast is in fact concretely revealed in *My Place*. Not as a cliché or as an ideological position, but as a deeply lived experience, Aboriginality in *My Place* manifests itself as an awareness of interconnection and mutuality that gives the self life only through love for the other. Self and other are in constant interchange in Aboriginal consciousness, creating an ongoing experience of community that challenges and overcomes the separations enforced by white patriarchal imperialism.

The fact that Sally's mothers keep alive this Aboriginal spirit is something of a paradox, a transgression of Aboriginal norms. Answering an interviewer who wondered about the strong presences of women in the text, Gladys asserts, "It's a bit of an Aboriginal trait, because when you look at any family, there's always the mother and grandmother there" (Wright, 100). Similarly, Sally claims, "It's a matriarchal society, and also, from what we can see going back, all the women in our family have been strong characters in different ways" (Wright, 100). Yet C. D. Rowley has observed that although "matri-focused authority" in "part-Aboriginal" families may be "traced back to the Aboriginal culture" (328), matriarchy was not clearly a feature of precontact Aboriginal society. While some tribes are matrilineal, "in Aboriginal society things pertaining to the flesh were assumed to come to the individual from the mother and through her; . . . the things of the spirit came through the father, whose responsibility it was to maintain the sacred ties with the country and the ancestral spirits" (163). In the absence of Aboriginal fathers, the mothers in Sally Morgan's family work to preserve the spiritual legacy of Aboriginality. These mothers allow the white fathers to govern "things pertaining to the flesh," while they maintain the more highly valued "things of the spirit." In this way, whether or not matriarchy was from the first "Aboriginal," it becomes a key feature of life in postcontact Aboriginal families. It is a matriarchy of the spirit, grounded in a life-saving denial of the flesh.

In coming to claim and to articulate both her Aboriginal flesh and her Aboriginal spirit, the well-mothered daughter reunites them, healing the wound administered by a white Australian policy of genocide. As she discovers and heals her self, Sally also accomplishes the healing of her mother and grandmother—even her great-grandmother. For while Gladys and Daisy strenuously resist Sally's efforts to learn the "secret" of their Aboriginal flesh, in the end they are each grateful for her efforts. Sally's quest allows both of them to own and acknowledge the parts of themselves they have denied. Nan admits that she thinks Sally is doing the right thing by recovering Aboriginal ties. Similarly Gladys confesses, when Sally's obsession to know the truth brings her back to meet her "mob" (the members of her family and tribal group who have remained on or near their original land): "To think I nearly missed all this. All my life, I've only been half a person. I don't think I really realised how much of me was missing until I came North. Thank God you're stubborn, Sally" (233).

During the same trip, Sally has a dream in which she sees Annie (her great-grandmother), Lilly (her great-aunt), Old Fanny (her great-great-grandmother), and Rosie (another great-aunt, who had died as a child). When Sally sees her mother the next morning, Gladys tells her that in the night she saw her standing with a group of Aboriginal women. Overwhelmed and in tears, Sally responds that their foremothers are happy. The implication is that Sally's quest and the family's return to the North have brought peace to their female Aboriginal ancestors.

In its demonstration of such a profound, ongoing reciprocity between mothers and daughters, speakers and listeners, givers and receivers, Morgan's text embodies what Sidonie Smith has called "a new kind of language and narrative form, perhaps even a new discourse" that "decenters all centerers and effectively subverts the patriarchal order itself" (59). To Smith's emphasis on the subversion of patriarchy, one must add the subversion of racism and colonialism, which join with patriarchy in Australia to create the devastating conditions of Aboriginal lives. *My Place* challenges not only the patriarchal order, but the racist and colonialist orders as well. Its "new discourse" is in fact something quite old, an expression of the Aboriginality repressed but not destroyed by a patriarchal, racist, colonialist society. Arthur Corunna, a healer, explains that his "power" to heal comes from above and that "you can't cure yourself. You got to use that power to help others" (213). Thus the autobiographical narratives in *My Place* must serve, not the autobiographer, but the audiences who listen and are healed by the stories. Sally proves her Aboriginality by healing her mother and grandmother and by effecting a healing in her readers. For the self Sally uncovers and records, in her own life as well as in the lives of her mothers, is a self constituted in community, a self whose power consists in giving power to others, a self that circulates in time—in other words, a "mother."

Although it steadily moves toward and concludes with an affirmation of Aboriginality and maternity, *My Place* begins with Sally Morgan's experience of her white father, Bill Gilroy. From the very first page, the world inhabited by this father, an alcoholic and violent war veteran who made only occasional appearances in their lives, is contrasted with the more stable and nurturing world of Nan and Mum. "Dad" in the first chapter is in the hospital, a place that Sally recalls as dust-free and newly polished. Here Sally feels herself to be "a grubby five-year old in an alien environment" void of "magic" (11). Sally associates magic with her mother's rainbow cakes, decorated with a swirl of pink and white chocolate, similar to, but significantly different from, the swirl of white in the hospital's green linoleum-covered doors.

The note of magic struck in those opening paragraphs is echoed a few pages later when Sally reports a reverie into which she drifts while sitting on the hospital verandah. She recalls how, just the day before, Nan had awakened her before dawn, to hear a special bird heard by no one but Nan. Cold, sleepy, but excited, Sally sat on the back steps, impatiently waiting. She remembers the awe she experienced when suddenly she heard the high trilling call of the bird. The magical music of Nan's special bird brought tremendous joy and energy to Sally. Looking back at that moment, she calls it "magical" and then laments the lack of magic in her father's shiny hospital room. In these two scenes, the opening chapter immediately establishes a highly charged, magical intimacy between Sally and her mother and grandmother, contrasting it with the more awkward and chilling relationship with her father.

In the second chapter, the alien worlds of Dad and the hospital are extended to the school Sally enters at age six. Like the hospital, school is a place without magic, without spirit. At school, which she calls the factory or the army, Sally quickly experiences herself as different from the other children, once again a "grubby offender" (26). In one embarrassing incident, she is publicly humiliated when she wets herself after a long struggle to get the teacher's attention. The teacher calls Sally a dirty girl and sends her out of the room, justifying Sally's description of the other children as "the spick and span brigade" (26). On another occasion, when asked to draw a picture of her parents, she does not realize until too late, amid the snickers of her classmates and the reprimand of her teacher, that she was supposed to draw them with their clothes on.

On a more positive note, Sally observes a difference in how she and her peers experience family life. While all the other children have their own beds, Sally regularly sleeps with her brother Billy and sister Jill;

sometimes both Nan and her brother David join them. Sally is afraid to tell her classmates about the times five of them share a bed, yet she considers the other students disadvantaged because of their apparent lack of family closeness. Even more significantly, she finds her classmates' attitudes to their brothers and sisters hard to understand. Sally explains that she and her sister and brother sought each other out at every opportunity on the playground at school and that they savored those contacts. Her classmates, on the other hand, seemed not to like their siblings. In her childhood sense of family, Sally demonstrates an "Aboriginal trait," though with no consciousness of its source or any sense of racial difference.

The children at school, however, have picked up something, and they challenge Sally's claim to being Australian. Sally turns to her mother, who works to deflect the question. When Sally's mother asks what her classmates think she is, she blurts out that they suspect she is Italian, Greek, or Indian. Her mother avoids telling the truth and instructs Sally to tell her classmates that she is Indian, thus silencing her for the moment and appeasing the children who suspect that Sally and her siblings are not Aussies. From that day, when she is six or seven, until she is fifteen, Sally believes herself to be Indian.

Sally's relationships with Mum and Nan—in contrast with her experience of Dad and the outside world—are characterized by indulgence, love, play, and security. When Dad is in the hospital, Mum and Nan take special steps to make home a happy place. After Dad commits suicide when Sally is nine, she notes that fear leaves them. Sally makes her mother vow faithfully never to marry again, and Mum takes three part-time jobs in order to provide for her five children and for Nan, who cooks, cleans, washes, irons, and mends, along with chopping the wood and tending the garden. Sally remembers the family sleeping in rough beds on the floor of the lounge-room, watching TV in front of a fire until the broadcast ended. She recalls the security and closeness she felt as the family told stories, laughed, and sang around an open fire. The Gilroy family, in a rented government house in a suburb of Perth, reproduces the Aboriginal lives of their ancestors in the bush.

Among the more striking features of the household is laughter: the children laugh constantly; Mum is often in a fit of giggles; even when Sally plays practical jokes on her, Mum somehow manages to see the humor of the situation. Above all, Mum is indulgent with Sally and the other children. After Bill's death, the house is filled with pets of all varieties, except wild creatures from the bush. And although Mum always insists that she will not tolerate any more, she inevitably succumbs to Sally's pleas about a dog, a sick bird, a stray cat. Deeply spiritual—with an ecumenical sort of faith—Mum takes the children to every religious meeting imaginable: Roman Catholic, Baptist, Anglican, Church of Christ, and Seventh Day Adventist. She asks the children to say the Lord's Prayer each night, but when Sally resists Mum simply sighs and tells her that perhaps she'll feel like it the next night. When Mum begins to make more money, her indulgence takes the form of unlimited candy and fruit.

Nan, too, indulges Sally. When Sally develops an aversion to school and learns to feign illness, Nan takes her side and says she must stay home—then allows her to play in the yard. Mum, who is not fooled by the deception, nevertheless goes along with it. At one point, Mum even encourages Sally to play hooky from school, taking her to a sale and lying to the school's head about the absence. Yet a conflict emerges over the importance of schooling; Sally dreams of becoming an artist and going to study in Paris. Her mother insists that she finish secondary school and attend college, so that she might become a doctor or a vet. Though Gladys is herself deeply distrustful of institutions and sympathetic to her daughter's resistance to regimentation, she wants her to have a secure job. Nan, typically, tells Gladys to take it easy on the child.

Yet Nan, in her distrust of outsiders and her commitment to alternative customs, often puzzles and frustrates Sally. In her final year at primary school, Sally notices that whenever the children bring their friends home to play after school Nan disappears. One afternoon, Sally walks with a friend into the kitchen—Nan's domain, from which the children were excluded—to find her making tea. Later, Nan chastises Sally for inviting her friends into their home. She explains that Sally's friends are never to see how they live because they will become the objects of ridicule. Sally acquiesces to Nan's request, though she is puzzled by it—as she is by Nan's behavior toward animals and plants. One day, Sally surprises Nan in the yard, tapping trees and placing her ear against them as though listening for something. When Sally asks what she is doing, Nan accuses her of spying and says that she was just checking on "them" to make sure that they were all right. She silences Sally by telling her that she has work to do. Sally, while confused, dismisses the mystery and says that there was much about Nan she did not understand.

Although for the most part Sally accepts Nan, she resists her imposition of the "Old Cures"—pepper as a treatment for wounds, kerosene to remove aches and pains, onions as an antiseptic. It is regarding the molding onions that, at fourteen, Sally has her first major disagreement with her grandmother. Sally is repulsed by the onions strewn around the house, noting that her friends' rooms don't stink the way hers does, and insists that there are to be no more onions. Mum tactfully tries to settle the fight, suggesting that Nan keep the onions out of Sally's room, though they soon reappear. Sally rants and raves, and the noisy conflict continues until Gladys purchases a spray product called Medic. Nan remarks that the spray seems to have some of the old cures in it and that she can feel it clearing her lungs. Sally reports that from that point on her room smelled of Medic.

Without revealing the secret of her Aboriginality, the opening chapters of *My Place* thus establish Sally's experience of difference as a child: difference between the world of her mothers and that of her father and difference between her family and the world of her friends and outside institutions. While she is growing up, Sally doesn't understand the nature or reason for that difference, nor, as she narrates her childhood, does she explicitly indicate that her father is more closely related to the outer world than are her mother and grandmother. Yet she offers enough details about the conflict between her father and mother/grandmother to account for her ultimate choice of her mothers' world; and she also provides a few hints of the nature of her father's difference. Dryly describing the family's visits to her paternal grandparents after her father's death, she notes that they would never allow the children into the house, because they seemed to worry about the heritage that came to the children from Daisy. And in the stories she narrates about her father's violence, she offers a parable of the relations between white men and black women in Australia.

Whenever her father had "bad fits," the family would seek refuge in a neighbor's house. Dad would yell abuse at his wife, mother-in-law, and children, while Sally, the eldest, would be sent forth to negotiate with him. Often Bill would agree to take his family back if Nan would promise not to return. Bill's hostility to Nan is not explained at this point in the narrative—Sally simply reports that he had a thing about Nanna—though later Nanna herself confesses: "'When Gladdie wasn't around, Bill used to call me a bloody nigger. . . . No one should call anyone a bloody nigger. I kept quiet 'bout that 'cause I didn't want to cause trouble, but it hurt me real bad to hear him say that'" (347). At the young age of seven or eight, Sally instinctively resists her father, not consciously aware of the racial dynamics at work. She insists that her mother would not agree, that Nan would have no place to go.

Still her father would press forward in his attack on Sally—and, ultimately, on Aboriginality—offering potato chips, her favorite treat, if she agreed to his terms: "Reaching behind his back and down the side of his bed, he pulled out three unopened packets of potato chips. Slowly, he placed them one by one in my lap. I could feel the pointed corner of one pack sticking through the cotton of my thin summer dress and into my thigh. Suddenly my mouth was full of water. 'You can have them all,' he said quietly, 'if . . . you stay with me'" (42) In this not-so-subtle temptation scene, Dad, the white man, asks Sally to abandon her dark grandmother and mother, echoing the scenes of sexual violation and separation of mothers from children that lie in the women's pasts.

As a child, Sally refuses the advances of her white father, though not without struggle. Later, when presented with a similar choice as an adult, Sally again experiences conflict, though now she is aware both of the stakes and of the real terms, and she makes her choice with greater assurance. The year is 1973, seven years after Sally first learns of her grandmother's "blackness" and hence her own (potential) Aboriginality. The journey to the final moment of choice had been long and arduous. One day, coming home from school, the fifteen-year old Sally had been astonished to discover Nan, crying as she sat at the kitchen table:

> "You bloody kids don't want me, you want a bloody white grandmother. I'm black. Do you hear, black, black, black!"
>
> For the first time in my fifteen years, I was conscious of Nan's colouring. She was right, she wasn't white. (97)

Stunned by this revelation, Sally asks her younger sister if she knew that Nan was black. Jill tells her of course she did and asserts that it is terrible to be Aboriginal.

Sally resists Jill's analysis, seeking an answer directly from Nan or Mum and entering a new phase in her relationship with her mother. She relentlessly pesters her mother, who skillfully dodges the questions about Nan's past. When Sally corners Nan, she discovers her intolerance for such questions. Nan's short fuse only makes Sally more determined. Mum finally orders her not to bother Nan, and Sally is left to puzzle through the meaning of Nan's blackness, confused by the consistent denials of both women. At one point, she questions Nan's habit of buttering up the rentmen, explaining to her that they do not need to worry about being evicted. Nan responds bitterly, telling Sally that she does not know what it's like for "people like us" (105). She likens her people to Jews, who are unjustly persecuted but who continue to survive. Yet Nan refuses to answer questions about the past and the identity of her people, and Sally remains confused by her grandmother's comparison of them to Jews.

For six years, Sally gropes for answers until one day, in a moment of inattention, Gladys admits the truth. Sally is by this time married, a student in psychology at the university, living with her husband and her sister Jill in a small house in South Perth. Mum has come over for her daily visit, and she and Sally are in the kitchen drinking tea. When Mum is in a relaxed and talkative mood, Sally very casually asks if they are Aboriginals. Her mother tells her they are before she realizes what she's saying. Though her mother tries to take back her acknowledgment, Sally challenges her to tell the truth. Once the truth is out, the wall between mother and daughter crumbles and the two women move closer to one another. Sally then applies for and receives an Aboriginal scholarship, even though the Repatriation scholarship granted to children of war veterans paid more than enough for her schooling.

A crisis develops when an anonymous classmate complains to the school authorities that Sally has obtained the Aboriginal scholarship under false pretenses. Called into the office, Sally is astonished by the accusation and becomes fiercely angry, refusing to bring forth any proofs. Although Sally's anger convinces the school official of her authenticity as an Aboriginal, Sally is shaken by the experience and begins to question herself, asking if she's been dishonest. She wonders what claims she can make to Aboriginality, given that she has never lived off the land as a hunter-gatherer. Nor has she participated in *corroborees* or heard stories of the Dreamtime. She admits that she hardly knew any Aboriginal people and that she had told everyone she was Indian. About ready to give up her claim to Aboriginality, Sally suddenly has a vision. While riding the bus home, she sees Nan standing in front of her, looking at her, and she begins to speak with her. Sally views this appearance as a sign that Nan wants her to retain the scholarship that links her to Aboriginality and to Nan. So Sally chooses to stay on her course in order to care for Nan, simultaneously discovering and affirming her Aboriginal spirit, her commitment to helping others with the power she has been given. Here Sally Morgan makes plain the nature of Aboriginality: a granddaughter's love for her grandmother—the same love she had expressed as a child when she resisted her father's desire to separate her from both Nan and Mum.

For while Nan had originally been singularly unimpressed with Sally's decision to apply for the Aboriginal scholarship, Mum and Sally had noticed a change in her during the year preceding the anonymous challenge. Nan began to take an interest in news about black people. At that time her favorite word became "Nyoongah," the name of the Aboriginal people of southwest Australia: "To Nan, anyone dark was now Nyoongah. Africans, Burmese, American Negroes were all Nyoongahs. She identified with them. In a sense, they were her people, because they shared the common bond of blackness and the oppression that, for so long, that colour had brought. It was only a small change, but it was a beginning" (138). Sally's life acquires a "new purpose," as she begins to hope that her identification as an Aboriginal will enable Nan to embrace her own identity as well. But even as she begins to express her affinity with other blacks, Nan continues to thwart Sally's efforts to learn more about her past. She does not tell her own story until 1983, a full seventeen years after her first outburst about being black.

In 1978, stimulated by the visits of Arthur, Nan's brother, who is not at all ashamed to admit that he is a "blackfella," Sally decides to write a book about the family. Mum supports her project, but Nan maintains that she will not share her secrets with others. To Arthur's claim that history needs to be rectified she responds with silence and anger. Sally pushes forward in her stubborn way, eventually eliciting stories from both Arthur and her mother. In the course of hearing these stories she finally comes to understand why Nan has been so reticent and develops an even deeper, ultimately healing compassion for her grandmother.

From Arthur, Sally first learns about the government policy of taking children away. Describing life at Corunna Downs, the "station" in the North owned by Alfred Howden Drake-Brockman, Arthur explains that all the people around there belonged to each other and were the tribe that made the station. But because Arthur is a "half-caste," born to the pure-blooded Annie Padewani and the white station owner, he is taken away at the age of eleven, purportedly to be educated. Arthur painfully recalls clinging to his mother while being ripped from her grasp. He never sees her again. Arthur's shattering experience of separation from the mother who was always good to him is not singular: it is an experience repeated in the lives of Daisy and Gladys. Yet while Arthur is taken away from his mother, he does not have his own children taken from him. Certainly he feels the pain of separation; but for Daisy and Gladys, the pain reverberates in multiple dimensions. This is why they find it more difficult to speak.

When Daisy decides to tell her story shortly before her death, the brutal separation of mother and child is at its core. As she says, "In those days, it was considered a privilege for a white man to want you, but if you had children, you weren't allowed to keep them. You was only allowed to keep the black ones. They took the white ones off you 'cause you weren't considered fit to raise a child with white blood" (336). She describes being taken from Annie when she was fourteen:

> When I left, I was cryin', all the people were cryin', my mother was cryin' and beatin' her head. Lily [her sister] was cryin'. I called, "Mum, Mum, Mum!" She said, "Don't forget me, Talahue [Daisy's Aboriginal name]!"
>
> They all thought I was coming back. I thought I'd only be gone a little while. I could hear their wailing for miles and miles. "Talahue! Talahue!" They were singin' out my name, over and over. I couldn't stop cryin'. I kept callin', "Mum! Mum!" (332)

She remembers when her own child, Gladys, was taken away. She recalls the pain and fear in the face of Gladys, who believed she was coming back. She tells of how she emptied her soul of tears for a child forcibly taken away from her. But even as she weeps for Gladys, she remembers and identifies with her own mother's pain: "She was broken-hearted, God bless her" (341).

Still more devastating than the separations she narrates is the unspeakable secret Nan refuses to tell fully: about a child she had before Gladys was born who was taken away from her in infancy, a child she has not seen since, but for whom she still suffers. She tells Sally that there are some things she just can't talk about.

The separations that have rent the lives of Gladys, Daisy, Arthur, and Annie threaten to reappear in the lives of Sally and her siblings. Gladys explains that she never left her abusive husband because he threatened to take the children away from her. The laws were on his side—Aboriginal women were not allowed to keep children fathered by a white man. Gladys sacrifices her peace and happiness in order to be able to remain with her children. When Bill dies, the fear is intensified, for Gladys and Nan believe that a government official might come and take the children away. After the visit of one welfare lady who becomes furious when she sees the family's sleeping arrangements, Gladys and Nan decide never to tell the children they are Aboriginal. Thus Mum tries to pass and Nan stays out of the way, her pain only erupting in moments such as the incident when she cries in the kitchen.

Yet the fear and pain of the mothers is never gone. On the first day of school, Sally's mother desperately abandons her to "The Factory." Sally's screams for her mother remind Gladys of her own forced separation from her mother. Like the women before her, Sally is terrified by this sudden wrenching from her mother; although Gladys knows that at the end of the day she will be able to retrieve her daughter, the ancestral fear recurs for her as well. Years later, when Sally wants to live in a boardinghouse near her college, Mum is horrified by the idea. After weeks of tearful arguments, she allows Sally to go and then embarks on frequent visits, always leaving in tears.

When Sally is separated from her mother at the ages of six and twenty, she does not know the family history—the secret of Aboriginal flesh and the wound to that flesh—that has shaped the lives of her mother and grandmother. Yet in her narration of her own experience—and in her quiet juxtaposition of that experience with those of her mother and grandmother—she demonstrates that the life of the Aboriginal mother is reproduced in the consciousness of the Aboriginal daughter. History is not past, for it shapes the lives of Aboriginal families in modern Australia, even after the abolition of black slavery and after the repeal of the law that mandated that "half-caste" children be taken away. The pain of mother-child separation reverberates throughout *My Place*, repeated in scene after scene; it is the wound Sally's story must both open and heal; it is the primal experience that underlies the existential and narrative emphasis on maternity.

In the final pages of the book, after yet another devastating "opening," the wound is at last healed, through Sally's care for Nan and Nan's acceptance of that care. Nan is ill with lung cancer and has spent a few days in the hospital, where she finds herself being treated like an animal. Nan tells of the countless doctors who thumped on her chest without regarding her as a human being. While she lay naked, they entered and exited her room without a kind word. Nan is certain that the doctors treated her with such callousness because she is black. Horrified, angry, feeling Nan's pain, the family decides that she will not go back to the hospital; she moves in with Sally and, among her great-grandchildren, tells her story into Sally's tape-recorder.

During these last days, Nan teaches her great-grandchildren words in her native tongue, letting down her guard about the old language. Every night, Sally's daughter Amber reads Nan a bedtime story about Aboriginal children in the Western Desert. Nan listens happily; when Amber finishes reading, Nan tells about her own childhood. Sally notices that as Nan speaks her language changes: she seems to be back there, reliving everything.

As Nan approaches her death, Sally gets closer and closer to her, caring for her intimately, in a repetition of the healing Nan performed when Sally had rheumatic fever. One night as Sally massages her grandmother with Vaseline, Nan smiles with delight and tells her that it feels good to be touched with tenderness. She admits to Sally that all of her life she has been treated like a beast of the field. Nan tells Sally that she can't help but feel like a dirty old "blackfella." Sally, feeling her heart breaking, begs her grandmother not to talk about herself like that. She tries to comfort Nan by telling her that the whole family loves her and would do anything for her.

The day before she dies, Daisy hears the Aboriginal bird, the same bird she had introduced Sally to as a child. She tells Sally that God sent him to tell her that she's going home soon, home to her own land and her own people, where they all will be waiting for her. The reader recognizes that Nan can at last go home because Sally, her granddaughter, has mothered her. For all the elder women's efforts to hide their blackness and their pain, Mum and Nan have nevertheless maintained and nurtured within Sally an Aboriginal spirit. And it is this Aboriginal spirit, the "power" passed on to her, that ultimately enables Sally to bring Aboriginal wholeness to her mother and grandmother. It is a wholeness she herself has achieved. After Nan's death, Sally too hears the bird call, "'Around and around': 'Oh, Nan,' I cried with sudden certainty. 'I heard it, too. In my heart, I heard it'" (358).

My Place's greatest meaning and impact emerges through close consideration of the Aboriginal/Australian context in which it takes shape. Yet many readers, Aboriginal or not, can hear the Aboriginal bird call, recognizing in it the voices of mothers and daughters working to hold fast to one another in a world that would pull them apart. In finding and claiming her place, Sally Morgan gives power to others who would make the same quest.

Works Cited

Gilligan, Carol. *In a Different Voice: Psychological Theory and Women's Development.* Cambridge: Harvard University Press, 1982.

Healy, J. J. "'The True Life in Our History': Aboriginal Literature in Australia." *Antipodes* 2, no. 2 (Winter 1988): 79–85.

Morgan, Sally. *My Place.* New York: Little Brown, 1990.

Rowley, C. D. *Outcasts in White Australia.* Canberra: Australian National University Press, 1971.

Smith, Sidonie. *A Poetics of Women's Autobiography: Marginality and the Fictions of Self-Representation.* Bloomington: Indiana University Press, 1987.

Trinh, T. Minh-ha. *Woman, Native, Other: Writing Postcoloniality and Feminism.* Bloomington and Indianapolis: Indiana University Press, 1989.

Wright, Mary. "A Fundamental Question of Identity: An Interview with Sally Morgan." *Kunapipi* 10, nos. 1–2 (1988): 92–128.

"My mother is here"

Buchi Emecheta's Love Child

PATRICIA LEE YONGUE

As a native African writer of the colonial and postcolonial eras, who has chosen to make her home and her living and raise her five children (three daughters and two sons) in England, Buchi Emecheta certainly attends to the pejorative processes of assimilation and dehistoricization at work among African communities in their native environs and in the West. She is fiercely loyal to the land, people, and historicity of her native Africa and to many of its traditions. Perhaps she is never so much so as in her narrative preservation of the stories (especially those told by women), tribal traditions, and ancestral and historical background of her people.

Emecheta is also fiercely feminist. As a woman, a mother, and a sociologist, she advances insightful perspectives on social and political realities, their origin, and change that are different from those of most male African writers who write in English and of the literary and cultural critics who still routinely ignore her—and the subjectivity as well as historicity of most of the women of Africa. Although she is an outspoken critic of imperialism, Emecheta refuses to sentimentalize tribal culture, to depict precolonial Africa, simplistically, as an Eden ransacked by Western imperialism; for a significant part of the told and untold history and story of tribal Africa is the oppression of women. One old Ibuza man's story of his life contains it all: "My first wife ran away . . . because I beat her up. My second wife died when she was having a child. My third one had to go, because I fed her for seven years and she bore me no child" (*BP*, 111).

Throughout her fiction—*The Bride Price* (1976), *The Joys of Motherhood* (1979), and *The Family* (1989) are treated here—Emecheta continually juxtaposes, with cynical irony, the natural developmental, transformative processes represented by and occurring within the womanly body with the transmogrifying procedures of both indigenous and imposed patriarchy. One of her favorite strategies is the decoding or rewriting of patriarchal myth and literature, whether tribal or Western, to disclose their own antifeminist strategies. She emphasizes the mother-daughter relationship as a particular target of sadistic patriarchal assault, for dividing mother from daughter severs woman from herself. One self becomes the man's woman and serves him obsequiously, as, say, Ariel, released from the cloven pine, serves Prospero in Shakespeare's *The Tempest*; the Other self, the complex unspeakable, unspeaking core of her womanhood that truly cares for itself, is imprisoned in its very repression and thus, according to the Kristevan thinking Emecheta often emulates, in the discourse of the Father. The one disperses and keeps at bay the man's enemies; the other goes mad, as young Aku-nna Odia in *The Bride Price* nearly does, from want of wholeness and her own speech. Both selves are primed and ironically unify to attack the daughter (or daughter surrogate): the one angrily to protect its own objectification; and the Other to cannibalize itself. The detachment within and without kills the woman (sometimes literally) and allows patriarchy to continue its killing and thus its tyranny over woman's body, which is host of man's discourse.

On the day that Aku-nna can no longer conceal from her mother the beginning of her menstruation—on what, according to Igbo tradition, should have been the happiest day of her life—she can no longer conceal from herself the underlying truth about women in her patriarchal, polygynous culture. All of the history and tradition of her sex that she has learned through "preoccupying" stories and admonitions, which gave even the admonitions glamor, is obliterated for Aku-nna by the immediacy into which that history and tradition converge. The lore, like the law, inscribes her own lack, her want of a say. Both have modified her behavior into that of an object. Her mother, long since objectified, ironically becomes the agent of that conversion.

A woman, as Aku-nna discovers on the official day of her womanhood, is merely commodity. In fact, the celebration of a Nigerian girl's coming of age is, depending on her marketability, one more celebration of a man's accession to wealth and prominence and of the mother's fulfillment of her responsibility to her husband. The very least a mother who has produced a daughter can do is to make the girl fit enough to obtain a healthy bride price and, optimally, a title for the father. Women who have many daughters console and congratulate themselves in terms of the expensive bride prices these daughters might bring. It comes as no surprise, then, that the name Aku-nna means "father's wealth" (10).

A woman's body is the only value she retains—chiefly in the hopes that it will bear sons whom it can then cook for and otherwise cater to, as it does for the adult men in her family—and that value works only in the economic and political interest of its current owner: in Aku-nna's Igbo community, the woman's father, his inheritor (through primogeniture), or her husband. All of its life, too, that body accommodates this hierarchy of men. Aku-nna's mother teaches her, for example, that "no woman should carry her father's glories to her husband's house. As soon as a good woman was married, she must learn to exult in her husband's accomplishments, however small they might seem in comparison with her father's" (125). Ma Blackie also teaches Aku-nna, and "loudly," that all her joy, especially any she receives from the difference of her own body, depends on and exists in terms of man; he is the "author" of woman's happiness (111).

Like the staple of the Nigerian diet, the yam, which females of a household spend many hours of their lives pounding vigorously into meals for their families, the woman is pounded by culture into a distortion of her womanly and differentiated self and, like the yam, ironically, becomes an inadequate source of nourishment for herself and her family. In the ordinary Nigerian household, it is, of course, the mother who teaches the skill of yam pounding to her daughters; so, in Emecheta's continuing irony, it is the mother who grooms daughters for this other substantive truth. She instructs her daughters how to pound themselves into a smooth pap, their bodies—and the feminine principle embodied—served up to and devoured by patriarchy (the psyche cannibalizing itself), so that in the dissolution of woman's difference the community starves. Its behavior becomes desperate.

Aku-nna Odia has, of course, been learning all along that the female body exists, menially and meagerly, to serve; when it is young, it does housework and defers its own nutritional needs to those of the father, brothers, and uncles. If it receives any particular care at all before it is married (always deemed indulgence, as Aku-nna is interminably reminded, even by her mother), this is due to the owner's awareness that it will be a unit of exchange, so that he needs to augment or at least maintain its economic value.[1] At the onset of menstruation, depending on its condition and the class of its family, it is capable of securing the promised bride price for its owner—in Aku-nna's case her deceased father's brother, Okonkwo Odia, who by his right as Ezekiel Odia's inheritor has taken Ma Blackie as his fourth wife. Because Aku-nna is not a son and in her culture therefore is thought to be a product of the mother's bodily weakness and/or the parents' passion (love is feminized into a weakness, as Emecheta explains in *The Joys of Motherhood*), she has until this day bided her time in relative obscurity. Now men and families owned by men will compete formally to possess her body. She has no say in this matter; no one, especially her mother, will listen. For this she should be happy!

Aku-nna's "predicament" is earlier antithesized for her one day, as she is crying her eyes out in the throes of first love, hidden at "the foot of an orange tree at the far end of the school field." "Encapsulated" by orange trees, she becomes privy to a natural ritual of life going on in a community above, where there is a weaving of difference into a home, rather than an exclusion of difference according to hierarchical and binary valuation: "The nest in the tree very near to where she was sitting was being built by two birds; sweethearts, perhaps. Their happiness, their ability to communicate so intimately with one another, brought home to her more vividly her predicament" (89). Instead of being on the verge of making a happy home and family, Aku-nna must wait quietly as one of her family's nest eggs.

Like Nancy Chodorow in America and Julia Kristeva and Luce Irigaray in Europe, Emecheta responds to patriarchy's psychic and societal repression of women as the reign of the phallic order which disconnects woman from her maternal being, except to serve the basic reproductive needs of the culture and economic and narcissistic needs of the male. This severance, conducted through the mother-daughter relationship, empowers an ideology of valuation of the separate, the fixed, and the permanent as opposed to flow, change, and continuance, the global modality to which the maternal body, inclusive of male and female substance, commits "from time immemorial." Ironically, perhaps, but logically, the severance of mother from daughter that becomes cultural practice is the internal factor that also promotes the disconnection of colonialized and Christianized Africans from their native (mother) culture, just as Africans themselves have been converted into commodity at the paying hand of British imperialism.

Playing with the myths of the Christian tradition (which she sees as but a troublesome exchange of one set of patriarchal superstitions for another, whose methodology is purely behavior modification), Emecheta intimates in *The Bride Price* that the menstrual stream originating in the mother and continuing in the daughter is like the biblical Red Sea, stanched and divided by patriarchal fiat—"lift up thou thy rod, and stretch out thine hand over the sea" (Exodus 14:16)—to insure the autonomy of the masculine against the feminine desire for connectedness and wholeness. During her menstruation, in fact, when a woman is "considered unclean" to the point of being unfit to enter "the household where the man of the family had either the '*Eze*' or '*Alo*' title," it is also "taboo to go to the stream" (*BP*, 93, 95). However, Nna-nndo, Aku-nna's brother, can blithely take out his fishing rod and go down to the stream anytime he chooses, as he does in a fit of pique over an empty water jar. In the abnormal separation of mother and daughter, in the distortion of maternity from process into production, there is dry ground, as there is for the Israelites walking in the midst of the sea—but it is a space that promises the sustained dehydration of the culture, as if it were a collective *ogbanje* (living dead), rather than its access to fertility.[2] The "rod that smoteth the river" has also struck itself a blow, and only reabsorption of the feminine can mitigate the violence.

According to Kristeva, misogyny or antifeminism not only endorses but also predicts and provides the model for racism and imperialism. The original fear and resentment of one's own otherness (separateness from the maternal body) that has been projected onto and objectified (pre-Oedipally) in the female, while the concurrent delight in one's individuality is retained, results in the societal practice of feminization and abjection of the Other.[3] The paradigms driving the economies and epistemologies of patriarchal cultures construct unity in one fixed way, by allowing that only masculine paradigms govern, and thus continue to advocate constructs of separatism and friction, consigning unity (permanence and fixedness) to the realm of the desirable but unattainable ideal. Constructions of deity, whether monotheistic or pantheistic, clinch the rule of the phallic; evil is usually constructed as emerging from or inhabiting the body, a mimicry of the maternal body, particularly one carrying a daughter. In Igbo culture, a woman, especially one who has not produced a live son and/or who has produced only daughters, does not achieve complete womanhood until her husband releases her from her enfeebled (or dangerously near evil) state by impregnating her with a son (*JM*, 53). A mother looks at her daughter partly as a reflection or sign of her own incompleteness.

Hence, if she is acutely responsive to the consequences of Western invasiveness, racism, and domination—"if you did not want trouble for yourself or your family, you abided by the laws of the white man" (*BP*, 87)—Emecheta nonetheless emphasizes that imperialism is historically no stranger to African behavior, for it is the law of the Father. In a very patent irony, the patriarchal dispositions of the Western world (later of the Muslim) have bonded, almost like a chemical process, with those already indigenous to African culture to intensify repression and thus the oppression of woman and the principle of the feminine, of the unified and continuously unifying self. Men "kill, rape and disgrace women and children, all in the name of the white man's money" (*JM*, 88). That "dark continent" that Freud imperialistically located in the womb (to "explain" what he did not understand about the sexuality of the female), which has subsequently become a metaphor used by the West to represent and feminize "primitive" Africa and the "condition of negritude," is not entirely discarded as an "imperialist trope" (Andrade, 92) but seems understood by Emecheta in the way Hélène Cixous understands it: as that repressed desire of and for the feminine (the wholeness of difference) which the maternal body inscribes.

Emecheta accepts the shared reality of antifeminism and seems, again like Kristeva and Irigaray, to understand its source in the complexity of human male and female difference. She writes oppositionally to those feminists and other cultural and postmodernist critics who seek adamantly to downplay, even to try to disgrace (in simplistic reductions that cooperate with patriarchy), the significance and signifying capacity of the woman's maternal body as both a physical and psychic source of the origination and sustenance of difference, transformation, and communion. Wherever it is appropriate, Emecheta counteracts such metonymic male-authored "lyrics" as those about "girls with mosquito legs, girls with breasts like pumpkins, girls with hair on their chests" (*BP*, 60) with lyrical metaphors of the maternal body, grounded in nature. At every opportunity, she emphasizes the significant breach between mother and daughter that needs to be healed. In *The Bride Price*, Aku-nna, who gets precious little nurturing from her mother, sighs at feeling the soft warmth of the late day sun, so different from the "fiery heat" of the afternoon: "its rays were gentle, caressing, like the touch of a tender mother" (26). Emecheta's celebration of the mother and the maternal body counteracts Aku-nna's dismal experience. This is feminine writing and feminism in its most radical expression (see Palmer).

African women, like women everywhere, have always had to deal with the fact that their bodies signify and are a means of male imperialist expansion. In a perversion, similar to the Western one, of a connection which Emecheta, like Kristeva and Irigaray, believes exists between the maternal body and the earth, women's bodies are territories and become "goods" which must produce other "goods" for the ruler. But insofar as they have lived in a polygynous culture, African women have been uniquely colonized.

Once sons are born, they leave the orbit of woman. As children, it is true, they are somewhat commodified. But they also accrue immediate privilege, such as greater access to food and water and approving words, than their mothers and sisters have. Consequently, each wife and her daughters unofficially compose a chattel unit dictated to by the husband but left to compete with other units and sometimes within their own unit for privileges and even sustenance. The wives' production of sons becomes the chief way of winning, of daughters the way of losing.

In *The Joys of Motherhood*—a novel elucidating tribal women's obsession with bearing sons, whose rights, as Nnu Ego is well aware, will allow them to starve their mothers and their sisters into anemia—a most poignant scene occurs at the birth of one of Nnu Ego's daughters. This birth takes place at a time in Nnu Ego's life when it is most important to her to have a son, lest she lose her preferred place among the wives of her husband, Nnaife. Nnu Ego is near middle age and has had to work exceptionally hard and, not for the first time, to endure nutritional privation during her pregnancy. The baby is stillborn.

> Nnu Ego stared at the picture she made [lying in a pool of her blood] with her dead daughter in horror. She felt like crying, but at the same time did not want to. She felt the loss of this little piece of humanity, this unfortunate little thing she had carried while climbing up to Zabo market, this thing she knew was probably being hurt as she had bent defiantly down to wash clothes for her sons. . . . Then she

> started to feel guilty. Had she wanted the child to die—was that the interpretation of the slight relief she had experienced when she had crawled to the dead child to check what sex it was? That it was a girl had lessened her sense of loss. Oh, God, she did not wish it. She would have been happy to have the child. (194–195)

Only later is she aware (the name Nnu Ego has to be a pun) of the horror of what patriarchy has done to her—and to her daughters. Earlier, Nnu Ego had tried to kill herself when her infant son died inexplicably. Then at a peak of her competition with Adaku, a younger wife, for the favor of a frenzied Nnaife (a pun as well) Nnu Ego contrasts her passivity and Adaku's response in a way typical of the antifeminism that causes her horror in the end: "Adaku had nothing to lose except her girl child, but she, Nnu Ego, had everything to lose" (133).

Although the wives try to unite out of both emotional and political need, their commodification and competition prevent true bonding. Female friends are to be made outside the family, with the wives and widows and daughters of other men. Similarly, mothers need their daughters for help in the struggle to maintain position, but at the same time they are required to view them as antagonists or to repeat the process of commodification with their daughters' bodies. Healthy bonding between mother and daughters has been difficult, particularly for daughters whose mothers were born before education was offered to girls and who were most torn between tribal belief and practice and whatever social constructs they acquired from Christian and British systems. For Emecheta, restoration of that bonding is necessary for women—and for the health of the community.

In *The Bride Price*, Aku-nna learns on the day of her womanhood that her mother, Ma Blackie, will betray her—has been betraying her, incrementally, from the start. The flow of womanly blood from mother to daughter that should be commemorated by a sacred rite of passage and inheritance of its own and that should ensure a continuous, strong, and unifying feminine principle in the culture is forced, under the conditions of patriarchy, to turn back against itself and become the host of the family's as well as woman's disintegration. Even the biological process is threatened, as both Aku-nna and Nnu Ego in *The Joys of Motherhood* are denied food in order that men might eat. During her pregnancy, months later, Aku-nna develops severe anemia, symptomatic of the vampirism patriarchy induces in mother and fetus (which is born female): "almost as if something or other were sucking her blood" (*BP*, 161). The half-starved Nnu Ego with her stillborn daughter surrounded by a pool of maternal blood is likewise a devastating image of that destruction.

Even though cultural practice is working all along to thwart her subjectivity, Aku-nna still possesses the normal human sense of herself as subject, as a willful being with desires and needs that command attention. Retaliating against the rules, out of her natural desire to be clean, to wash herself during her menstruation, for example, she uses up the water her brother presumes is for his use. However, her lie to explain to Nna-nndo why the water in the jar is gone, a consequence of concealing her menstruation from her mother, reveals that at some level she already knows her mother is "lost" to her and will not defend her position. The lie itself, that her mother may have used up the water before she went to market (95), contains the real truth: in the course of living out the rest of her own li(f)e as a commodity, Ma Blackie has consumed her daughter's half of the water of purification and fertility. Aku-nna soon begins "to hate her mother for being so passive about it all" (116).

Aku-nna is somewhat consciously and conscientiously her father's daughter, for she resembles him physically and mentally. But, like all daughters, unconsciously she relies on her mother's loyalty to her as a source of love, certification, and identity (Chodorow), even though she realizes that by Ezekiel Odia's death she "had not only lost a father, she had also lost a mother. Ma Blackie found herself so immersed in the Okonkwo family politics, and in making ends meet, that she seldom had time to ask how the world was with her daughter" (82). This passivity toward her daughter transforms into a culturally deliberate act of betrayal. More than her father's death—which motivates the surface plot of *The Bride Price* by transplanting Aku-nna from a more to a less sensitive and sophisticated societal and paternal environment, from Lagos to Ibuza, her ancestral home—it is the discovery of maternal disloyalty which is the critical occasion for Aku-nna. In Nigerian society, this whole process is invisible—which is why Emecheta gives it visibility—because "when you have lost your father, you have lost your parents. Your mother is only a woman, and women are supposed to be boneless" (28).[4]

On the night of this same celebratory day Aku-nna also learns perhaps the most personally tragic of all truths about woman: that patriarchy has manipulated the body of her mother, whom she had always heard would be her best friend, into being her enemy. Aku-nna realizes "officially" what she has already suspected: that Ma Blackie's elation over her daughter's menses is short-term and economically induced. As Aku-nna discovers, Ma Blackie is pregnant by Okonkwo, and Aku-nna's body, translated into a bride price, will "see her through her period of confinement. She knows that Ma Blackie would let Okonkwo have his way [choosing the husband for Aku-nna] now that he had made her dream of becoming a mother once more come true" (122–123).[5] Emecheta predicts that both the biological and cultural process of menstruation will end in death rather than life, because the mother, on the word of the father, feeds her daughter on her own body. Okonkwo gives Ma Blackie "a hen that had been protesting violently in his clutch. He told Ma to kill the hen and make some hot Nsala soup for her daughter who had now grown into a woman" (115).

In Okonkwo's behalf, Ma Blackie rescinds her support of Aku-nna's growing affection for her teacher, Chike Ofulue, the son of a slave, who, despite his father's achievement of affluence, could only bring discredit upon Okonkwo's family, deprive him of a coveted title, and disrupt his future opportunities to negotiate for profit.[6] But Aku-nna still possesses the human will to resist tyranny. She also represents Emecheta, the woman writer who must resist wherever she can the unnatural, killing demands of patriarchy and compose a new text more suitable to her own individual and sexual difference. So Aku-nna refuses to eat portions of the hen killed especially for her and, in the matter of Chike, is angry that Ma Blackie does not consider her a person who should be able to make important decisions about her own life. She is also experiencing the anxiety of her imposed situation and a great deal of menstrual pain (intensified by poor nutrition), both of which dispel her appetite but compel hunger pangs for a situation society disallows her. Not only is Aku-nna considered valuable because of her body, but that body itself has no right to its own needs. The ritual must proceed, regardless of the pain.

The scene in which Ma Blackie ceases to sympathize with her daughter, or even her daughter's body which mirrors her own, and begins publicly to demand that Aku-nna submit to sexual humiliation is horrific and clear. Emecheta gives it the rhythm and ruthlessness of a tribal ritual. In fact, in these several scenes circumscribing Aku-nna's official passage into womanhood, Emecheta's stark presentation evoking the immediacy of film imposes an even more ritualistic behavior on the already ritualistic behavior of her cast.[7]

To set the stage for maternal betrayal, Okoboshi Obidi, a "foul-mouthed" classmate, has begun to harass Aku-nna. Unlike the good and handsome Chike, Okoboshi, a fair-skinned boy who walks with a limp, does not love Aku-nna; he merely lusts. Chike himself has been a predator of women, for his father "had passed on to [him] all the maleness a man could want" (105); his own transformation into a loving and sensitive young man, who helps Aku-nna through her menstruation infinitely more than her mother does, is important and is connected to his Western education and to his own experience of "Otherness" within his race. But into the repellent Okoboshi, who rebuffs schooling, Emecheta infuses the grotesqueness and lameness of patriarchy. In her characterization of him she parodies tribal ritual and myth in order to represent the foulness of patriarchal practice. Okoboshi desires Aku-nna for his wife because she is something of a prize in this world where women are chattel. She was raised in more cultivated environs than she now inhabits in Ibuza and has the well-bred manners as well as physical grace of her more privileged upbringing. Unlike the dark, muscular, and rough girls of Ibuza, who have grown used to carrying *akpu* baskets and to hearing only folk stories, Aku-nna is light-skinned, delicate—her smooth body is free of scars—and educated in white ways and language. Ironically, Okonkwo's family and Okoboshi's family resent her for these same characteristics. Her own mother resents her as well; she feels she has made many concessions for Aku-nna to get an education, but only because the education will enhance the bride price.

On the night of Aku-nna's debut into womanhood, as the prospective suitors take their place in the hut, waiting for her to enter dressed so that her breasts will tantalize them into wooing, Aku-nna is in agony, both from her menstrual cramps and from the open hostility between Chike and Okoboshi. Suddenly, Okoboshi approaches Aku-nna and seizes her roughly by her shoulder; he grabs at both her breasts and starts to squeeze and hurt her (120). Chike retaliates.

When Ma Blackie hears her daughter cry out—the cry "not of a girl having fun with her suitors but the cry of a girl in agony"—she rushes into the hut and "intervenes." However, in the instant between responding as a mother to what she knows is her daughter's pain and entering the hut to find Okoboshi on the floor, blood dripping from his mouth, an awful transformation occurs. Ma Blackie turns on her daughter. The menstrual blood, so precious to the human race and so definitive of woman, should form a special bond between mother and daughter. But it does not. Ma Blackie allies herself with Okoboshi and the few drops of blood he has shed in behalf of lust and greed. The moment is spectacular and specular.

"Mother," Aku-nna begged, "please don't say anything [to Chike]. Okoboshi was hurting me, he was. . . ."

"You mean you have nice breasts and don't want men to touch? Girls like you tend to end up having babies at their father's houses, because they cannot endure open play, so they go to secret places and have themselves disvirgined. I will kill you if you bring shame and dishonour on us. How can he hurt you with all these others watching?" (121)

In the end, Ma Blackie does kill Aku-nna, much as she discovers she loves her daughter, by her continued endorsement of those cultural practices that kill women. By the time she decides to defend Aku-nna, neither the witch doctors nor the God of the Christians can compensate for the damage.

After Aku-nna is kidnapped by the vindictive Okoboshi, Ma Blackie sits on her mud couch, stunned, now quite worried about her daughter, who does not even know half the customs of Ibuza, but equally drained by the futility of her efforts to groom Aku-nna for Okonkwo's advantage. The family carries out rituals of searching and crying.

Aku-nna does gain her freedom from Okoboshi and, with the direct help of her pregnant mother (not of witch doctors or the Christian God), escapes from Okonkwo's wrath and marries Chike. The marriage is a happy one; but when Aku-nna becomes pregnant, the force of her undernourished life, the lateness of her mother's care and bonding, unleashes itself on her body in the toxic anemia so common among Nigerian girls. She has a difficult pregnancy, and in her sixth month she begins to fail. Chike's brother, a gynecologist who tries to help, tells the couple that "bad feeding in their youth" combined with poor health care kills many pregnant girls. Their bodies do not physiologically mature and strengthen enough to endure pregnancy; Aku-nna herself, at sixteen, looks like a fourteen-year-old.

Aku-nna dies in a hospital, incapable of bearing her own physical struggle, let alone that of the baby moving within her, but not before giving birth to a daughter. When she finds out from Chike that she has had a girl, Aku-nna smiles peacefully. To commemorate their love and this Other child (and to give Kristevan *jouissance* a practical expression), she and Chike name the little girl Joy (167).

This conclusion to *The Bride Price*, seemingly simple and sweet despite the tragedy of Aku-nna's death, is deceiving. The celebrated birth of the daughter, representing the rebirth of the mother, begins the process of cultural rehabilitation because it begins the process of human rehabilitation—of unification, which the maternal body signifies. But that celebratory birth does not and will never happen as an idyll, in a world untouched by physical, evolutionary, and sociopolitical realities. The entire biological process of maternity, from menses through delivery, though at times "sweet," is difficult and painful, a reality of woman's difference patriarchal practice refuses to appreciate and most often trivializes. According to *The Bride Price*, this is, in effect, the premier political action against women because it is an oppressive, murderous act, a gynocide, which sets woman physically and emotionally against her own maternal body and her daughter's.

In *The Family*, Emecheta identifies patriarchal oppression more intensely than she has ever done before with the specific and terrible desecration of the female body that distills into the separation between mother and daughter (and of course into yet another unnatural relationship with the sons). This separation likewise causes the decentralized, nomadic experience of the Other, but particularly the Other woman, described so well by writers such as Audre Lorde and Zora Neale Hurston. Emecheta dedicates *The Family* to "that woman in the Diaspora who refused to sever her umbilical cord with Africa," who embodies the continuity of mother and daughter necessary to the fertile continuance of culture. The woman is both mother and daughter; the one becomes the other, continuously.

Gwendolen Brillianton is placed in the care of her Granny Naomi, when her mother, Sonia, decides to leave Jamaica for England to be with her husband, Winston, who has taken a job in London. Sonia promises to send for Gwendolen, but two years elapse before she does. During that time Gwendolen has received only four letters from Sonia, a manifestation of woman's lack of communication and voice. Once Gwendolen and her mother are reunited, it does not take long for communication between them to break down and for Gwendolen to learn that the reason for her mother's silence and her own call to England is that Sonia has had two sons and needs a housekeeper and babysitter. "You stay all day at dat school doing nutting," Sonia chides Gwendolen, who has just asked her mother for some study time at home so that she might move out of the remedial reading class, "and when you come home, you have to help. You understand? Dat's why me send fe you to come, not just for education!" (84). If one might understand the economic circumstances forcing Sonia to abandon her daughter to household drudgery, one cannot understand Sonia's spite and lack of sympathy. On the day her mother left for England, Gwendolen had felt a sense of nascent rupture: "Gwendolen had never seen [Sonia] so happy. . . . it looked as if her Mammy was happy to leave her behind, giving her the impression she was not really wanted" (18).

Gwendolen's family status as part slave—every free minute at home is assigned to housework or child care—extends back to her early childhood in Jamaica in a horrible way that anticipates her later experiences. Emecheta's outrage at patriarchy and at woman's cooperation in the enslavement of women, principally by her betrayal of her daughters and the body they share, is felt in Gwendolen's subjection to sexual molestation and incest. When she is eight, and in Granny Naomi's care, her Uncle Johnny begins to visit her bed at night and to molest her, preying on the little girl's need to please her elders, on her immature sexual drive, and on her awareness that what is happening is decidedly wrong. Gwendolen is driven to private despair and to bedwetting and subjected to public humiliation. "Once [Granny Naomi] was so angry that she made Gwendolen carry her soiled beddings around their yard to shame Gwendolen into stopping" (27).

Out of desperation rather than trust, Gwendolen finally tells Granny Naomi what Uncle Johnny has been doing to her. Granny Naomi believes her, but thinks that such behavior is not unusual. Granny Naomi gets Uncle Johnny to stop, for his behavior is considered bad in both tribal and Christian value systems. However, instead of also consoling Gwendolen and trying to help her overcome her pain, she begins accusing her granddaughter of every trivial offense and takes these occasions to beat her mercilessly. Gwendolen is only nine at the time.

Daddy Winston starts molesting her when she is an adolescent, while her mother is in Jamaica for two years after her mother Granny Naomi's death. In a reverse repetition of Gwendolen's early feeling that her mother did not mind deserting her, Sonia had an uneasy feeling, before her departure for Jamaica, that Winston was beginning to favor their daughter over her. "There was something new and she guessed it was Gwendolen. She could not put a name to what exactly it was that suddenly made her inadequate. But she felt it. It was there" (88). Although Sonia remains in Jamaica far beyond the normal mourning period, because she has found her independent life attractive (135), Emecheta intimates that she has sacrificed her daughter, tendered her over to another child molester. She has used a "logic" mothers under patriarchy have learned to disconnect from their daughters and to transfer self-hatred.

Winston Brillianton's rape and impregnation of his daughter has, like Sonia's set-up of it, the semblance of ritual. Sonia's expression of her own grief for her dead mother, which is truly "hysterical" and also the prescribed practice of womanly wailing, suggests the social and psychic divisiveness between herself and her mother and between herself and her daughter. At the very end of *The Family*, Sonia's recognition that her daughter's daughter is also her (step)daughter forces her to react in the way she has acted all her life: "almost like a puppet whose strings had suddenly been pulled tight" (239). Her voice—uttering her final words, "Winston Brillianton!"—"had the finality of a closed door."

Emecheta represents Gwendolen's recovery from the morass of her family's life not only as an affirmation of the maternal body but also as an interracial relationship. Gwendolen meets and has sex with Emmanuel, a white boy who himself has known social and family oppression. He is of Greek descent and is becoming increasingly alienated from his family, who do not approve either his career choice or his black girlfriend. Emmanuel is further repudiated by Sonia; Gwendolen, in her last attempt to preserve some family order, lets her think that he is the father of her unborn child (Winston Brillianton has died, possibly suicidally, in a fire which mirrors his own spent life of provincialism, racial subjugation, and incest).

Although he is not as sensitive or smart as Aku-nna's Chike, Emmanuel is more caring than his girlfriend's mother. Here Emecheta is not being insensitive to woman's predicament and the way a mother is sabotaged by patriarchy into withholding love from her daughter. Mothers of Sonia's generation, like her own mother and Nnu Ego in *The Joys of Motherhood* and Ma Blackie in *The Bride Price,* are probably ill-equipped psychologically, because of their situation with respect to old and new influences, to fight their conflict with much success. The generation after Gwendolen and Aku-nna need not be so defeated.

Gwendolen represents the onset of a new capability of modern woman, through greater education and health care, to begin to bring about some shifts in the system and to restore the natural process of development and connections. Emmanuel, like Chike, represents a latent sensitivity and sensibility—in more Kristevan terms, a repressed (outlaw and outsider) desire for wholeness that can issue in love and compassion and caring. Both Gwendolen and Emmanuel and Aku-nna and Chike accept their newborn daughters. But while Aku-nna wants to give her daughter the Anglo name Joy, to celebrate her as the issue of marital love, Gwendolen, who has had more direct Anglo experience, gives her daughter the Yoruba name Iyamide, which her mother calls an "uncivilized African voodoo name" (237). But the name is glorious, and the family portrait of Gwendolen, Emmanuel, and Iyamide—so different a picture from Nnu Ego and her stillborn daughter in a pool of Nnu Ego's blood in *The Joys of Motherhood*—displaces all the Christian and African lore that has made Sonia a "puppet." Iyamide means "my mother is here."

Given the history, the thousands of years of patriarchal mutilation of women, recovery of the mother-daughter bond through regard for the reality and meaning of the maternal body—which is necessary for cultural renewal—does not come simply from pure sensitivity. Change from psychic, social, and even biological enslavement emerges gradually, and with a struggle, from the mutual education of women and men, just as it does for Aku-nna and Chike in *The Bride Price* and for Gwendolen and Emmanuel in *The Family.* At times, it requires women to isolate themselves from men so that integration, when it occurs, will benefit from their strength.

In this context, Emecheta observes that the colonialization of Africa produced at least three "goods" which appreciably aided women and which therefore probably added another, but this time masked, dimension to male anger against imperialism—for males wished to continue their domination of women. The primary benefit was the greater access through education and literacy to different modes of thought and knowledge. As in the case of Aku-nna, whose teacher (and later husband) Chike Ofulue becomes an agent of her release, it is the education of women that motivates their liberation and that becomes central in Emecheta's fiction to the process of their awareness. Despite the "philosophical" lessons that young girls learn from tribal stories (*BP*, 23–24)—Emecheta coyly does not say what such lessons are—they learn from their mothers how to subjugate themselves to men and how to mistrust other women. Only women who have been exposed to Western education can make some move toward intellectual and physical and even financial independence (Frank, 23). Even when mothers encourage their daughters to go to school decoratively, for the sake of increasing their bride price rather than their capacity for self-definition, as Ma Blackie does, daughters may learn enough and find themselves personally enriched enough, as Aku-nna does, to want and begin to pursue autonomy.

Equally important to women's struggle for equality was the introduction of more informed health care and nutrition. Women's gynecological and obstetric needs had been negotiated chiefly by tribal superstition as well as by misogyny, resulting in many stillbirths, infant deaths, and life-threatening and fatal pregnancies, especially among young mothers, like Aku-nna, whose youth should have been their greatest defense. Emecheta places no magical or sentimental value on Western medicine, however; its practice can fail in diagnosis and treatment and sometimes it exists to treat conditions inflicted by Western exploitation of Africans, as in the case of Aku-nna's father, Ezekiel Odia. Aku-nna's own fatal pregnancy, however, is purely a consequence of tribal practice. One swift but pointed example of tribal idiom bespeaks all the misogyny affecting pregnant women psychologically and physically: Aku-nna's supposedly sensitive father tells her that her Uncle Uche "was as lazy and as sluggish as a woman expecting twins" (17). In teaching her that food went first to all men in the family and last to women, Ma Blackie taught Aku-nna literally to starve herself, to turn menstrual blood into a killing, anemic blood.

Westerners were, of course, no less patriarchal in their attitudes toward women. Even though Christian missionaries (notably women) kindly insisted that pregnant and nursing mothers take care of themselves nutritionally, for the sake of the children, Christian practice still taught women to support their husbands at all other physical (not to mention, emotional) cost to themselves. But Western medicine (and Christian practice) in very practical ways helped women in particular to recover from tribal customs which deferred to care of the male body and reflected tribal misogyny.

Male African writers and critics would charge that the Western invader always constru(ct)ed native African culture and behavior ethnocentrically and assessed it according to its own beliefs and imperialist practice—Western critics would read African literature, indeed colonize it, in terms even of their own social neuroses and "universal-humanoid abstraction," said Wole Soyinka (x). Few (if any), however, observed openly that women in colonial Africa were assisted at the very basic level of literacy, education, and health to understand their bodies and/or to seek knowledge and understanding of menstruation, pregnancy, and childbirth. Many have been quick to condemn as negligible or culturally irresponsible and politically naive what they have construed as African women's endorsements of the West. Their own sustained political oppression and cancellation of women, even in their texts and epistemologies, they quickly forget.

Learning the Western ways of commerce, of buying and selling for profit, was another boon for tribal women, as they often became the major providers for their families, particularly after 1929, the year when the Great Depression in the West began, which affected the colonial African economy, and also the year of the Igbo Women's War (see Van Allen). Often daughters learned these skills from their mothers and, like their mothers, used them simultaneously both to implement traditional practice and to achieve nontraditional independence. Many tribal males who had themselves learned to pursue money under the degrading white colonialist domination, like Nnaife in *The Joys of Motherhood*, merely intensified their own domination of women; as a "grass-cutter at the railway compound," Nnaife is proud that he can "now even afford to beat [his wife, Nnu Ego] up" (117). By contrast, the women who learned white ways with capital used their money to help their families and/or to create more opportunities of independence for themselves and their children. Adaku, Naife's younger wife who cannot produce a living son, eventually takes her daughters and moves away from the family to start a family of her own, where her daughters are free of male psychological and physical abuse. Unlike Nnu Ego, who is more committed to Nnaife because she wants to remain his favored wife and because she has some access to that status owing to her sons, Adaku becomes a successful businesswoman with plans to educate her daughters.

If there is any lesson to be learned from Emecheta, who clearly does want to teach, it is that mothers especially need to go against the grain of patriarchal tradition and to teach their daughters to pursue education—not as a festoon of commodification, which it is in many societies (in the West as well as in Africa), but as a core of personal enrichment, growth, and freedom. That this education itself is structured according to patriarchal (and Western) paradigms and discourse poses a problem at some levels, of course, but not an insurmountable one, especially for the intellectual and writer who must become a teacher. Emecheta herself writes—teaches—out of her own maternal body. This is what she must do for her daughters, and for her sons.

Emecheta remains relentless and powerful in her representation of the maternal body as significant and signifying at the individual and social levels. She writes, I think, in the face of increasing surges of anti-essentialist feminism, most riding on the premise that woman's distinguishing biological capacity has only biologically reproductive meaning and contributes virtually nothing to human knowledge, perception, valuation, and what Gayatri Spivak calls "soul making" (in Gates, 263). In fact, some accuse essentialism of being not a human but a Western and Eurocentric social paradigm and therefore unacceptably "nontheoretical" and imperialist and conceding to patriarchy's imprisonment of women within the gendered maternal role. But Alice Walker notes—sharply, intending every connotation of her words—Emecheta's unusual stance with respect to her writing self: Emecheta writes because of her children, not in spite of them (66–70).[8]

Notes

1. Emecheta does not let this irony go by. To compensate for such "privileges," the girl is often made to do more work or take a beating or go without some delicacy, a compensation which can, of course, harm the girl and decrease the very bride price the privileges are meant to increase.
2. Emecheta dedicates *The Bride Price* to her mother, Alice Ogbanje Emecheta.
3. For her remarks on the construction of a racist (anti-Semitic) discourse, see Kristeva, *Powers of Horror: An Essay on Abjection*, 174–187.
4. In *Nigerian History and Culture*, ed. Richard Olaniyan, an otherwise helpful text, women receive virtually no treatment at all, even in explanations of family life and ritual. Women are written out. Male roles only are defined and discussed and maleness is attributed to acknowledged forces of power. For example, the meaning of the name for God in Edo, Osanobwa, is "the source-being who sustains and carries the universe" (237); yet the author continually refers to this being as "he," when sex is not prescribed and when the description seems more appropriate to female experience. In the same essay, regarding the introduction of Islam into the culture, the author reckons that the "impact" of Islamic émigrés to Nigeria was achieved in part through "their ability to make both women and cultivated lands productive" (241).
5. Ma Blackie's "dream" of becoming a mother again is in her case only a cultural construction imposed on her by patriarchy. Ma Blackie realizes that, at forty plus, her only value to Okonkwo is the bride price her daughter will obtain and her ability to produce a son. Emecheta shows bitterness at the absurdity, the tautology of Okonkwo's logic. Man has decided what makes woman happy and then congratulates himself on fulfilling the desire he has imposed on her.
6. According to Nigerian belief and practice, once a slave, always a slave, no matter how prosperous the person or descendants become. Even Chike's father, who is affluent, submits to that belief and does not encourage Chike to pursue Aku-nna.
7. See Yemi Ogunbiyi, "The Performing Arts in Nigerian Culture," in *Nigerian History and Culture*, ed. Olaniyan, 318–340.
8. Emecheta's essentialism is potent and necessary. For two exceedingly fine, more theory based, commentaries supporting essentialism, see Naomi Schor, "This Essentialism Which Is Not One: Coming to Grips with Irigaray," 38–58; and Diana Fuss, "Reading Like a Feminist," 77–92.

Works Cited

Andrade, Susan Z. "Rewriting History, Motherhood, and Rebellion: Naming an African Women's Literary Tradition." *Research in African Literatures* 21 (Spring 1990): 91–110.

Benjamin, Jessica. *The Bonds of Love: Psychoanalysis, Feminism, and the Problem of Domination*. New York: Pantheon, 1988.

Chodorow, Nancy. *The Reproduction of Mothering: Psychoanalysis and the Sociology of Gender*. Berkeley: University of California Press, 1978.

Cixous, Hélène, and Catherine Clement. *The Newly Born Woman*. Trans. Betsy Wing. Minneapolis: University of Minnesota Press, 1986.

Emecheta, Buchi. *The Bride Price*. New York: George Braziller, 1976.

———. *The Family*. New York: George Braziller, 1989.

———. *The Joys of Motherhood*. New York: George Braziller, 1979.

Frank, Katherine. "Women without Men: The Feminist Novel in Africa." In *Women in African Literature Today*, ed. Eldred Durosimi Jones, 14–34. London: James Currey, 1987.

Fuss, Diana. "Reading Like a Feminist." *Differences* 1 (Summer 1989): 77–92.

Gates, Henry Louis, Jr., ed. *"Race," Writing, and Difference*. Chicago: University of Chicago Press, 1985, 1986.

Irigaray, Luce. *This Sex Which Is Not One*. Trans. Catherine Porter. Ithaca: Cornell University Press, 1985.

Kristeva, Julia. *Powers of Horror: An Essay on Abjection*. Trans. Leon S. Roudiez. New York: Columbia University Press, 1982.

Olaniyan, Richard, ed. *Nigerian History and Culture*. Essex, Eng.: Longman, 1985.

Palmer, Eustace. "The Feminine Point of View: Buchi Emecheta's *The Joys of Motherhood*." *African Literature Today* 13 (1983): 38–57.

Schor, Naomi. "This Essentialism Which Is Not One: Coming to Grips with Irigaray." *Differences* 1 (Summer 1989): 38–58.

Soyinka, Wole. *Myth, Literature and the African World*. Cambridge: Cambridge University Press, 1976.

Van Allen, Judith. "'Aba Riots' or Igbo 'Women's War'? Ideology, Stratification, and the Invisibility of Women." In *Women in Africa*, ed. Nancy J. Hafkin and Edna G. Bay, 59–85. Stanford: Stanford University Press, 1976.

Walker, Alice. *In Search of Our Mothers' Gardens*. New York: Harcourt Brace, 1983.

(Re)claiming the Race of the Mother

Cherríe Moraga's *Shadow of a Man, Giving Up the Ghost,* and *Heroes and Saints*

JULIA DE FOOR JAY

Cherríe Moraga's courageous voice first emerged in the 1980s and has since become a significant one for Chicana, feminist, and lesbian studies. It has been heard in several genres: poems, fiction, essays, and plays,[1] sounding the theme of betrayal, informed by various myths and legends in the Chicano / Chicana culture. She focuses, in particular, on the myth of La Malinche. In the pattern of Malinche, a woman who does not conform to prescribed roles is labeled La Vendida, the "sell-out," or La Chingada, the "traitor" (also slang for "the violated one"). Moraga attacks this encoding, arguing that women have been socialized by male-centered, heterosexual-centered ideologies into "selling out" or betraying their own daughters, apprenticing them for submission and servitude. In her plays *Shadow of a Man, Giving Up the Ghost,* and *Heroes and Saints,* Moraga explores this process of socialization and its effects on mothers and daughters in the Chicano / Chicana community, finally rendering a vision of revolution, led by courageous *vendidas,* as the only recourse to (re)claim the race.

Moraga begins her exploration of the Chicano mother-daughter relationship by focusing on *la familia,* a locus of multiple oppressions, "wounds," that relate to a larger sociopolitical context. She states, "My identity as a Chicana, a lesbiana, a mujer always had to do with the relationship between my deeply personal side and the whole political construct. I had to look at my family, at the contradictions and the mixed messages . . . the good stuff and the negative stuff" (quoted in Lovato, 23). Having been born and reared in a family with an Anglo father and a Chicana mother, Moraga had been encouraged to emphasize her "whiteness." In "La Güera" she writes, "It was through my mother's desire to protect her children from poverty and illiteracy that we became 'anglocized'; the more effectively we could pass in the white world, the better guaranteed our future" (*Loving in the War Years*, 50). Passing also meant appropriating the language of the dominant culture; therefore, Moraga spoke English, filtering out her mother's fluent Spanish.

Not only had Moraga attempted to pass as an Anglo, but she also had attempted to pass as a heterosexual, these two disguises becoming equally oppressive. This oppression was not lifted until Moraga heard Ntozake Shange read her poetry and experienced a profound "revelation," in which she realized that she had denied "the brown in me," that she had denied the language that spoke to the "emotions in my poems," and that she had denied "the voice of my own brown mother" (*Loving in the War Years*, 55). At this point she began her quest for a more authentic self and a more authentic poetic voice. In "A Long Line of Vendidas," she asserts, "To be a woman fully necessitated my claiming the race of my mother" (*Loving in the War Years*, 94).

Claiming the race of the mother meant claiming its myths and legends and acknowledging the codes and signs of the dominant ideology, its institutions and institutional practices. According to Nancy Saporta Sternbach, Moraga "draws upon, conjures, reinvents, and reinterprets Mexican myth and pre-Hispanic heritage" (52). In particular, Moraga draws upon the myth of La Malinche.[2] However, while most writers concentrate on Malinche herself, Moraga focuses on Malinche's mother—the mother who sacrificed herself for men and the mother who betrayed the daughter by colluding with the dominant ideology. In one version of the myth, Malinche's mother wanted her son by a second marriage to inherit the estate so she sold her daughter into slavery (Mirandé and Enríquez, 24–25). Moraga explores this legacy of betrayal in her works—not just betrayal by the mother but betrayal by any woman of another. In an interview with Mirtha N. Quintanales, she discusses this theme and links it with her search for the meaning of love: "And for me, the conditions [for love] have always had something to do with the issue of separation—

leaving and the consequences of leaving" (12). She admits that she has a "deep racial memory that the Chicana could *not* betray a sister, a daughter, a compañera in the service of the man and his institutions if somewhere in the chain of historical events and generations, she were allowed to love herself as both female and mestiza" (*Loving in the War Years*, 136).

To Moraga, Malinche, because she was a woman, had very little choice in her situation; therefore, her association with the downfall of her people is unjustified. Denigrating her, and by association denigrating all women, is a political act of a patriarchal system. In fact, several extant accounts mention her sensitive and loving nature. According to one chronicler, Malinche showed no vindictiveness when she encountered her mother and half-brother years later; instead, she treated them with mercy and love (Del Castillo, 126). Adelaida R. Del Castillo argues, "No one, not Cortés, not the Catholic Church, nor her own husband, not even history itself, nor the mestizo nation she gives birth to realize the great injustice they have done her by obscuring her in defamation" (143). By labeling her a traitor, "man is attempting to submerge the female character in negativism and Mexican culture does it through demeaning the character of Doña Marina—La Malinche" (146). Norma Alarcón asserts, "Her almost half century of mythic existence, until recent times mostly in the oral traditions, [has] turned her into a handy reference point not only for controlling, interpreting or visualizing women, but also to wage a domestic battle of stifling proportions" (182).

Moraga's mother also became a Malinche figure, a traitor, because she married an Anglo. Moraga herself, because she refuses to marry and serve any man, becomes the worst traitor or "malinchista" of all (Sternbach, 53). She reasons in "A Long Line of Vendidas":

> My mother then is the modern-day Chicana, Malinche marrying a white man, my father, to produce the bastards my sister, my brother, and I are. Finally, I—a half-breed Chicana—further betray my race by *choosing* my sexuality which excludes all men, and therefore most dangerously, Chicano men.
>
> *I come from a long line of Vendidas.* (*Loving in the War Years*, 117)

Sternbach observes that "her [Moraga's] conclusion brings her back to her people, the people of her mother. . . . although she is obviously giving a new and perhaps reclaimed meaning, if such a thing is possible, to the word *vendida*" (55).

The myth of La Malinche works in various combinations with two other myths: La Virgen de Guadalupe and La Llorona.[3] All are images of motherhood. The Virgin of Guadalupe is the virgin mother, sexless and pure, whereas Malinche is "the violated mother" (Paz, 85), sexual and adulterated. La Llorona, historically linked to Malinche, is the suffering mother: she suffers, according to one legend, because she has deviated from her proper role as "good" wife and mother. Like the Virgin of Guadalupe and La Malinche, La Llorona "reflects a cultural heritage that is relentless in its expectations of feminine roles" (Mirandé and Enríquez, 33).

The two contrasting figures of Malinche of Tenépal and the Virgin of Guadalupe, or the polarities of whore or virgin, linked with La Llorona, the Weeping Woman, have become entrenched in the Mexican and Chicano cultures, providing major stumbling blocks to women in their quests for self-determination. To avoid being labeled *mujer mala*, a woman must adhere to certain prescriptions: she must serve the males, take care of the home, mother the children, and give priority to the sons. Moraga states, "You are a traitor to your race if you do not put the man first" (*Loving in the War Years*, 103). She must give her allegiance not only to the institution of *la familia* but also to the institution of the Catholic Church, for "familial restrictions share close covenant with the Catholic faith" (Feyder, 5). For Moraga, embracing the mother means acknowledging the mother's roles in the society and the effects of those roles on her—and her daughter's—racial/sexual identity.

Somewhat autobiographical, *Shadow of a Man* focuses on *la familia*, examining how betrayal works in the context of the family structure. Hortensia, a traditional wife and mother, has allowed the dominant ideology to define her totally; she exists primarily to serve others, especially her husband and son. She is a prime example of the mother who "sells" her daughters into patriarchal slavery. Gloria Anzaldúa asserts, "I abhor some of my culture's ways, how it cripples its women, *como burras*, our strengths used against us, lowly *burras* bearing humility with dignity. The ability to serve, claim the males, is our highest virtue" (21). During the course of the play, Hortensia cooks, serves meals, folds clothes, and dresses and undresses her husband, Manuel. But still she feels that she is invisible to Manuel and demands that he see her: "Yo existo. (Pause.) Manuel, yo existo. Existo yo" (32).

Mainly, Hortensia exists for her children, defining herself primarily as mother. Even her husband is a little boy to her. She tells her youngest daughter, Lupe: "Funny, when a man is asleep, tha's when you really get to know him. You see the child's look on his face, before he wakes up and remembers he's a man again. In his half dream, tiene la voz de un niño." She admits, however, that her children, not her husband, receive her allegiance: "But your husband really isn't your child. He di'nt come from your body. Y no matter cuántas veces le das el pecho, tu marido no es tu hijo. Your blood never mixes. He stays a stranger in his own home" (44).

Her primary allegiance, though, is the one she bestows on her son. Moraga comments on the Chicana mother's preference for sons:

> Ask, for example, any Chicano mother about her children and she is quick to tell you she loves them all the same, but she doesn't. *The boys are different*. Sometimes I sense that she feels this way because she wants to believe that through her mothering, she can develop the kind of man she would have liked to have married, or even have been. That through her son she can get a small taste of male privilege, since without race or class privilege that's all there is to be had. The daughter can never offer the mother such hope, straddled by the same forces that confine the mother. (*Loving in the War Years*, 101–102)

Irene I. Blea concurs: "Even at birth Chicano females and males do not start out the same. Boy babies are still preferred" (127). In a scene that reveals her phallocentric view, Hortensia tells her daughters: "Mira, qué lindo es [the baby's penis] . . . like a little jewel. Mi machito. Tha's one thing, you know, the men can never take from us. The birth of a son." Leticia retorts, "Well, I don't see you getting so much credit." "But the woman knows," explains Hortensia. "Tú no entiendes. Wait until you have your own son" (29).

Having internalized the belief that men are superior to women, Hortensia perpetuates these attitudes in her relations with her two daughters, indoctrinating them into a dualistic behavior system. The son, a fledgling *macho*, may venture from the home to test his wings and to develop a masculine identity (Mirandé and Enríquez, 114), but the daughter may not leave freely. When Leticia wants more freedom—like the males in the culture—Hortensia tells her: "If God had wanted you to be a man, he would of given you something between your legs." Rejecting this assessment of woman as "lack," Leticia responds, "I have something between my legs" (44). However, Hortensia perpetuates the double standard within the culture and defines women as dirty and whorelike if they desire the same privileges as men.

At one point Hortensia defines herself as whorelike, impure and unclean. After being abused and rejected by Manuel, she proclaims, "¡Estoy cochina! ¡Filthy!" She pours vinegar over herself and informs her daughters: "Tu padre thinks I stink, pues now I stink for sure" (34). Unable to feel "clean," she almost murders her daughter Lupe, her child by her husband's friend Conrado. Years before, in a classic "exchange of women among men" personal (and ultimately political) act, Hortensia had been offered to Conrado by Manuel as a sexual partner for one night. Lupe is the product of that liaison. Consumed by guilt, Hortensia symbolically renames herself *la chingada*—the traitor (also "the violated one").

Lupe, the twelve-year-old youngest daughter, internalizes the mother's "teachings" and assumes a caretaker's role. Following her mother's example, she waits upon her father, existing in his "shadow" and literally and symbolically sitting at his feet (69). Betty Garcia-Bahne, in "La Chicana and the Chicano Family," discusses this "modeling" and its effects upon Chicano women. She points out several "myths" that bolster the Chicano family structure and shows how they establish women's dependency and "mitigate against the development and exercise of self-determination" (43). One of these myths is that family members can be assured of well-being if they are under the leadership of a male. Garcia-Bahne argues that this type of hierarchical construct undermines the woman's sense of worth and potential. It also places too much responsibility and pressure on the male (44). By modeling the mother's behavior, Lupe enters into the traditional configuration of the family and, by extension, other umbrella institutions.

One of those institutions is the Catholic Church, which casts a long shadow over the bodies and psyches of the women. Lupe, identifying with her mother, takes on the negativism of Malinche, confusing the family's "secret" with her own secretly budding sexuality. In the first image of the play, Lupe appears wearing a Catholic school uniform and holding a votive candle under her chin. Only her face is seen, staring into a mirror. On the wall the shadow of a crucifix can be seen. She reflects, "I have x-ray eyes. . . . I can see through her [Sister Genevieve's] habit. . . . She has a naked body under there. . . . I think there's something wrong with me" (30) She tries to confess to the priest but is unable to reveal her sexual dilemmas. She realizes: "No matter how many times I make confession, no matter how many times I try to tell the priest what I hold insida me, I know I'm still lying. Sinning. Keeping secrets" (12). Yvonne Yarbro-Bejarano posits that "Catholicism in its institutionalized form . . . inculcates in [women] the need to sublimate the body and its desires, as captured in the image of Lupe's disembodied head illuminated by a candle in the shadow of the cross" ("Cherríe Moraga's 'Shadow of a Man,'" 99–100).

Lupe's identity quest in the context of family, culture, and institutional religion is the controlling element of the play (her monologues begin and end the production). At one point, she considers her new confirmation name, vacillating between Cecilia and Magdalena—one burned at the stake, the other considered a prostitute—women who encode the dualities. Finally, eschewing all female saints, she decides on Frances, a masculine name she appropriates in order to align with a rebellious female friend. In the last image of the play, Lupe stares at the mirror, again speaking to her reflection: "I've decided my confirmation name will be Frances 'cuz that's what Frankie Pacheco's name is and I wanna be in her body. When she sits, she doesn't hold her knees together like my mom and the nuns are always telling me to. She jus' lets them fly an' fall wherever they want . . . real natural-like . . . like they was wings instead of knees" (49). With this decision, Lupe begins to rebel against the systems that have constrained and repressed her, represented by the mother and the church.

In the last action of the play, Lupe covers the mirror, a signifier with multiple references, with a rebozo, a black shawl. The family is on the way to the father's funeral, and Aunt Rosario instructs Lupe to cover the mirror because she does not want Lupe's father to come back and try to take them with him. In *Borderlands/La Frontera,* Anzaldúa discusses the multiple symbolism of the mirror in Chicano culture. The mirror is "a door through which the soul may 'pass' to the other side." It is also "an ambivalent symbol, reproducing images but also containing and absorbing them. In addition, it is a path to knowledge, a way of 'seeing through' an experience" (42). In Freudian/Lacanian terms the mirror reflects patriarchal ideology that she cannot enter. By taking on both "masculine" and "feminine" aspects and by taking on a name that blurs the dualities, thereby adding a new sexual dimension, Lupe threatens and challenges the existing power structure, based on male privilege and heterosexuality.

Another daughter who threatens and challenges the existing order is Lupe's older sister, Leticia, called the *política* by her mother. From the outset of the play, Leticia is a radical feminist, fighting oppression, not only for women but also for the *raza*. She has no respect for male-centered power structures, often countering her mother's phallocentric views. When her mother refuses to allow her the freedom she allows her brother Rigo, Leticia, in frustration, declares: "Es hombre. Es hombre. I'm sick of hearing that. It's not fair." Hortensia returns, "Well, you better get use to things not being fair. Whoever said the world was goin' to be fair?" Leticia proclaims, "Well, my world's going to be fair!" (18). When her mother tries to convince her that having sons is a sublime experience, Leticia pronounces, "Who knows? Maybe I won't have kids" (29). Choosing not to have children constitutes a challenge to male-based ideologies that control women through marriage and motherhood—a choice that is an attempt "to undo the power men everywhere wield over women, power that has become a model for every other form of exploitation and illegitimate control" (Rich, "Compulsory Heterosexuality and Lesbian Existence," 202).

In another act of defiance, Leticia gives away her virginity, taking away the power of the patriarchy to use her as a commodity. When her mother asks her, "Why you give your virginidad away for nothing?" Leticia responds: "I was tired of carrying it around . . . that weight of being a woman with a prize. Walking around with that special secret, that valuable commodity, waiting for some lucky guy to put his name on it. I wanted it to be worthless, Mama. Don't you see? Not for me to be worthless, but to know that my worth had nothing to do with it" (45). By the end of the play both Lupe and Leticia refuse to be sold out by the mother and the race, and both refuse to have their sexuality repressed or exploited.

Giving Up the Ghost, also somewhat autobiographical, focuses on betrayal in the family context but extends the examination into personal relationships. The mother is absent from the text, but her influence is omnipresent. Significantly, the epigraph of the play is a song Moraga's mother sang: "If I had the wings like an angel / over these prison walls / I would fly" (3). One of the "prisons" to which Moraga refers is the prison of rigidly defined sexual roles, set up by patriarchal ideologies to bolster power structures. Adrienne Rich calls this prison "institutional heterosexuality" and points out that it is "a major buttress of male power." In

1979, in *On Lies, Secrets, and Silence,* she called for a close scrutiny of the "indoctrination of women toward heterosexuality" and for "a politics of *asking women's questions,* demanding a world in which the integrity of all women—not a chosen few—shall be honored and validated in every aspect of culture" (17). Moraga takes up this challenge in *Giving Up the Ghost.* In the opening scene, Marisa (Moraga), the daughter, writes in a sketchbook that she is going to consider "the question of prisons / politics / sex" (6). In "A Long Line of Vendidas," Moraga writes: "The one aspect of our identity which has been uniformly ignored by every existing political movement in this country is sexuality, both as a source of oppression and a means of liberation" (*Loving in the War Years,* 109).

One of the main points the play makes is that heterosexual relations are often harmful to the body and spirit and that lesbian relations are often restorative and healing. Historian Linda Gordon writes, "For women . . . heterosexual relations are always intense, frightening, high-risk situations which ought, if a woman has any sense of self-preservation, to be carefully calculated" (quoted in Rich, *On Lies, Secrets, and Silence,* 196). Marisa's goal is to fight institutional heterosexuality. At the beginning of the play, she speaks directly to the audience: "My mother was a heterosexual, I couldn't save her. My failures follow thereafter" (8). In *Giving Up the Ghost,* Marisa also attempts to save Amalia, a mother figure, from institutional heterosexuality. Paradoxically, Amalia feels like a failure, too. Her first words are "I am a failure" (8). But Amalia's lack of self worth stems from patriarchal neglect and abuse. Marisa insightfully recognizes this in her mother and then later in Amalia. Her failure to rescue these women, both the mother and the mother figure, depresses and angers her. Later in the same scene, she states, "I wanna talk about betrayal, about a battle I will never win and never stop fighting. The dick beats me every time" (9). Moraga, in *Loving in the War Years,* proclaims, "I love women to the point of killing for us all" (117). As a result, Mary K. DeShazer calls Moraga a "sister in arms" because of her fight against multiple oppressions, noting that her battle cry is "neither hyperbolic nor malevolent; it reflects instead the historical, ideological, and affective locus from which she speaks" ("Making *Familia,*" 282). It reflects her love and commitment to Chicanas, grounded in her love for her mother.

Marisa's love of Amalia is a transferal from the love of the mother to the love of an older woman.[4] Although heterosexual at the beginning of the play, Amalia connects sexually and spiritually with Marisa as the play progresses. According to Teresa de Lauretis, in "Sexual Indifference and Lesbian Representation," "the play itself [moves] away from any simple opposition of 'lesbian' to 'heterosexual' and into the conceptual and experiential continuum of a female, Chicana subjectivity from where the question of lesbian desire must finally be posed" (175). According to Alarcón, "Moraga puts into play the concepts 'man' and 'woman' (and the parodic 'butch/femme'), with the intuitive knowledge that they operate in our subjectivities, so that it is difficult to analyze them, except in the way she has done" (156).

The use of a split subject, Marisa/Corky, and the blurring of time and sequence contribute to Moraga's quest to dismantle limiting concepts of Chicana identity. The split subject, moving back and forth through time, avoids a unified subject and narrativity. In "The Female Subject in Chicano Theatre: Sexuality, 'Race,' and Class," Yarbro-Bejarano notes, "The juxtaposition of past and present in the text reveals the cultural construction of female identity, specifically through the restricted gender roles of masculine/feminine, active/passive, subject/object, penetrator/penetrated defined in Chicano-specific cultural terms through the myth of *La Malinche* and the *chingón/chingada* polarity" (147).[5] "The chingón," writes Octavio Paz, "is the macho, the male; he rips open the chingada, the female, who is pure passivity, defenseless against the exterior world" (77).

Giving Up the Ghost presents this "defenseless" position of women in the culture. Corky, Marisa's twelve-year-old self, assumes a male-identified persona in order to escape the oppression she witnesses in the culture. Her mother's powerlessness in the face of sexism and racism contributes to her sexual determination. Sue-Ellen Case contends that Corky can only inhabit a subject position in society if she enters as "male-identified" (132).

However, when she is raped, Corky is forced "to confront her internal split between her identification with the subjugating male and her repressed self-knowledge as female" (Yarbro-Bejarano, "Cherríe Moraga's *Giving Up the Ghost*," 116). For example, the rape episode reveals that Corky has internalized societal attitudes. At one point, she decides: "I knew I musta done somet'ing real wrong / to get myself in this mess" (28). In "A Long Line of Vendidas," Moraga discusses the historical practice of blaming the rape victim and links it to the Malinche myth: "In the very act of intercourse with Cortés, Malinche is seen as having been violated. She is not, however, an innocent victim, but the guilty party—ultimately responsible for her own sexual victimization" (*Loving in the War Years*, 118). Alarcón points out that "because Malintzin aided Cortés in the conquest of the New World, she is seen as concretizing women's sexual weakness and interchangeability, always open to sexual exploitation." She writes, "Indeed, as along as we continue to be seen in that way, we are earmarked to be abusable matter, not just by men of another culture, but all cultures including the one that breeds us" (184). The rape also confirms Corky's "femaleness" because she feels absent, objectified: "I suddenly feel like I'm floating in the air / my thing kina attached to no body / flapping in the wind like a bird a wounded bird" (28). When she is penetrated, Corky cries, "He made me a hole!" (29). This declaration of nothingness and despair is a rite of passage for Corky/Marisa, for she realizes that she is vulnerable in the society. Yarbro-Bejarano maintains that "the rape brings home Corky's sex to her as an inescapable fact, confirming her culture's definition of female as being taken" ("The Female Subject in Chicano Theatre," 147). María Herrera-Sobek, in "The Politics of Rape: Sexual Transgression in Chicana Fiction," posits that Moraga encodes in *Giving Up the Ghost* the construct in the act of raping, of making (i.e., of "en-gendering"), women: "In this process of engendering, fabricating, that is, making a gender, the end result is a hole and absence: women as invisible, voiceless, worthless, devalued objects." She further notes that women are "silent entities dominated by ingrained patriarchal vectors where the Name of the Father is Law, and years of socialization to obey the Father's Law transforms the female subject into a quavering accomplice in her own rape." Women, then, betray themselves as well as other women: "Women are socialized into being participants in their own [and other women's] oppression" (172–173).

Women in the culture are socialized to betray each other because of the culture's directive to put the male first. This process occurs between mothers and daughters such as Lupe and Leticia in *Shadow of a Man* and occurs between women friends and/or lovers. Marisa bears the wounds of these betrayals: "The women I have loved the most have always loved the man more than me, even in their hatred of him" (14). Consequently, she fears that Amalia will leave her. Moraga's dramatization of Marisa's jealousy and pain illuminates the complexities of their relationship.

Marisa's decision to battle for women, to save them, begins with the physical and psychical "wounding" she experiences during the rape. Partly, Marisa relates to Amalia because Amalia has also been wounded by men. Marisa believes, "It was not natural or right that she got beat down so damn hard, and that all those crimes had nothing to do with the girl she once was two, three, four decades ago" (35). Also, Marisa relates to Amalia because Amalia's wounds remind her of her mother's. Healing Amalia, then, by extension, means healing the mother. Using her hands as "weapons of war," Marisa attempts to restore Amalia, "making her body remember, it didn't have to be that hurt" (35). Together, the women heal each other. Spiritually, they connect, suggesting "the possibility of mutual salvation" (Yarbro-Bejarano, "Cherríe Moraga's *Giving Up the Ghost*," 118), their love for each other becoming a religious experience. When Amalia tells Marisa, "You make love to me like worship," Marisa wants to say, but does not: "Sí, la mujer es mi religion" (34). Temporarily, the women find salvation not in God but in each other. Yarbro-Bejarano notes that "for Moraga the lesbian couple is the microcosm in which the dynamic of faith works itself out, becoming a metaphor for feminism" ("Cherríe Moraga," 173–174).

Partly, Marisa relates to Amalia as a way to embrace the race of the mother. Ultimately, embracing the mother's race means embracing, or accepting, one's mestiza heritage, one's Indian roots, in particular. The longing to connect with the mother's culture is finally a longing for community. In turn, Amalia, longing for her Indian roots, finds a connection to them in Marisa's mestiza features. Moraga dramatizes the women's connection to the past through the dream sequences, in which the women are Indians, dancing or making tortillas, clapping them together in time to indigenous music. The most significant sequence is the one in which Amalia dreams that they are Indians and have broken some taboo in the village. Amalia is afraid until she realizes that "it is *you* who have gone against the code of our people." She also realizes that she does not fear punishment from "los dioses"; instead, she fears the breaking of the taboo—the fact that "the taboo *could* be broken." She concludes, "And if this law nearly transcribed in blood could go, then what else? What *was* there to hold to? What immutable truths were left?" (33). Amalia represents the culture's fears when laws are broken, laws that provide the glue to hold the society together. Ultimately, she fears the downfall of the entire race. If a lesbian, the worst traitor or "malinchista" of all, could break the culture's sexual mandate, then the culture itself could be in danger of unraveling. Embedded in this dream vision is Moraga's hope of a new, liberating cultural configuration.

Overall, in *Giving Up the Ghost*, Moraga addresses the continuum of mother-daughter love. She implies that daughters receive a legacy of love from the mother that is nourishing and healing, unlike the legacy from the father that is often demeaning and damaging. To Moraga, women should tap into this source of sustenance in order to heal and save each other. Marisa draws from this source but is unable to convince other women, including Amalia, to eschew heterosexual relationships.

The ending of *Giving Up the Ghost* is somewhat despairing. Marisa states, "I am preparing myself for the worst" (35). However, the beginning is hopeful (the play is not linear in form). In a flashback, Marisa writes that her love for Amalia was a "blessing" that convinced her that she was not "trapped" (7). On a personal level, Marisa finds love that transcends the material. On a political level, she wages a war to redeem women, including her mother, from the "prison" of institutional heterosexuality.

In *Heroes and Saints*, which is "an unusual blend of realism, surrealism, and political theater" (Gelb, 518), Moraga extends the issue of betrayal beyond the somewhat insular family sphere to the more all-encompassing Chicano community. In order to demonstrate this, she draws two different mother figures: one who perpetuates institutional beliefs and practices, the Catholic Church, in particular, and one who challenges them.

Dolores, like Hortensia in *Shadow of a Man*, perpetuates institutional ideologies, her racial/sexual identity having been shaped by an oppressive and relentless socialization process, grounded in traditional Catholicism. "It is a faith," assesses Linda Feyder, "that has placed taboos on female sexuality making the Hispanic woman ashamed of her own body" (5). In the main, Catholicism is the overriding belief system that informs her identity. By colluding with this belief system in the socialization of her own daughters, she betrays them, limiting their potential, sexually and politically. According to Hal Gelb, "The mother is reactionary, a sexually and otherwise repressive, fatalistic figure who must be overthrown" (519).

Dolores, the traditional, self-sacrificing mother, is coded as the mother of La Malinche, who sells her daughter into servitude and submission, and La Llorona, who weeps for her lost children and grieves for her "sins." Motherhood is not only her "work," as she proclaims, but it is also her identity. In the words of Garcia-Bahne, "Women accept this definition of themselves because of some security that comes with the role, but this acceptance lends itself to a subtle but pernicious undermining of women's self-esteem" (39). For example, she loses this identity, this sense of selfhood, when she loses her children: "It doesn't matter," she relates, "how old they get or how far away they go, son tus hijos and they always take a piece of you with them. So you walk around full of holes from all the places they take from you." Also, to Dolores, motherhood is a sacred vocation, one she equates with saintliness: "El Dios es el único que nos llena" (130).

One of her sacred missions is to protect her daughters from the "outside" world. She does this by keeping them voiceless, sexless, and invisible. The house, or the traditional family structure, is another one of Moraga's "prisons" or "cages." Dolores literally imprisons her youngest daughter, Cerezita, inside the house, never allowing her to be seen or heard. Although political and social turmoil is occurring in the community, Dolores does not define herself as a member of a community but as a mother of an insular traditional family unit. Garcia-Bahne postulates, "The Chicano family can thus be seen as a vehicle which incorporates those strengthening qualities that are necessary for social units to survive under exploitive conditions and paradoxically embodies those values which mitigate against the development and exercise of self-determination" (43).

Amparo is the nontraditional mother figure, coded as La Malinche because she challenges institutional beliefs and practices. She is considered a "bad" woman, a deviant, because she has "assertive social skills and self-confidence" (Garcia-Bahne, 41). With this particular character, Moraga offers a new definition of mother and nurturer. Amparo, although married, has no biological children, but she and her husband have "adopted" all of the community's children, "show[ing] the guts to fight para sus niños" (130) and organizing the Mothers and Friends of McLaughlin. Unlike Dolores, who believes the home is a safe, nurturing place, Amparo believes the home has become a "prison"—unsafe and life-denying. Also, unlike Dolores, Amparo rejects traditional Catholicism, informing her: "I don' even go to church no more, ni recibir comunión . . . coz I'm tire of swallowing what they want to shove down my throat" (102). Her rejection of the institutions of the traditional family and church is a movement away from oppressive, closed systems and a movement toward liberating, expanding definitions of *la madre* and *la familia*.

Yolanda, the oldest daughter, represents the unmarried mother, still trapped in the traditional home. Her baby daughter's illness and death from pesticide poisoning marks her transformation from stasis to action. First, she rejects the church, telling her mother: "He's [God's] forgotten you and me and everybody else in this goddamn valley." Secondly, she rejects the veiling and silencing of women, exposing herself to the men in the helicopter and daring them: "Take me!" (131). In despair, she asks her mother: "Don't you see, 'amá? I gotta find her killer. Put a face to him, a name, track him down and make him suffer the way we suffer. I want to kill him, 'amá. I want to kill some . . . goddamn body!" (132). With this declaration, Yolanda aligns with Amparo and joins the protests.

The youngest daughter, Cerezita, born without a "body," is a multiple referent. Because she has been wounded by pesticide poisoning, she is a reference to the children who are sick and dying in the Chicano community. Her severed head designates the separation of body and mind, and the "decapitation" of women or the denial (or "cutting off") of sexual desire by repressive cultures. It also represents her "virgin-like," "saint-like" state, prompting her mother to name her "virgencita" (137). In addition, the privileging of the head is a visual attack on the biologism that ultimately bolsters the privileging of the body. Furthermore, it is an attack on those who attribute lesbianism to biological factors. Significantly, Moraga attributes lesbianism "to social factors and/or luck—certainly not to physiology" ("Algo secretamente amado," 151).

Cerezita's mother, a proxy for institutional heterosexuality, indoctrinates her daughter in several ways. When she removes the anatomy books in order to eliminate worldly temptations, she is mimicking church teachings: "The biggest sins are in the mind" (113). When she prevents her from going outside and from looking out the window, she is attempting to repress her sensuality and to curb her quest for self-determination. In addition, when she attempts to "cut off" her tongue, a multiple signifier of sensuality, sexuality, and language (108–109), silencing her in order to "protect" her, she is molding her to comply with societal norms. This conditioning of Cerezita's mind and the condition of her body demonstrate how the mind and body are controlled by church and state. Rich writes, "This culture of manipulated passivity, nourishing violence at its core, has every stake in opposing women actively laying claim to our own lives" (*On Lies, Secrets, and Silence*, 14).

When Cerezita rejects her mother's socializing methods and aligns with Amparo's social activism, she also rejects the reductive appellation "virgencita" and aligns with the liberating signifier La Virgen of Guadalupe.[6] At the conclusion, she offers herself as a sacrifice, not as a traditional self-sacrificing mother but as a new liberated and liberating mother, "Madre . . . Libertad" (148). When Cerezita appropriates the Virgin's image, clothing herself in the signifier, she gives the political act a spiritual dimension. In "A Long Line of Vendidas," Moraga observes that a movement's effectiveness often depends on "a spiritual imperative. Spirituality which inspires activism and, similarly, politics which move the spirit—which draw from the deep-seated place of our greatest longings for freedom—give meaning to our lives." She maintains that "such a vision can hold and heal us in the worst of times, and is in direct opposition to an apolitical spiritualist view of the world or a totally materialistic perspective" (*Loving in the War Years*, 130).

Moraga's examination of the La Malinche legacy and its effect on the mothers' and daughters' racial/sexual identities is a political act to challenge, and ultimately to dismantle, patriarchal systems, based on institutional heterosexuality. In all three of her plays, she looks closely at the ways mothers (and mother figures) and daughters interact during the socialization process. All of the women are at different stages of self-realization and self-actualization. All are "betrayers," either "selling out" the daughters by preparing them to serve the patriarchy or "selling out" the culture by daring to criticize it. The lesbian is the most daring of the *vendidas* or *chingadas*, for she not only "sells out" the cultural contract, but also blurs the distinctions between the dualities, threatening the very foundations of the power structures. In her last play, *Heroes and Saints*, Moraga takes her characters into the realm of the absurd to magnify the physical and psychical wounds women have borne under repressive institutions and to render a vision of revolution. This revolution, however, not only (re)claims Chicana women but also (re)claims the race.

Overall, Moraga dares, in these dramatic works, to critique the Chicano culture, ironically becoming *la vendida* in the process. But she argues, in "A Long Line of Vendidas," that "to be critical of one's culture is not to betray that culture" (108); in fact, not to critique the culture would be an "act of self betrayal" (112), as well as a betrayal of her mother and, by extension, all Chicanas. To critique the culture, then, is an act of love, an act of reclamation. She writes, "It is the daughters that can be relied upon. Las hijas who remain faithful a la madre, a la madre de la madre" (*Loving in the War Years*, 139).

Notes

1. In 1986 she received the American Book Award from the Before Columbus Foundation for *This Bridge Called My Back: Writings by Radical Women of Color* (1981), which she co-edited with Gloria Anzaldúa. *Loving in the War Years: Lo que nunca pasó por sus labios*, a compilation of her poems, short stories, and essays, was published in 1983. This book contains two seminal essays that inform Moraga's works: "La Güera" and "A Long Line of Vendidas." Although she calls herself primarily a poet, she has written several plays: *Giving Up the Ghost: A Stage Play in Three Portraits* (first staged reading 1984; first produced 1987); *La extranjera* (1985); *Shadow of a Man* (first staged reading 1989; first produced 1990); and *Heroes and Saints* (first staged reading 1989; first produced 1992). *Shadow of a Man* is a recipient of the Fund for New American Plays Award.
2. According to Adelaida R. Del Castillo, in "Malintzin Tenépal: A Preliminary Look into a New Perspective," Malintzin Tenépal (her Aztec name), also known as La Malinche and Doña Marina, was sold to the Mayans by her mother in tandem with her second husband; she was later given to Hernán Cortés as a gift, along with several other young women. A brilliant woman who could speak several languages, she became invaluable to Cortés as an interpreter and guide. Partly, she assisted him because she believed, as many Aztecs did, that he was the god Quetzalcoatl, whose arrival had been predicted on the very day Cortés and his men came ashore. Because of her strong faith, Malintzin became the first Indian to be baptized as a Christian in her native land. Although she and Cortés had a son, he eventually married her off to another Spaniard, Don Juan Jaramillo. After Malintzin's death at the age of twenty-two (probably from smallpox), Jaramillo tortured and robbed her children of their rightful inheritance.
3. Octavio Paz, in *The Labyrinth of Solitude: Life and Thought in Mexico*, relates that the Virgin appeared in 1531, about ten years after the Spanish conquest, to an Indian, Juan Diego, on the Hill of Tepeyac, where a temple had stood in pre-Hispanic times dedicated to the Aztec goddess of fertility, Tonantzin, known to the Indians as "Our Mother" (84). In "The Virgin of Guadalupe: A Mexican National Symbol," Eric R. Wolf explains that to the Indians, and later to the mestizos, this revelation linked their ancient gods and goddesses to the new order, validating their existence and assuring them salvation. (During the time

of the conquest, Spanish officials debated whether the Indians were worthy or capable of being saved. If they were subhuman, then there was justification for oppression and exploitation.) The Virgin of Guadalupe represents on one level maternal warmth, life, hope, and health. She also represents a sexless, yet motherly state, the ideal to which Chicanas should aspire. On another level she represents major political aspirations: "The myth of the Guadalupe thus validates the Indian's right to legal defense, orderly government, to citizenship; to supernatural salvation, but also to salvation from random oppression" (37).

In *La Chicana: The Mexican-American Woman*, Alfredo Mirandé and Evangelina Enríquez offer several versions of the La Llorona myth dating back to pre-Columbian times. All reflect the culture's attitudes toward women. Prior to the arrival of Cortés, her voice was heard, crying for her lost children. Later, she was associated with La Malinche. Legends surrounding her have migrated to the southwestern United States; California and Texas have their own unique versions. In all the interpretations, she is a woman who has transgressed in her proper role as "mother, wife, mistress, lover, or patriot" (31–33).

4. In *Loving in the War Years*, Moraga writes about her profound love for her mother, the source from which her love for other women emanates. In her poem "La Dulce Culpa," she asks,

> What kind of lover have you made me, mother
> *so in love*
> with what is left
> unrequited. (15)

Provocatively, Adrienne Rich states, in "Compulsory Heterosexuality and Lesbian Existence," "If women are the earliest sources of emotional caring and physical nurture for both female and male children, it would seem logical, from a feminist perspective at least, to pose the following questions: whether the search for love and tenderness in both sexes does not originally lead toward women; *why in fact women ever redirect that search . . .*" (182).

5. *Chingón* and *chingada* have multiple meanings in Spanish, Mexican, and Chicano cultures; basically *chingón* refers to an active, aggressive male; *chingada* to a passive, violated female (Paz, 77).
6. The image of the Virgin carried on banners united farmworkers during strikes and demonstrations in California and Texas (Anzaldúa, 29).

Works Cited

Alarcón, Norma. "Chicana's Feminist Literature: A Re-vision through Malintzin/ or Malintzin: Putting Flesh Back on the Object." In *This Bridge Called My Back: Writings by Radical Women of Color*, ed. Cherríe Moraga and Gloria Anzaldúa, 182–190. Watertown: Persephone, 1981.

———. "Making *Familia* from Scratch: Split Subjectivities in the Work of Helena María Viramontes and Cherríe Moraga." In *Chicana Creativity and Criticism: Charting New Frontiers in American Literature*, ed. María Herrera-Sobek and Helena María Viramontes, 147–159. Houston: Arte Público, 1988.

Anzaldúa, Gloria. *Borderlands/La Frontera: The New Mestiza*. San Francisco: Spinsters, 1987.

Blea, Irene I. *La Chicana and the Intersection of Race, Class, and Gender*. New York: Praeger, 1992.

Case, Sue-Ellen. "From Split Subject to Split Britches." In *Feminine Focus: The New Women Playwrights*, ed. Enoch Brater, 126–146. New York: Oxford University Press, 1989.

de Lauretis, Teresa. "Sexual Indifference and Lesbian Representation." *Theatre Journal* 40 (May 1988): 155–177.

Del Castillo, Adelaida R. "Malintzin Tenépal: A Preliminary Look into a New Perspective." In Sánchez and Cruz, 124–149.

DeShazer, Mary K. "'Sisters in Arms': The Warrior Construct in Writings by Contemporary U.S. Women of Color." In *Writing the Woman Artist: Essays on Poetics, Politics, and Portraiture*, ed. Suzanne W. Jones, 261–286. Philadelphia: University of Pennsylvania Press, 1991.

Feyder, Linda, ed. "Introduction." In *Shattering the Myth: Plays by Hispanic Women*, 5–8. Houston: Arte Público, 1992.

Garcia-Bahne, Betty. "La Chicana and the Chicano Family." In Sánchez and Cruz, 30–47.

Gelb, Hal. "Heroes and Saints." *Nation* (Nov. 2, 1992): 518–520.

Herrera-Sobek, María. "The Politics of Rape: Sexual Transgression in Chicana Fiction." In *Chicana Criticism: Charting New Frontiers in American Literature*, ed. María Herrera-Sobek and Helena María Viramontes, 171–181. Houston: Arte Público, 1988.

Lovato, Roberto. "Yo Existo: The Woman of Color Breaks the Silence." *City* (Nov. 1990): 23–24.

Mirandé, Alfredo, and Evangelina Enríquez. *La Chicana: The Mexican-American Woman*. Chicago: University of Chicago Press, 1979.

Moraga, Cherríe. "Algo secretamente amado." In *The Sexuality of Latinas*, ed. Norma Alarcón, Ana Castillo, and Cherríe Moraga, 151–156. Berkeley: Third Woman, 1993.

———. *Giving Up the Ghost: A Stage Play in Three Portraits*. Albuquerque: West End, 1994 (all references to the play are from this source).

———. *Heroes and Saints*. In *Heroes and Saints and Other Plays: Giving Up the Ghost, Shadow of a Man, Heroes and Saints*, 85–149. Albuquerque: West End, 1994 (all references to the play are from this source).

———. *Loving in the War Years: Lo que nunca pasó por sus labios*. Boston: South End, 1983.

———. *Shadow of a Man*. In *Shattering the Myth: Plays by Hispanic Women*, ed. Linda Feyer, 9–49. Houston: Arte Público Press, 1992 (all references to the play are from this source).

Paz, Octavio. *The Labyrinth of Solitude: Life and Thought in Mexico*. Trans. Lysander Kemp. New York: Grove, 1961.

Quintanales, Mirtha N. "Loving in the War Years: An Interview with Cherríe Moraga." *off our backs* (Jan. 1985): 12–13.

Rich, Adrienne. "Compulsory Heterosexuality and Lesbian Existence." In *Powers of Desire: The Politics of Sexuality*, ed. Ann Snitow, Christine Stansell, and Sharon Thompson, 177–205. New York: Monthly Review, 1983.

———. *On Lies, Secrets, and Silence: Selected Prose 1966–1978*. New York: W. W. Norton, 1979.

Sánchez, Rosaura, and Rosa Martinez Cruz, eds. *Essays on La Mujer*. Los Angeles: University of California Press, 1977.

Sternbach, Nancy Saporta. "'A Deep Racial Memory of Love': The Chicana Feminism of Cherríe Moraga." In *Breaking Boundaries: Latina Writing and Critical Readings*, ed. Asunción Horno-Delgado et al., 48–61. Amherst: University of Massachusetts Press, 1989.

Wolf, Eric R. "The Virgin of Guadalupe: A Mexican National Symbol." *Journal of American Folklore* 71 (Jan.–Mar. 1958): 34–39.

Yarbro-Bejarano, Yvonne. "Cherríe Moraga." In *Chicano Writers: First Series*, ed. Francisco A. Lomeli and Carl R. Shirley, 165–177. Vol. 82 of *Dictionary of Literary Biography*. Detroit: Gale, 1989.

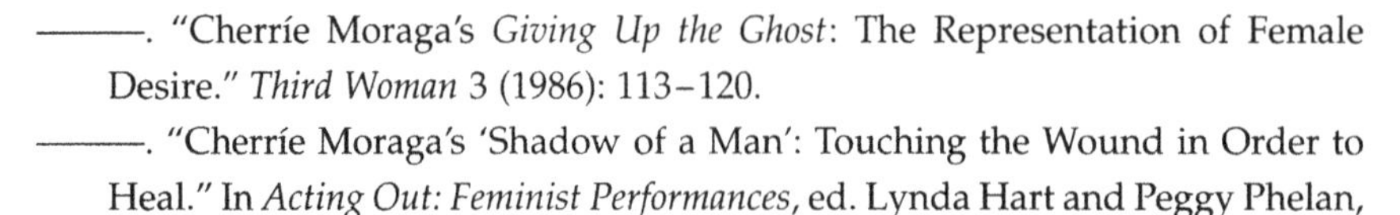

———. "Cherríe Moraga's *Giving Up the Ghost*: The Representation of Female Desire." *Third Woman* 3 (1986): 113–120.

———. "Cherríe Moraga's 'Shadow of a Man': Touching the Wound in Order to Heal." In *Acting Out: Feminist Performances*, ed. Lynda Hart and Peggy Phelan, 85–104. Ann Arbor: University of Michigan Press, 1993.

———. "The Female Subject in Chicano Theatre: Sexuality, 'Race,' and Class." In *Performing Feminisms: Feminist Critical Theory and Theatre*, ed. Sue-Ellen Case, 131–149. Baltimore: Johns Hopkins University Press, 1990.

The Poetics of Matrilineage

Mothers and Daughters in the Poetry of African American Women, 1965–1985

FABIAN CLEMENTS WORSHAM

"The image of the mother," according to critic Andrea Benton Rushing, "is the most prevalent image of black women" in African American poetry ("Afro-American," 75). These images have been developed through a long and distinguished literary history, reaching back through the diaspora to ancient African cultures in which "the African woman is associated with core values" and is revered as "guardian of traditions, the strong Earth-Mother who stands for security and stability" (Rushing, "African," 19). These values, passed down through an oral tradition in which women have played a major role, as well as through the medium of print, continue to define the ways black women are represented in African American literature and the ways they perceive themselves and their daughters and act upon these perceptions. Christine Renee Robinson argues that "self-reliance, independence, assertiveness, and strength are inherent characteristics of Black women which are passed on to Black girls at a very early age" (Nice, 68). And it has been widely noted that, contrary to the experience of most white women, black mothers and daughters prosper through relationships that are mutually loving and supportive (Nice, 197; Washington, 148). A recent landmark study by Vivian E. Nice not only points out the relevance of these literary images to sociological and psychological explorations of black motherhood, but also suggests the possibility of using these artistic representations of relationships between black mothers and daughters as models of the kind of supportive, interdependent relationships possible between mothers and daughters of any race once freed from the distorting influences of patriarchal culture.

The writings of African American women hold particular interest for Nice and other feminist theorists who seek to replace the Freudian model of female adolescent development (which emphasizes conflict) with a model based on interdependency and "growth through relationships" (Nice, 66), thus fostering stronger positive bonds between all mothers and daughters and between members of the larger community of women. Nice is aware, however, that ambivalence and conflict will be part of even the most loving relationships, and she applauds contemporary black women writers for revealing ambivalence "in all its glory." In the works of the contemporary poets she cites, there exists "the connection between mothers and daughters and the legacy of strength between them without denying the anger, guilt, and difficulties in communication which can also exist and the fact that connection and anger can in fact co-exist" (187).

In African American poetry, however, there have been at least three forces working to limit the depth of characterization and fullness of description in representations of black mothers and daughters:

1. the symbolic nature of the mother in the African American tradition;
2. the dominant white culture's insistence on what it identifies as universality;
3. the necessity of promoting "positive images" of blacks in order to achieve social change.

With regard to the first of these forces, Rushing notes that "women often symbolize aspects of black life that are valued by the race"; she claims that "that usually unconscious thrust has been something of a straightjacket" ("Afro-American," 74). She calls these symbolic images "epic," "heroic," or "archetypal" ("Afro-American," 82). In another instance, she reflects that poetry may not be a suitable instrument for creating realistic characters ("African," 24). Nan Bauer Maglin agrees that these depictions are often symbolic, but she emphasizes the legitimacy of symbolic representation:

In the literature of matrilineage often the strength of the women in our past is sentimentalized or is magnified so that our own strength appears to be negligible—

especially in terms of the hard physical and social conditions of the past. Sometimes our genealogical and historical mothers become not persons but symbols (which we need) and lose their multidimensionality. (263)

Maglin cites Lucille Clifton's "My Mama Moved among the Days" as an example of such symbolization, but she argues that Clifton's depiction is "not simplistic" since the poem reveals the mother's fear as well as her strength (263).

Taking a different approach, Arnold Rampersad in his article "The Universal and the Particular in Afro-American Poetry" writes of the dominant white culture's insistence on universality and its equally vehement insistence that the particulars of black experience cannot be construed as universal. Such strictures led to the propagation of "raceless virtues" as black writers attempted to "elevate" their writing while effectively binding it in shackles. Rampersad says of this verse that it "is sometimes executed in glorious fashion, but in many instances it is much like the efforts of a man bound and gagged who is trying to get one's attention" (9). True universality is rooted in the specifics of everyday life; false universality (that prescribed by the dominant culture) "thrives on vagueness; it abhors the specific in any form that stresses concrete experience" (8). Rampersad identifies Amiri Baraka as the poet who, in the 1960s, initiated "a violent assault on the obsessively universal in Afro-American writing" (14).

Finally, the necessity of promoting "positive images" of blacks in general and of black women in particular may have contributed somewhat to the limiting range of characterization of mothers and daughters (for references to the need for positive images, see Ward, 189; Giovanni, 40; Parker, xxx). The projection of positive images, of course, is essential to the development of black pride and self-worth and is a key element in countering stereotypes such as "the Mammy" and "Sapphire." However, this inherently good and useful prescription for change may have produced a somewhat paradoxical side effect: a positive stereotype. As Rushing observes, "in almost all the mother poems, mother is above criticism, the almost perfect symbol of black struggle, suffering, and endurance" ("Afro-American," 76). Ward warns, though, of the problems inherent in judging the adequacy of these representations:

Whether visions of Black women in literature are positive or negative, true or distorted, good or bad, real or surreal, satisfying or inadequate is relative. Evaluation of the vision depends in part on some understanding of the cultural imperatives that governed its creation and in part on whether those imperatives (linguistic, social, psychological, etc.) are constant with our own. (188)

In the intensely autobiographical poems of contemporary African Americans, such as Alice Walker, Lucille Clifton, Carolyn Rodgers, Audre Lorde, and Colleen McElroy, images of black mothers and daughters have achieved a fullness and depth of representation which indicate the individuality of black women and the diversity of their experience. Although the poems are at times more abstract and symbolic, at times more concrete and specific, taken together they provide the model of interdependency which Nice speaks of, with its welter of love, ambivalence, admiration, and anger.

An impressive example of the strong traditional mother appears in Alice Walker's sequence "In These Dissenting Times" (Adoff, 475–480). In carefully crafted, spare verses, Walker employs incremental description to build, piece by piece, an image of a woman of her mother's generation, a mighty gold-toothed woman who dragged her children to church. The third poem in the sequence is entitled "Women," and it is here, primarily, that Walker consciously creates an iconography of traditional black motherhood. As is apparent from the poem's title, Walker has no intention of creating individualized, idiosyncratic portraits of these women. Here she continues the generalized, fragmentary descriptions begun in the prologue. She describes the women's voices as husky, their steps as stout, and their hands as fists. And she shows the women acting not in isolated, separate incidents, but in actions which have become mythologized, embedded in the cultural consciousness of African Americans because of their persuasiveness and the intense emotion—the pain, the humiliation, and the fortitude—which those actions symbolize. The persona notes that these "Headragged Generals" (477) demolished barriers and marched across mined fields to secure an education for their children. Yet when her purpose is individual representation, she does that equally well. In the fourth poem of the sequence, "Three Dollars Cash," she particularizes a representation of her own mother by retelling the story of how her family paid the midwife who brought her into the world. Most of the poem is spoken by the mother, and the diction and cadences of the mother's speech further particularize the poem. The mother's language also creates a casual, informal atmosphere, as does Walker's use of the word "Mom" rather than "Mother."

Whether Walker speaks symbolically or specifically, throughout the sequence she restricts herself to the idealized representation of black motherhood. According to Mary Burgher,

> Values specifically attributed to Black mothers include the belief that there is a promised land beyond this life of bondage and oppression, that one has within oneself the natural wit and resourcefulness to find strength in apparent weakness, joy in sorrow, and hope in what seems to be despair, and that the love of a mother cannot always be determined by physical presence or material gifts. (116)

The faith and determination of these women is shown in their insistence that life will be better for their children, even if that involves physical hardship and sacrifice for themselves. Burgher emphasizes these qualities: "It is not she separately who is significant and it is not what she attains personally and immediately that matters; instead it is what the future brings from the ideas she expresses, the consciousness she reflects, the action she takes" (120).

In much of the poetry of these contemporary writers, the mother is a figure of such mythic proportions that her life haunts her daughters through the duration of their own lives. Lucille Clifton, whose mother died in mid-life (at age forty-four), has written extensively upon this theme. In her poem "Breaklight," she speaks of her own intellectual and spiritual growth, which culminates in a new understanding of her mother. She says that when her mother's fears approached her she listened as they explained themselves to her. The persona notes with certainty, "And I understand" (*An Ordinary Woman*, 85). These experiences of mystical enlightenment culminate in a very intense, personal understanding. It is useful, in considering this poem, to look at Clifton's "My Mama Moved among the Days" (Adoff, 308). Part of what Clifton finally "understood" in "Breaklight" may have been what she was unable to understand earlier: her mother was able to get them "almost through the high grass," but seemingly turned around and ran back into the wilderness. The mother here is loved and yearned for, but is not idealized, even though the language is highly symbolic. She has not fully carried out her responsibilities to her daughter. These may be particular responsibilities which remain unnamed and which the mother left undone out of fear or they may simply be her obligation to live and to nurture her daughter, which she was unable to do. Both poems are dreamlike: Mama moves "like a dreamwalker in a field," the disembodied fears knock at the door, trying to "explain themselves." In coming to understand her mother's fears through these dreams, Clifton resolves the bewildering unfinished relationship (at least momentarily, to the extent that poetry can serve that therapeutic function) and assuages her pain.

In a poem commemorating the twenty-first year of her mother's absence ("february 13, 1980"), she speaks again of her grief and pain, naming her mother "the lost color in my eye" (*two-headed woman*, 15). Clifton, whose middle name is Thelma, after her mother, feels that her mother's name has continued to protect her despite her mother's physical absence. She says that she has worn her mother's name like a shield. Her complex feelings are apparent when she notes that the shield has both ripped her up and safeguarded her. And since her mother's absence has come of age, Clifton determines that she must now accept the responsibilities that go along with womanhood. But she assures her absent mother that although she has grown into a self-sufficient woman, she nonetheless remains spiritually close to her. Her mother, though dead, is a continuing presence in her life; lest she disappoint the lingering spirit, the daughter must reassure her that she is still loved and needed.

Approaching the age at which her mother died, Clifton ruminates more darkly upon her mother's death in two poems, "the thirty eighth year" and "poem on my fortieth birthday to my mother who died young." In the first one, the tone is resigned and melancholy, as Clifton reflects upon her life and finds herself merely "an ordinary woman." Implicitly, she compares herself to her mother, finding herself inadequate. She says that she had expected to be more than she was. Instead she views herself as "plain as bread" (*An Ordinary Woman*, 93). In contrast, she remembers her mother as very wise and beautiful. Despite these perceived differences, she identifies strongly with her mother, saying that she has surrounded herself with memories of her mother so that her mother's dreams could be fulfilled through her. The persona clearly sees herself as a continuation or replication of the mother. The implication is that daughters cannot truly find voice until they validate their mother's voice or experiences. Having rescued her mother from death by living for her, she now faces the death which swallowed up her mother. She associates life with images of Africa and death, in contrast, with images of Europe. The prospect of death creates in her an intense loneliness which she had not anticipated; if she is coming to the end of her life, she asks that she be allowed to come to it without fear and loneliness. She says that before she dies, she wants to come "into [her] own" (95). Here she is not seeking to escape from her mother's life (and thus from death), but to emerge from her mother's life equipped with the emotional resources which will allow her to live her own life fully before it ends.

The image of "turning the final turn" derived from the footrace is used again in "poem on my fortieth birthday" (*two-headed woman,* 14). Here the tone is not at all melancholy; rather than growing more abject as the fateful date nears, Clifton (perhaps drawing upon the emotional resources she has inherited and cultivated) seems to rally as she approaches the homestretch. Defiant, strong, goal-oriented, she informs her mother that she intends to keep running. Yet she is not convinced of victory: "if I fall / I fall." The vortex of her mother's death continues to pull her into its spiral.

A truly grueling example of this intense mother/daughter identification is Carolyn Rodgers's "The Children of Their Sin," a double narrative in four parts (21–25). Three of the parts relate the daughter's decision to change seats on a public conveyance; one part tells of the mother's being mugged. As the mother's and daughter's experiences are interwoven, the daughter's changing seats becomes even more intense, violent, and emotionally wrenching than her mother's mugging.

In the first section of the poem, Rodgers explains that she decides to change seats on a bus (or possibly a train) because the man who sat down next to her seems unsavory. Because she has money in her pockets (and because she bears her mother's experience in mind, as is revealed later), she moves to a seat by a stylishly dressed white businessman. Yet as she does so, she "smother[s] faint memories and / shadows and things." The dramatic and passionate narration of the mother's mugging (by a "mean nigger") in section two is followed in section three by the riveting protest of the shadows which she had "smothered" in section one. While she fears that this poor, hungry black brother might mug her, she is reminded by a coliseum of black women ancestors of all the atrocities that white slaveholders heaped upon blacks. These ancestors scream to her to remember the whips, the bodies hanging from trees, the women who were raped and whose children were sold away. The poem moves toward a crescendo of anguish and guilt as Rodgers hears her mother's desperate screams juxtaposed against the agonies of the black race at the hands of white slaveholders. Identifying with her mother, she chooses white over black (she changes seats). Although at first she is only vaguely uncomfortable at this decision, ultimately she understands that her choice is a true act of treason against her race.

Produced at the heart of the Black Arts Movement and promoted by Dudley Randall's Broadside Press, Carolyn Rodgers's work is widely known and often discussed. Her poems "Jesus Was Crucified, or It Must Be Deep" and a companion piece, "It Is Deep," in which Rodgers refers to her mother as "a sturdy Black bridge that I / crossed over, on," are well known (8–12). Rodgers is especially skilled in the depiction of conflict, whether internal or interpersonal. In "Jesus Was Crucified," the points of contention between mother and daughter are apparent: the mother does not approve of her daughter's rejection of religion or her association with revolutionaries (whom she accuses of being Communists); the daughter resents the mother's complacency and lack of political awareness. The daughter's tone throughout is sarcastic and sassy; the mother appears backward and ridiculous, and there is little in this poem to indicate that the daughter has any compassion for her. In the collection *how i got ovah*, however, this poem is followed by "It Is Deep," which serves as a sort of retraction and reconciliation. This poem indicates a complete shift in the daughter's awareness; suddenly she understands that despite their differences they are united by their love and strengthened by the hardships they have come through together.

Discussions of these poems are included in studies by Maglin (265) and Nice (187). Both critics recognize that these poems show the ambivalence characteristic of any intense, enduring relationship, and both recognize the relationship depicted as a model of their ideal mutual support and interdependency. Maglin also notes that "It Is Deep" "articulates some of the themes of the literature of matrilineage: the distance between the mother and daughter; the sudden new sense the daughter has of the mother; the realization that she, her mother, is a strong woman; and that her voice reverberates with her mother's" (265).

Although Maglin and Nice focus on a pair of poems in which conflicts are neatly worked out, in a growing number of mother-daughter poems conflicts are not resolved so neatly, and some are not resolved at all. Despite the tendency for relationships between black mothers and their daughters to be supportive, there are individual exceptions, and some of them are poets. Audre Lorde appears to be one of these, though her struggle to understand her mother is evident in her poems. One of them, "Story Books on a Kitchen Table" (*Coal*, 27), opens, "Out of her womb of pain my mother spat me / into her ill-fitting harness of despair."

Lorde's diction here is sharp and effective; the connotations of *spat*—disgust, disdain, and filthiness—in this context, the act of giving birth, are intended to shock and offend. The child is immediately harnessed—confined—in the mother's despairing world view. The mother undoubtedly fears that her child will shame her by not turning out properly, that she will reject her mother's views and values. Her mother leaves her, for reasons unstated, in the care of "iron maidens." Needing the warmth and tenderness of a "perfect" mother, the child is left with emotionally distant old women. She is (mal)nourished on European witch tales rather than stories of her African-Caribbean heritage. The table is empty, the mother vanished. The poem suggests that there are mothers who seek to control and manipulate; when their daughters resist, the conflict intensifies. The child's loneliness and desperate needs are manifested as heartache—the ache of the ill-fitting harness, a despair like her mother's.

In the poem "Prologue" (*From a Land*, 43–46) Lorde says that in her mother's attempts to teach her survival strategies she tried to beat her whiter every day. She refers to her mother's "bleached ambition" as her motivation for teaching her children about her mother's errors. In her integrity and determination to speak the truth as she understands it, Lorde does not minimize the mother's error; yet the insertion of one word, *survival*, associated as it is with the fabric of oppression, clarifies the complexity of the situation. The mother is not infallibly good or innately evil. And as her mother tried to beat her into whiteness, Lorde recalls her "loving me into her blood's black bone." Here the paradoxical identification of physical punishment with love and Lorde's recognition that she and her mother are bound the more strongly for it are evident. Lorde's attempts to understand her mother are also revealed in "Black Mother Woman," where she imagistically represents the process of this understanding: she has peeled away her mother's anger "down to the core of love" (*From a Land*, 16).

Another contemporary black woman who has written exceptional poems on the theme of mother-daughter conflict is Colleen McElroy. The image she presents of the mother in the poem "Bone Mean" could not in any way be construed as positive. The persona notes that the mother has stacked the world against her daughter. Intentionally mean and vindictive, this mother serves mint-flavored ice cream at the child's birthday party, fully aware that the child dislikes it. As her daughters have matured, she has "pruned and pinched / them into bonsai symmetry" (*Queen*, 25). A harsh, domineering, cronelike woman, she seeks to control everything around her, until her daughters have no voices and no wills of their own.

Although such a poem is not politically useful in the interests of feminism or race struggle, it is nonetheless a valid and skillfully constructed work of art. If one insists that all art is political, then this poem might be construed as misogynist. If one holds, however, that a poem should be the artist's representation of the truth of her experience as she conceives it, then this poem is a work of integrity, and perhaps also of courage, for the view presented here has not been "politically correct" since the mid-sixties.

Intense, unresolved conflict is the theme again in McElroy's poem "Ruth" (Stetson, 287–288). The daughter has been haunted for twenty-seven years by her memory of her mother falling down a flight of stairs during one of their arguments. She remembers the terror she felt as she was unable to prevent her mother from falling. Immobilized, she felt like the famous statue of Venus (the Aphrodite of Melos) without arms to catch her mother. Here imagery reveals her complex feelings: on the one hand, the mother is "larger than life," "a great vulture"; on the other, she is "fragile . . . plunging in wingless flight." McElroy has been unable to write about this incident for twenty-seven years, all attempts thwarted by the memory of her mother's angry words. Nonetheless, her relationship with her mother has been an obsession, as is evident in the countless unfinished verses about her mother which she has stuffed away in closets. Writing the poem, she has finally recognized the cycle of pain and blood in which she and her mother (and all women) are trapped. She has been unable to see herself in her mother, to recognize the forces that unify them, including perhaps their shared oppression. And she understands that she will someday continue the cycle in her relationship with her own daughter. However, the ending of the poem does not indicate a complete reversal—anger and bitterness have not completely been replaced by love and understanding. Modifying the words of the biblical Ruth, McElroy says, "Wherever I go you have gone." Not only does she see her mother as having prepared the way for her, but she cannot find a path that is uniquely hers—a path her mother has not taken before her—and she finds this frustrating. The persona is in search of a space to call her very own, perhaps, one in which she will be able to break the cycle of pain and begin a new legacy which includes joy.

As is apparent in quite a few of these poems, including this one, feelings are complex. They result from a lifetime of experience and, like thunderheads, are continuously roiling. The poems about mothers and daughters reflect the shifting configurations of feelings.

McElroy's poems do not exclusively present conflicts, though she does that with great skill. Perhaps the most beautiful poem she has written is "Mother," a birth poem rich with the imagery of the African jungle (*Music*, 34–35). The poet imagines her mother, sedated while giving birth to her, dreaming of "emerald green forests," "queleas and touracos." The mother's dream of Africa symbolizes her role in the generational continuity of the black race. Her daughter, the poet, sits in an easy chair, happy and comfortable, trying to remember what it was like to be in her mother's womb. Continuity of lineage is emphasized as the daughter hums her mother's song while her own children watch her.

Two other notable birth poems are Audre Lorde's "Now That I Am Forever with Child" and Lucille Clifton's "light." Lorde's poem deals with the birth of her daughter, including the experience of pregnancy, her thoughts about the baby's prenatal development, the birth itself, and (in a brief conclusion) the child's individuation. Clifton's poem is about her own birth, particularly her mother's choice of the name Lucille for her, and includes the story of her ancestor whose name she is given. All of these birth poems are romantic, magical representations.

According to Nice, "there is much less written by mothers than by daughters on the mother-daughter relationship" (70). Indeed, this is true with regard to poetry. Outstanding poems by mothers on daughters are rare, the strongest having been written by Audre Lorde. Several have also been produced by Alice Walker. These poems focus on misgivings and insecurities which the mother experiences as she attempts to raise her daughter.

In "What My Child Learns of the Sea," Lorde ponders the intellectual growth of her daughter, who, despite what Lorde has passed on to her, will one day be a "strange girl . . . cutting my ropes" (*Coal*, 22). Yet Lorde herself will feel responsible for her daughter's view of the world, her optimism or pessimism. In "Progress Report" Lorde deals with her daughter's adolescence and, despite the apparent love between the two, the growing distance between them. When her daughter asks her about love, Lorde doesn't know whether to recommend "a dictionary / or myself" (*From a Land*, 13). She feels unsure whether she has taught her daughter enough about blackness and she knows that behind the closed door of her room her daughter is reading secret books. Lorde's respect for her maturing daughter, her acceptance of her as an individual, is obvious throughout the poem. She appreciates the child's strength of spirit, tenderness, and fearlessness, qualities she admires; and she remembers to knock before entering her daughter's room.

Alice Walker's poems about her daughter are very different from Lorde's—more direct and less evocative. Nonetheless, they reveal similar insecurities. Only a few lines of the poem "Mississippi Winter III" focus on her daughter, but what emerges clearly is Walker's anticipation of her daughter's adolescence, even though the child is only four. Walker is "alarmed" that her little daughter already "smells / of Love-Is-True perfume" (*Horses*, 38). This experience leads Walker to muse upon her own preference to avoid romance. "My Daughter Is Coming!" (*Horses*, 38–39) shows Walker frantic as she prepares a room for her daughter, who has been living far away in the custody of her father. Joyous, excited, and insecure, she worries that her daughter will only notice the torn curtains. Poems of this kind, in which mothers reveal their feelings about their daughters and illustrate the difficulties of motherhood, prove to be a valuable resource in understanding the mother's role.

Poems in which the poet deals with her role as both a mother and a daughter are especially rare. However, it is in these poems that the continuity of generations can be seen most clearly. Colleen McElroy's "In My Mother's Room" not only reveals the linkage of women from generation to generation within her own family, but also points to the connection of all women within a larger women's culture (*Queen*, 5–6). McElroy's images of her mother are not idealized, yet they achieve symbolic power. Her unflattering description of her mother's vulnerable naked body, with its childbearing scars, her mouth sagging open, suggests that this is a woman of flesh and blood and that McElroy is able to see beyond her role as mother to her physical existence as a woman. Though they are torn by conflict, she and her mother are "shadows of black into black," and she expects to follow her mother in "age-old patterns." Her connection with her mother and with all women is apparent in her assertion that she will follow the path of her foremothers in childbirth. Thus, here again as in "Ruth" is the "cycle of blood and pain" with its connection to fertility, childbirth, the continuation of one's genetic line, and the propagation of one's race. Though McElroy's daughter is innocent about what lies ahead for her, the poet understands that her continuation of this female role is inevitable.

Lucille Clifton also links three generations of women in her family in her poem "i was born with twelve fingers" (*two-headed woman*, 4). Using the extra fingers which she, her mother, and her daughter were born with as a symbol of magical power and generational continuity, she says that members of their community were afraid that they would learn to cast spells. Here Clifton alludes to the mythological woman of power, the African conjurer. Although the fingers were surgically removed, the power is not so easily excised. She speaks of the missing fingers as ghosts with powerful memories. This line of women remains powerful: "we take what we want / with invisible fingers." And she closes the poem with a beautiful image of the three women—one dead, two living, linking those amazing hands across the boundaries of death.

Contemporary African American women poets, whose cultural traditions have primed them for this task, are speaking of these connections between women and in doing so are creating a poetics of matrilineage. The simple direct verses of Alice Walker, the terse, mystical writings of Lucille Clifton, the passionate lines of Carolyn Rodgers, the evocative encodings of Audre Lorde, and the richly imagistic poems of Colleen McElroy are diverse representations of black women as mothers and as daughters. These writers are "beginning to piece together the story of a viable female culture" (Washington, 147). A part of that culture will be a full understanding of what it means to be the mother of a daughter or the daughter of a mother. Additionally, these poets are finding ways to see beyond those relationships, to see their mothers and their daughters as unique, individual women within a larger community of women. The mother-daughter poems produced by these talented and wise black women suggest that both mothers and daughters grow spiritually when they recognize and valorize each other's experiences as women.

Works Cited

Adoff, Arnold, ed. *The Poetry of Black America: Anthology of the Twentieth Century*. New York: Harper and Row, 1973.

Bell, Roseann P., Bettye J. Parker, and Beverly Guy-Sheftall, eds. *Sturdy Black Bridges: Visions of Black Women in Literature*. Garden City, N.Y.: Anchor Doubleday, 1979.

Burgher, Mary. "Images of Self and Race in the Autobiographies of Black Women." In Bell et al., 107–122.

Clifton, Lucille. *An Ordinary Woman*. New York: Random House, 1974.

———. *two-headed woman*. Amherst: University of Massachusetts Press, 1980.

Giovanni, Nikki. *Re:Creation*. Detroit: Broadside Press, 1970.

Lorde, Audre. *Coal*. New York: W. W. Norton, 1976.

———. *From a Land Where Other People Live*. Detroit: Broadside Press, 1973, rpt. 1983.

Maglin, Nan Bauer. "Don't never forget the bridge that you crossed over on: The Literature of Matrilineage." In *The Lost Tradition: Mothers and Daughters in Literature*, ed. Cathy N. Davidson and E. M. Broner, 257–267. New York: Frederick Ungar, 1980.

McElroy, Colleen J. *Music from Home: Selected Poems*. Carbondale: Southern Illinois University Press, 1976.

———. *Queen of the Ebony Isles*. Middletown, Conn.: Wesleyan University Press, 1984.

Nice, Vivian E. *Mothers and Daughters: The Distortion of a Relationship*. New York: St. Martin's, 1992.

Parker, Bettye J. "Introduction." In Bell et al., xxv–xxxi.

Rampersad, Arnold. "The Universal and the Particular in Afro-American Poetry." *CLA Journal* 25, no. 1 (1981): 1–17.

Rodgers, Carolyn. *how i got ovah: New and Selected Poems*. Garden City, N.Y.: Anchor Press / Doubleday, 1975.

Rushing, Andrea Benton. "Images of Black Women in Afro-American Poetry." In *The Afro-American Woman: Struggles and Images*, ed. Sharon Hartley and Rosalyn Teborg-Penn, 74–84. Port Washington, N.Y.: National University Publications-Kennikat Press, 1978.

———. "Images of Black Women in Modern African Poetry: An Overview." In Bell et al., 18–24.

Stetson, Erlene, ed. *Black Sister: Poetry by Black American Women 1746–1980.* Bloomington: Indiana University Press, 1981.

Walker, Alice. *Horses Make a Landscape Look More Beautiful.* New York: Harcourt, 1984.

Ward, Jerry D. "Bridges and Deep Water." In Bell et al., 184–190.

Washington, Mary Helen. "I Sign My Mother's Name: Alice Walker, Dorothy West, Paule Marshall." In *Mothering the Mind: Twelve Studies of Writers and Their Silent Partners,* ed. Ruth Perry and Martine Watson Brownley, 142–163. New York: Holmes and Meier, 1984.

The Mother as Other

Orientalism in Maxine Hong Kingston's *The Woman Warrior*

SHERYL A. MYLAN

In the time since Edward Said's *Orientalism* was first published in 1978, the investigation of Western society's attempts to contain and represent non-Western cultures has become even more important. Postcolonialist studies have increased attention to the imperialist and ethnocentric spirit which underlies the discourse of so-called advanced societies. Since such discourses mask their ideological intentions to dominate, it is essential that they be interrogated to see the ways in which non-Western societies are cast into the role of Other. Denigrating non-Western belief systems, the West sets up its own values and standards as right and natural, which justifies its will to power. Long before Said, anthropologist Francis Hsu speculated about why Western society was governed by its need to dominate: "Can Americans afford to allow any other people, especially a non-Western people, to better them in any way? My conclusion is that they probably cannot because active superiority over others is essential to a people with the individual-centered way of life" (98). The Western sense of individuality is bound up with the need to vanquish. It is odd to think that someone who has suffered the misrepresentations of monoculturalism might regard her own heritage from such an interpretive position. In a sense, however, that is what happens between the Westernized daughter, Maxine, and her Chinese mother in *The Woman Warrior*.

Just as Britain, France, and the United States represented non-Western cultures in ways to assert their cultural hegemony, Maxine portrays her mother in a way to gain strength over her. Although Edward Said's *Orientalism* focuses on the Anglo-Franco experience with Arabs and Islam, it discusses characteristics of Orientalism which work well to describe Maxine's view of her mother, who represents all that is baffling and repugnant about Chinese culture to her daughter. Said states that "Orientalism was the distillation of essential ideas about the Orient—its sensuality, its tendency to despotism, its aberrant mentality, its habits of inaccuracy, its backwardness" (205). He is interested in Orientalism as a school of interpretation in which the culture, its history, and textuality intersect and by which non-Western cultures are studied and judged. As such, these large cultural issues may seem to bear little relation to the personal struggles of a daughter and her mother. However, if the personal and public are inseparable and if all acts are political and public expressions, then Orientalism can be seen in everyday struggles as well as in global contexts. Then it no longer will seem so odd to accuse the heroine, Maxine, of such a Western monocultural perspective. Out of ignorance and misunderstanding of her mother's life in China, Maxine constructs a framework by which to judge her; her standards for judging her mother are, if not manifest Orientalism, at least latent or unconscious demonstrations of Orientalism.

To admit the possibility that Maxine sees her mother and the Chinese culture she represents as the Other helps to explain the negative responses *The Woman Warrior* received from Asian American critics like Katheryn Fong, Benjamin Tong, and Frank Chin. It also reflects the continuing concern in the Asian American community about who has the right to represent their experiences. Complaining about the fakery of the text and its complicity in a racist, imperialist enterprise in "This Is Not an Autobiography," Chin argues for the authentic representation of Chinese culture. Tong agrees with Chin that Hong Kingston sold out with her exotic stereotypes, created to please a white audience. Certainly such critics are right in decrying the misrepresentations and caricatures of the Chinese as a superstitious, enigmatic, and devious people; these stereotypes have a lengthy history in American writing, not only in the popular press, but even among respected writers such as Bret Harte, Jack London, and John Steinbeck (Kim, Ch. 1). However, Hong Kingston never intended *The Woman Warrior* to be a documentary portrayal of Chinese culture and insists that it is "an American book"; she also states that her own "American-ness" has often been ignored and misinterpreted ("Cultural

Mis-readings by American Reviewers," 58). While some Western writers have represented Asian cultures as Other to dominate and appropriate, it is a mistake to view Hong Kingston primarily as a Chinese writer who willfully misrepresents and betrays her cultural legacy.

In part, this problem of the Asian-Americanness of *The Woman Warrior* stems from reading the text as Western autobiography, with its demands for factual accuracy. It is not merely that the West, unlike more communally based cultures, has different concepts of individuation, the self, and the individual's relation to the community, as Margaret Miller has demonstrated in "Threads of Identity in Maxine Hong Kingston's *The Woman Warrior*." Miller's points about autobiography are important, but it is also important not to overlook the fact that Hong Kingston planned to publish the work as a novel—which, in itself, counters classical Chinese literary tradition and its devaluation of fiction. However, she was convinced by her publishers to market the text as an autobiography, which has obviously led some readers to confuse the main character with the writer. The result of this confusion is that instead of seeing that Maxine behaves like a Eurocentric American who exoticizes Asian culture as a means of containing the threat of its power, some critics equate Hong Kingston with Maxine the daughter. Such an equation easily leads to the charges of inauthenticity and cultural betrayal against which Hong Kingston has protested. She is trying to capture the truth of her own psyche, to the extent that this is ever possible, not the documentary truth of Chinese culture. If Hong Kingston is allowed her rights as an author, though, and Maxine is read as a fictional construct, then the monoculturalism she exhibits is less a willful rejection of Chinese heritage than an unconscious way of subduing her mother's power over her.

Besides the charge of cultural distortion, another problem results from equating Maxine's monoculturalism with Hong Kingston's presentation of it. This is the complication of the mother-daughter relationship which arises because Maxine, the fictional character, is the autobiographer in Hong Kingston's "autobiography." Lynn Z. Bloom analyzes the dynamics of such relationships in women's autobiographies, noting that the autobiographer/daughter figuratively becomes her own mother as well as the "recreator of her maternal parent and the controlling adult in their literary relationship. . . . This may be an unfamiliar position for the daughter; it is certainly a reversal of the power and dominance" that has plagued her during the formation of her identity as a young woman (292).

Maxine as autobiographer has a vested interest in presenting her mother in such a way that her power is diminished. No undistorted presentation is ever truly possible, despite the desires for cultural accuracy; writers are always re-presenting. It must be noted that Maxine is a writer, re-presenting her mother and her stories. Orientalizing her mother and Chinese culture is one such way for Maxine to create her own self. Although it is certainly true that all people struggle to create a separate identity from their parents, as Nancy Chodorow has demonstrated, it is more difficult for girls since they identify with their mothers longer than boys do.

Making the break is even more complicated for young women whose cultural legacies are in sharp conflict. Amy Ling notes that "a minority individual's sense of alienation results not only from rejection by the dominant culture but also rejection of parental strictures" (123). Because of Maxine's need for personal autonomy, she aligns herself with Western culture, even though the West will always stigmatize her on the basis of race. It certainly seems strange that Maxine, in effect, takes up with the enemy and rebels against her mother, the one who tries to provide examples of strong Chinese women. It would seem more reasonable for Maxine to rebel against the patriarchal, patrilineal, and patrilocal Chinese culture—still alive in her Asian American community—which devalues women. After all, the important kinship relations, *liu ch'in,* all involve men—relationships between fathers and sons, between brothers, and between the brothers' children, their grandchildren, and their great-grandchildren (Yang, 7–10). She should also take aim at the Confucian doctrines which oppress women, such as the three obediences—a woman's obedience to her father, then to her husband, and finally to her sons when she is widowed—and the four virtues—woman's ethics, teaching a woman her place, woman's speech, telling her to speak little, woman's appearance, telling her to please her husband, and woman's chores, teaching her to do her housework (Shih-Shan, 157). But instead, Maxine makes her mother the target. She sees her as Other to carve out some psychic space for herself, both as a young Chinese American woman and as an artist.

To distance herself from her mother and her Chinese ways, Maxine must come to terms with sexuality, an excess of which, as Said demonstrates, has long been ascribed to non-Western cultures. In the first story, "No Name Woman," Maxine is a young woman on the verge of her own sexual awakening. She may be inexperienced and unknowledgeable about sex, but she is very curious and imaginative. Her mother tries to give her some advice by telling Maxine her aunt's story. Maxine, however, rejects the lesson—or, rather, she recasts it into her own version of Chinese sensuality. It is important to remember that this is an orientalized version of uncontrolled passion since romantic love is a Western concept, which even required the "linguistic creation of the term lien ai" (Hsu, 42).

Brave Orchid's version for Maxine is the simple account of her aunt's adultery and the murder of her newborn baby, whom she held when she leapt into the well to her death. She tells her daughter this story of suicide and murder as a cautionary tale to prevent Maxine from disgracing the family. Although widows' suicide among the gentry brought honor, especially for a childless woman who would no longer be of any value to her husband's family and whose only other option would be a second marriage to a man of lower status, such was not the case here. No-name aunt was from the country, and, as Margery Wolf notes, "among peasant women the act is not exotic" (112). It brought only horror, disgrace, and a warning that redounds on her niece fifty years later and in a different culture. The fact that Brave Orchid's warnings are so dire is some indication of the power of sexuality, once unleashed. Brave Orchid, whom Maxine sees as motivated by necessity, rather than as driven by passion, constantly presents a culture in which sexuality is a danger to be guarded against.

Maxine says she has difficulty imagining her aunt being sexually uninhibited, yet she immediately imagines her aunt at her dressing table, trying to arrange her hair in "heart-catching tangles" (9) to attract her lover's gaze. Maxine embellishes her mother's simple tale, perhaps imagining her aunt as more wild and sexually unrestrained than she was. Whether or not the picture is accurate is irrelevant. Accuracy and knowledge of a culture count for nothing in Orientalism, which makes it particularly pernicious. The Other culture is appropriated—restructured and re-presented to fit the so-called advanced culture's need for superiority and domination. So, even though Maxine views her aunt as a kindred spirit—passionate and rebellious—when she recasts her story, sexualizing it more than her mother does, she is commenting pejoratively both on Chinese culture and on her mother.

In "White Tigers," Maxine sexualizes the ancient story of Fa Mu Lan as another effort to distance herself from her mother. The story of Fa Mu

Lan or Lady Mulan has constantly been retold in genres as different as the ballad and the opera; it appears during the seventh to ninth centuries of the Tang dynasty with its great flowering of literature and art, during the fourteenth to seventeenth centuries of the last such ruling family, the Ming dynasty, and during the modern period. Various versions exist, with different characters and events. One of the biggest changes in this version—the lengthy apprentice-training in martial arts, deriving from *wuxia xiaoshuo*, the martial arts novel—emphasizes woman's power; the most important change, though, is the new combination of mother and soldier here, because it bespeaks Maxine's fascination with power and motherhood. Attitudes toward menstruation and childbirth, in particular, are a crucial part of the story for Maxine. When Fa Mu Lan begins to menstruate, the advice she receives from her surrogate mother is quite different from the warning Maxine received from her own mother when she learned the story of her no-name aunt. Instead of using the occasion to tell Fa Mu Lan not to disgrace her family by getting pregnant, her surrogate mother merely asks her to delay having children so that she can fulfill her role as warrior. She tells her not to worry about the blood, but to let it flow.

In many of the traditional versions of the story, Fa Mu Lan reveals to her fellow warriors only in the final moments that she is a woman. In the version Maxine relates, soldiers agree to fight alongside Fa Mu Lan, even after they learn that she is a woman. Though she is dressed as a man and wearing armor, the crowds cheer her on as a beautiful woman. The detail devoted to her pregnancy and the first month of her son's life further sexualizes the story. Note, for instance, how Fa Mu Lan regards her pregnant shape: "Now when I was naked, I was a strange human being indeed—words carved on my back and the baby large in front" (39–40). When the baby is born, Fa Mu Lan and her husband discuss what they should do with the umbilical cord, deciding to tie it to a flagpole to dry so they can save it in a box, just as their parents had done with their children's.

Fa Mu Lan's story is not only so fantastic that Maxine cannot use it as a model for her own development, but also so eroticized that she can dismiss her mother and her Chinese culture along with the story. She dismisses it so thoroughly, in fact, that it remains forgotten until long into her adulthood, although mother and daughter had chanted it together as they worked around the house. Brave Orchid had told Maxine the story of Fa Mu Lan—a name which is translated Sylvan or Wood Orchid, emphasizing their sisterhood—to help her daughter grow up as a powerful woman, despite her fears that Maxine wouldn't be able to avoid becoming a wife and a slave. Her fears about slavery are realized when Maxine is too weak to resist the racism of her boss, when he tells her to order "nigger yellow" paint and to book a banquet hall being picketed by CORE and the NAACP (48).

Maxine's inability to combat racism stems, in part, from orientalizing her Chinese culture, which leaves her with no inner resources upon which to draw. It is little wonder then that she whispers her protest to her boss, her "voice unreliable" (49). By regarding her Chinese heritage as Other, she has effectively silenced her own voice. In telling Maxine the story of Fa Mu Lan, Brave Orchid was trying to give her daughter a precious gift to inspire and strengthen her. In trying to find strength apart from her mother, Maxine rejected this story as inapplicable to the racist power struggles of the twentieth century. As a young woman trying to form her own identity, she finds that the story of Fa Mu Lan simply does not translate well, unlike the story of Ts'ai Yen—the second-century poet, scholar, and musician held captive for twelve years—whose songs of both barbarian and Chinese culture "translated well" (209). Before Maxine gets to the point where she can appreciate how two cultures—or two very different people—can meet in a spirit of mutual appreciation, she has to come to terms with her own needs to orientalize her Chinese heritage.

One of the needs Orientalism fulfills is the need for dominance. Power is gained by seeing the non-Western culture as weak and female, for implicit in Orientalism, Said notes, is a male "power-fantasy" (207). Through her interest in a woman warrior such as Fa Mu Lan, Maxine shows her desire for power. But by re-presenting a powerful and more sexualized Fa Mu Lan who, at the end of the story, nevertheless returns to her village, gives her son her helmet and swords, kneels before her in-laws, and assumes her duties as housewife and the bearer of more sons, Maxine thwarts her acquisition of genuine power. Brave Orchid was once a scholar and doctor, but now lines up with transients, alcoholics, and drug addicts for part-time farm work in addition to working long hours in the laundry. Looking at her mother as an example as well as the stories she tells, it is little wonder then that Maxine is conflicted about her real possibilities for power. She wants nothing so much as to get away from the chief reminder of what a Chinese woman is—her mother.

One way that this conflict is manifested is Maxine's desire to be like a boy. Constantly aware of the privileges of manhood, she rebels against traditional female tasks. She won't cook for her family, and she breaks dishes when she is forced to wash them. Her mother's reprimands for this behavior please Maxine; after all, "Isn't a bad girl almost a boy?" (47) She questions why there are elaborate month-long celebrations for the birth of a boy and none for the birth of a girl. When Maxine and her sisters visit their three cousins, the girls' great-grandfather screams at all six of them, calling them maggots and reproaching them for not giving him grandsons, but Maxine, who wants the privileges accorded to men, is nevertheless quick to condemn such patriarchal views. When her cousins explain that their great-grandfather behaves that way at every meal, Maxine and her sisters console them by saying, "Our old man hates us too. What assholes" (191). When she grows up and attends Berkeley, she refuses to be passive and marches for political causes, but still, "I did not turn into a boy" (47). Although as an adult Maxine continues to long for the independence which she associates with being male, her disgust with someone calling girls "maggots" shows her appreciation for female worth. Her readings in anthropology teach her that the Chinese believe that "'girls are necessary too'" (52), although she says that no Chinese she ever met conceded this point. But still she is willing to allow that "perhaps it was a saying in another village" (53). This growing acceptance of her own femaleness and her admittance of the possibility that not all Chinese disregard women reflect her movement away from Orientalism, which sees non-Western culture as sensual, feminine, and weak.

It is interesting, though, that Maxine usually associates China with femaleness and dependency since her mother, who represents everything Chinese that she wants to flee, is so strong. In some ways, Maxine views her mother as despotic—another characteristic of Orientalism. Perhaps the incident which best reflects the tyrannical power Maxine invests her with is the cutting of her daughter's frenum. With the understandably characteristic ambivalence of an Asian person who orientalizes her culture, she says, "Sometimes I felt very proud that my mother committed such a powerful act upon me. At other times I was terrified—the first thing my mother did when she saw me was to cut my tongue" (164).

Perhaps this mutilation subconsciously reminds Maxine of the mutilation most associated with the Chinese—footbinding, a practice introduced during the Five Dynasties period of the tenth century among court dancers (Kazuko, 11). Men praised the "golden lotus," finding it erotic to see women sway like willows. And so, for a thousand years, breaking the arches and bending the foot so that it would curve into a three-inch bow was a sign of gentility, soon imitated by all but lower-class villagers who had to work. By the late nineteenth century, intellectuals saw it as an "outmoded vestige of the past which crippled half the population and caused loss of 'international face' "; Natural Foot Societies started springing up in the early twentieth century (Croll, 45, 47). Still, footbinding is an image that resonates in Maxine's mind: "Even now China wraps double binds around my feet" (48). Like footbinding, the mutilation that Brave Orchid inflicts on Maxine suggests that her mother wants to help break her power—to destroy her voice. Just as footbinding suggests contradictory images of women, the cutting of her frenum causes Maxine to feel ambivalent. Kay Ann Johnson notes that in Chinese culture "while women were seen as naturally weak and submissive, they were also often portrayed as dangerously powerful" (17). So the image of binding and the actual cutting of her frenum coalesce in Maxine's mind, making her feel that her mother is trying to weaken her, despite her reasonable explanations.

Maxine is unable to accept Brave Orchid's reasons for cutting her frenum. She tells her daughter that she cut it so that she would not be tongue-tied and so that her tongue would be able to move in any language. Despite this explanation, Maxine repeatedly asks her mother to explain her motives and questions why she didn't cut her brothers' and sisters' tongues. Maxine believes her mother is lying to her; in fact, any explanation Brave Orchid gives her daughter is immediately suspect: "If my mother was not lying she should have cut more, scraped away the rest of the frenum skin, because I have a terrible time talking. Or she should not have cut at all, tampering with my speech" (165). Although Maxine often accuses her mother of being irrational and finds her actions incomprehensible, she is the one who is behaving irrationally in rejecting her mother's explanations. Instead of believing that her mother is acting on her behalf, Maxine attributes her difficulty speaking to her mother's mutilation of her tongue, an action which she can only read as willfully cruel.

This cruelty could have only one objective, according to Maxine—to dominate and silence her. As proof, she recalls her early years when she found it almost unbearable to speak. She thinks about how, even as an adult, her voice cracks and she feels dumb when she speaks. But her youth was the worst: she was silent at school for a year; for three years both she and her sister were completely silent, Maxine's only expression being her totally black paintings. She associates this domination with

Chinese culture, observing that the other Chinese girls were also silent, so she knew the silence had to do with being a Chinese girl. Maxine struggles with English at school, where she speaks it for the first time. When she recites in class, her voice sounds splintered. But it is not merely that English is a new language for her. One of her classmates whispers, "You can't entrust your voice to the Chinese, either; they want to capture your voice for their own use. They want to fix up your tongue to speak for them" (169). Despite her mother's statement that she wants her daughter to communicate freely, Maxine is silenced both in English and in Chinese.

Because Maxine cannot overpower her mother, she dominates one of the girls in school. She torments a girl who cannot even speak up in her Chinese school, perhaps because in the girl's timidity Maxine sees an image of her own powerlessness. By torturing another Chinese American girl, Maxine reveals her own self-contempt. Frank Chin and Jeffrey Chan note that such "self-contempt is nothing more than the subject's acceptance of white standards of objectivity, beauty, behavior, and achievement as being morally absolute, and his acknowledgment of the fact that because he is not white, he can never fully measure up to white standards" (67). So Maxine—barely able to communicate herself—pinches the girl, squeezes her face, pulls her hair, and demands that she talk. Maxine tells her to say her name, to call for her sister, to ask Maxine to leave her alone, to say anything—even "a" or "the"—and she promises she will relent. But the girl can only sob and make choking noises. Finally, in language that partially echoes her mother's admonition to Maxine when she tells the story of her aunt, she tells the girl that she is doing this for her own good and that she must never tell anyone she has been bad to her. She badgers the girl to talk. But the girl never really does talk; even as an adult, she remains sequestered in her family's home. The prospect of being silent and closed up—one of the crazy women that Maxine imagines every Chinese house has—increases her desire for independence from the oppressive Chinese culture her mother represents.

Unless she breaks away, Maxine knows she will go crazy. This prospect terrifies her because she has seen craziness up close in her aunt, Moon Orchid, as well as in the mad Chinese women in her neighborhood. Like the moon, her aunt is a reflective surface, but what she reflects are the traditional Chinese beliefs about women and their relations to their families, which Maxine finds so repellent. When Moon Orchid comes to the United States to reclaim her husband, Maxine sees a cultural clash which convinces her more than ever that China is the Other. At her sister Brave Orchid's prodding, Moon Orchid begins her quest. Her husband abandoned her and her daughter thirty years ago. Now, however, Brave Orchid persuades her that she can once again enjoy her status as first wife, although her prosperous physician-husband is married to a Westernized nurse and has a son. The plans, so incomprehensible from a Western point of view, but so reasonable to Brave Orchid, leave Moon Orchid humiliated. She begins her descent into madness. Soon she has paranoid fantasies; she thinks that Mexicans are plotting to kill her, so she stays in the house, with the windows and drapes closed and the lights off. When she refuses to let anyone else leave for fear they will turn into ashes, Moon Orchid is finally institutionalized. The plight of her aunt is not lost on Maxine. To be Chinese is to go mad; it is to be trapped in an alien, irrational world. Not surprisingly, Maxine notes that all of Brave Orchid's children decided to major in science or mathematics.

Maxine values the orderly, rational world represented by science since, through the lens of Orientalism, she sees nothing but irrationality in Chinese culture. A prime example is Brave Orchid as shaman. The song of her experiences at the To Keung School of Midwifery should serve as an example to Maxine of an independent woman with her own career. Certainly she is a model to the group of students who are like daughters to her as well as to her colleagues and friends. Instead, her experiences set her further apart from her daughter. Of all the incidents that surely happened at the medical school, the ones Maxine focuses on are all supernatural, like Brave Orchid's exorcism of a ghost. Dared by the other students, Brave Orchid sleeps in a haunted room where she battles a sitting ghost: "She grabbed clutches of fur and pulled. She pinched the skin the hair grew out of and gouged into it with her fingernails. She forced her hands to hunt out eyes, furtive somewhere in the hair, but could not find any. She lifted her head to bite but fell back exhausted" (69).

Although a knife is just beyond her reach, Brave Orchid defeats the ghost not through physical violence but through words. She speaks to the ghost throughout the night, insisting that it has no power over a strong woman. When the students gather around her the next morning to find out what happened, her story becomes even more strange and wonderful. She tells them that she was gone twelve years in all, during ten of which she was lost. She says that she walked back to the To Keung School from the Gobi Desert and that once she died. Had she not willed the monster to shrink, it would have fed on both her and the others. Finally she says that it waits to feed on them unless they attack it first. After they burn it out, one of the students finds a piece of wood covered with blood.

After retelling this story of her mother's medical training, Maxine says, "She had gone away ordinary and come back miraculous, like the ancient magicians who came down from the mountains" (76). Once she becomes Doctor Brave Orchid, her experiences are hardly the sort that would make her a credible scientist in the West. When she goes to work in the villages, she sees ghosts falling out of trees and coming out of cervixes because "medical science does not seal the earth, whose nether creatures seep out, hair by hair, disguised like the smoke that dispels them" (83). One night she encounters an ape-man which has escaped; she is undaunted, though, telling it to go home. Supernatural events like these do not trouble her because she "was midwife to whatever spewed forth . . . sometimes babies, sometimes monsters" (85).

Most irrational of all is the fact that Brave Orchid refuses to treat people who are dying. This, however, only improves her reputation and increases the number of her patients. She will not deal with the dying because she insists on bringing only health from house to house. The last picture of Brave Orchid as doctor is her turning her back on a woman who has been stoned by her villagers. Fearful of strafing by Japanese airplanes in 1939, they are alarmed by the village crazy lady, who has put on a headdress with small mirrors. As she dances, the light glints off these mirrors, which the villagers fear are signaling the planes. They stone her to death while Brave Orchid turns and walks to the mountains. Neither these experiences nor her medical expertise would be valued, much less comprehensible, in the West.

In fact, in the United States Brave Orchid's medical skills completely fail. It is not merely that her Chinese diploma is not recognized: she cannot even help her family. She tells Maxine that her diet is too yin, which is causing her to catch colds so frequently. In fact, she mistakenly thinks one of Maxine's cold pills is LSD but takes it anyway. Maxine tells her mother it is a simple over-the-counter cold tablet and also reprimands her for taking pills that are lying around. It is curious that a medically trained person would need to be told such things, but she does. Brave Orchid's medical expertise obviously does not translate well into the Western world that Maxine knows and accepts as right and normal. So, although Brave Orchid's knowledge and professional accomplishments should connect mother and daughter, they do not. Because the experiences are so alien to Maxine's cultural perspective, they make the chasm between mother and daughter even greater.

Not only are Brave Orchid's experiences in medical school and as a doctor alien, but so is her behavior in ordinary life, which Maxine finds baffling. When a delivery boy from the drug store mistakenly brings some pills to the Hong household, Brave Orchid is enraged and swears vengeance. She forces Maxine to go to the store and demand that they stop the curse. She feels their house has been tainted by the medicine and can only be remedied by free candy. Maxine recognizes that the druggist will no doubt think she is begging. But since her mother will not be dissuaded, she tells the druggist, "'My mother said you have to give us candy. She said that is the way the Chinese do it'" (170). Interestingly, she does not say, "That is the way we do it." She separates herself from what she sees as her mother's bizarre ideas and behavior. When the druggist presses her further—"'Do what?'" he asks—she responds, "'Do things.' I felt the weight and immensity of things impossible to explain to the druggist" (171). After that discussion, he does give the family candy, but it is leftover candy from holidays just past. Brave Orchid thinks she has triumphed, but Maxine is sure that the druggist is merely taking pity on them. The confrontation that is supposed to show power and victory only reinforces Maxine's belief that the Chinese way is weak, inappropriate, and irrational.

As if these traits were not enough to stigmatize the Chinese culture and its people as Other, its inaccuracy, another characteristic of an orientalized culture, troubles Maxine. The West, with its penchant for dominating the world through definition, precision, and fact, rejects ambiguity, imprecision, and mystery. It is not surprising that Maxine, in her efforts to reject her mother, is so bewildered and frustrated by her mother's inattention to fact. For example, when they are discussing age, Brave Orchid tells her daughter that the last time she saw her she was still young, but now she is old. Maxine tries to point out to her that they visited only a year ago. But her mother won't change her opinion; she simply notes that during that year Maxine became old. Then, talking about death, she mentions that she is eighty. Maxine says that according to her papers she is seventy-six. They argue about the exact age for a while; Brave Orchid says that her papers are wrong and that she's eighty, eight-one in Chinese years. She says she may be seventy or eighty and that numbers do not matter. To her, exactness is simply unimportant. There is a truth beyond fact, and a way of knowing beyond reason. Brave Orchid's is a different way of knowing, but Maxine makes no room for alternate visions of reality.

Nor does Maxine recognize that she sometimes mistakes ambiguity for inaccuracy. It is only as she develops, both as a person and as a writer, that she sees that there can be richness and beauty in ambiguity, especially in the Chinese language. As an adult she begins to look up the meanings of "Ho Chi Kuei," which immigrants call her and the others who have lived in the United States for a while. She does not know Chinese, but instead of orientalizing the culture to reject it, she begins exploring the language—the basis of any culture. She learns that "Ho Chi Kuei" translates in various ways, from one of a number of insects to "non-eater," a term which relates to Brave Orchid's notions of heroism (204). But she does not make this realization, which allows her to move away from her Western monoculturalism, until adulthood.

As a girl, she also fails to recognize that there might be serious, practical reasons for the inaccuracy, outright lies, and "the secrecy of the Chinese" (183)—not *our* secrecy—which she detests. "Don't tell" is her parents' constant refrain, although, as Maxine notes, "we couldn't tell if we wanted to because we didn't know" (183). As an adult, of course, Maxine recognizes that "they would not tell us children because we had been born among ghosts, were taught by ghosts, and were ourselves ghost-like" (183). But when she was growing up and trying desperately to divorce herself from her mother and her Chinese heritage, she did not realize how serious the possibility of deportation was and, therefore, how great the need for secrecy about one's background was. Although the worst of the deportation fear was over by the 1950s when Maxine was a girl, the fearful memories from earlier years surely must have remained strong in the tightly knit Chinese communities. The Immigration Act of 1924, passed to halt further Japanese immigration, also prohibited Chinese wives from coming to the United States to join their husbands. This act effectively stopped the growth of Chinese families, which typically had from six to a dozen children. Women who tried to enter the country were detained at Angel Island Immigration Station in the San Francisco Bay, where they might be held up to two years (Yung, 42). The

Chinese had good reason for guarding their identities even from their children, who might blurt out information that could lead to deportation for their families, but all Maxine could see was a legacy of lies, of which she wanted no part.

Maxine sees the Chinese as inaccurate or deceitful not only in matters with potentially serious consequences, but also in ordinary situations. She says that she and the other children in the family never really had a sense of when holidays occurred. There was no anticipation or excitement, only a vague awareness that they had eaten a certain food which deemed it a holiday. If anyone had the temerity to ask for explanations the adults got angry and evasive and silenced the annoying child. Maxine finds all the secrecy about these events doubly puzzling. She is confused not only about the actual dates of holidays, but also about how Chinese traditions, which her mother seems so insistent about honoring, are ever maintained or how they maintained a continuous culture for five thousand years. Once again, it is interesting to see that she refers to the Chinese as "they"—the Other—to distance herself from a culture that seems irrational from a Western perspective.

Though Maxine is often curious about how a culture that seems so strange to her could have lasted for so long, she also says she has no desire to understand it. In fact, she says that "if you don't figure it out, it's all right. Then you can grow up bothered by 'neither ghosts nor deities'" (185). But, of course, she is tormented by Chinese ghosts. Although Maxine may have learned from Brave Orchid and other members of the Chinese American community to refer to all non-Chinese people as ghosts—Meter Reader Ghosts, Garbage Ghosts, Urban Renewal Ghosts, Public Health Nurse Ghosts, Burglar Ghosts, and Wino Ghosts—for her, the real ghosts are Chinese, those shadowy, inexplicable presences that haunt her life. And she expends considerable effort to understand why her mother uses language in a way that bewilders rather than clarifies.

One such instance regards the birth of babies, who must be named and described as other than they are in order to protect them from the jealous gods. Despite her avowed desire for accuracy, Maxine is, however, pleased when her mother calls her "Little Dog," even though she, like her mother, is a Dragon. "Little Dog" is "a name to fool the gods" (109). This name signifies a loving connection, rooted in a cultural heritage that Brave Orchid hopes her daughter will eventually accept with pride. This sense of connection, however, will come only in time. When she is younger and prone to orientalize Chinese culture, Maxine is frustrated to the point of rage by what she regards as duplicity.

Maxine's frustration leads to one of the most memorable battles between mother and daughter. Because she believes Brave Orchid does not really know her, Maxine feels compelled to recite a list of "over two hundred things . . . so that she would know the true things about me" (197). She wants the truth to bring them closer, but unlike Brave Orchid, who wants their Chinese heritage to unite them, Maxine wants their union grounded in a Western sense of fact and accuracy. So she says, "If only I could let my mother know the list, she—and the world—would become more like me, and I would never be alone again" (198). One night when mother and daughter are alone in the laundry, Maxine begins to tell her the items on the list—how she killed a spider, how she hinted to a girl that she wanted a doll. When Brave Orchid doesn't respond to these revelations, Maxine thinks she must be more explicit. But to Brave Orchid, such precision and details are not the means to truth. In fact, telling her to go away, she adds, "I don't feel like hearing your craziness" (200). What is taking place in this scene is a clash of cultures arising from two different ways of knowing. Viewing her mother from a Westernized perspective, Maxine misunderstands what her mother values as truth. Consequently, she sees her disregard of the "truth" as a sign of Chinese primitiveness and inferiority, from which she must dissociate herself. Maxine recalls that she had to leave home to view the world logically, as a place filled with simplicity and without ghosts. She equates the West with order, logic, and rationality—a way of knowing superior to the byzantine complexities of a culture that she herself has orientalized. It is a way for her to escape her ghosts, for it is the Chinese culture which seems foreign to her. She also equates China with darkness, the West with a light that can illuminate the error of non-Western societies.

But Chinese society is only "backward" from a Eurocentric point of view in which progress is the domain of the West. The stories about her mother's cooking and eating as a strategy to combat ghosts are one such case in point. Maxine attributes Brave Orchid's ability to win over the sitting ghost to her ability to eat anything; "all heroes," she says, "are bold toward food" (89). Maxine notes that her mother kills and cooks raccoons, snakes, and skunks for her family and gives them five-day-old leftover squid eyes. She doesn't want to know the reasons why her mother cooks the kinds of food that she does; she evidently does not realize the privation which the Chinese suffered for many years and which had driven them to the United States since the 1850s. So thrift and inventiveness in the face of privation, which would ordinarily be praiseworthy qualities, do not make such a cuisine acceptable to her. Her rejection is far more than children's usual dislike of exotic foods, though. It is the exotic culture represented by the foods which Maxine rejects. This is suggested by her linking her mother's cooking with the fantastic stories of warriors who are heroic eaters: Kao Chung, "who in 1683 ate five cooked chickens and drank ten bottles of wine that belonged to the sea monster," Chou Yi-han, who ate a fried ghost, and Wei Pang, who ate a "ball of flesh entirely covered with eyes" (89).

Maxine makes the sorts of equations that set up China as Other, which she can then reject. She thinks that all she is rejecting is weirdness, not heroism. Out of ignorance, she is cutting herself off from a tradition of courage. Sau-ling Wong discusses the semiotics of eating in Asian literature, the importance of the ability to "eat unpromising substances and to extract sustenance, even a sort of willed enjoyment, from them; to put it symbolically, it is the ability to cope with the constraints and perceptions Asian Americans have had to endure as immigrants and racial minorities" (25). But rather than really face these problems, Maxine would rather ally herself totally with Western culture. In fact, so total is her denial that she refuses to cook for others and apparently cooks very little for herself, since her mother is so concerned that Maxine hasn't fattened up. But Maxine wants nothing to do with the heroics of eating. After recounting the mythic stories about eating, she says she would live on plastic, a perfect metonym for the greed and unnaturalness of Western society.

Eventually, however, Maxine rejects the plastic society of the West, but, more importantly, she rejects her Orientalism. She realizes that she understands little of her Chinese legacy, but now, instead of exoticizing it so much that she can dismiss it out of hand, she longs to discover this part of her culture. She knows now that to fix one particular image of a culture is to falsify it; she is open to fluid interpretations which allow and appreciate cultural difference. Though she once said she never wanted to go to China, she ultimately changes her mind and plans a visit as she continues to sort out what was real and what was imagined.

The Woman Warrior concludes with a collaborative talk-story by mother and daughter. Brave Orchid begins the story, telling about her grandmother and how she foiled thieves that struck the homes of theater patrons who were watching plays. Leaving the doors and windows open, the family went to the play. Because the bandits struck at the theater, the family's home and their possessions were safe. This segues into Maxine's portion of the story. She begins: "I like to think that at some of those performances, they heard the songs of Ts'ai Yen, a poetess born in A.D. 175" (207). For twelve years, Ts'ai Yen was a captive of a barbarian chieftain by whom she had two children. At night the barbarian warriors played music on their flutes—a high, disturbingly beautiful music that contrasted with the deathly music of the arrows which flew during the daytime. Ts'ai Yen begins singing in a voice which matches the flute music, her pain and anger about being separated from her family and China evident in her song. When she is ransomed, she brings her "songs back from the savage lands" (209), one of which is "Eighteen Stanzas for a Barbarian Reed Pipe," a song that the Chinese sing to their own instruments. Maxine notes that the barbarian songs translated well, a comment usually seen as a reconciliation of the conflicts that have divided mother and daughter. But such a reading is in danger of sentimentalizing the reconciliation, of making it seem that the two cultures can meet in a happy fusion or assimilation. Maxine's Chinese heritage is not neatly compatible with her American culture, as suggested by the fact that mother and daughter each tell different stories with only the slightest of connections. The two cultures can only touch; each must stand separate, its difference accepted rather than stigmatized as Other.

More importantly, Maxine is no Ts'ai Yen, a sojourner in barbarian cultures, longing to return to her native land. The United States is her native land, not China. Like Ts'ai Yen, she is, of course, an artist, reinterpreting the stories her mother tells her in the light of her American experiences. As Frank Chin notes, it is important to distinguish between being Chinese and being Chinese American. In a racist society, both are lumped together because of skin color and physical characteristics. But, Chin notes, "We're not interchangeable. Our sensibilities are not the same" (*Bridge* 2, 30). It is Maxine's mother, Brave Orchid—also a consummate storyteller—who has spent long years away from her homeland in an alien culture. Unlike Ts'ai Yen, though, she is not returning home. And even if she were to try, it would not be the China she knew—but instead a tissue of the fact, fantasy, and endlessly retold myths that would form her own memoir among ghosts. Though mother and daughter's collaborative talk-story does not signal an assimilation of Chinese and American cultures—which would not be desirable, even if it were possible—it does suggest that Maxine has stopped duplicating the hegemonic cultural values and assumptions of the West. She is free to find meaning in a cultural heritage that has a vital presence in her life and, finally, can put to rest the ghosts of her past.

Works Cited

Bloom, Lynn Z. "Heritages: Dimensions of Mother-Daughter Relationships in Women's Autobiography." In *The Lost Tradition: Mothers and Daughters in Literature*, ed. Cathy N. Davidson and E. M. Broner, 291–303. New York: Frederick Ungar, 1980.

Chin, Frank. *Bridge* 2 2 (Dec. 1972): 30–31.

———. "This Is Not an Autobiography." *Genre* 18, no. 2 (1985): 109–130.

Chin, Frank, and Jeffrey Paul Chan. "Racist Love." In *Seeing Through Shuck*, ed. Richard Kostelanetz, 65–79. New York: Ballantine Books, 1972.

Chodorow, Nancy. *The Reproduction of Mothering: Psychoanalysis and the Sociology of Gender*. Berkeley: University of California Press, 1978.

Croll, Elisabeth. *Feminism and Socialism in China*. London: Routledge and Kegan Paul, 1978.

Fong, Katheryn. "To Maxine Hong Kingston: A Letter." *Bulletin for Concerned Asian Scholars* 9, no. 4 (1977): 67–69.

Hsu, Francis L. K. *Americans and Chinese*. New York: Doubleday National Historical Press, 1953, 1970.

Johnson, Kay Ann. *Women, the Family and Peasant Revolution in China*. Chicago: University of Chicago Press, 1983.

Kazuko, Ono. *Chinese Women in a Century of Revolution 1850–1950*. Ed. Joshua A. Fogel. Stanford: Stanford University Press, 1989.

Kim, Elaine. *Asian American Literature: An Introduction to the Writings and Their Social Contexts*. Philadelphia: Temple University Press, 1982.

Kingston, Maxine Hong. "Cultural Mis-readings by American Reviewers." In *Asian and Western Writers in Dialogue: New Cultural Identities*, ed. Guy Amirthanayagam, 55–65. London: Macmillan, 1982.

———. *The Woman Warrior*. New York: Vintage Books, 1975.

Ling, Amy. *Between Worlds: Women Writers of Chinese Ancestry*. New York: Pergamon Press, 1990.

Miller, Margaret. "Threads of Identity in Maxine Hong Kingston's *The Woman Warrior*." *Biography* 6, no. 1 (1983): 13–32.

Said, Edward. *Orientalism*. New York: Pantheon Books, 1978.

Shih-Shan, Henry Staid. *The Chinese Experience in America*. Bloomington: Indiana University Press, 1986.

Tong, Benjamin. "Critic of Admirer Sees Dumb Racist." *San Francisco Journal*, May 11, 1977, 6.

Wolf, Margery. "Women and Suicide in China." In *Women in Chinese Society*, 111–141. Stanford: Stanford University Press, 1975.

Wong, Sau-ling Scything. *Reading Asian American Literature: From Necessity to Extravagance*. Princeton: Princeton University Press, 1993.

Yang, C. K. *The Chinese Family in the Community Revolution*. Cambridge: MIT Press, 1958.

Yung, Judy. *Chinese Women of America: A Pictorial History*. Seattle: University of Washington Press, 1986.

Love and Conflict

Mexican American Women Writers as Daughters

MARIA GONZALEZ

Contemporary Mexican American women prose writers depict in their texts female characters preoccupied with the conflicts inherent in the relationship between mothers and daughters who are members of a community that receives its cultural values from two worlds often in conflict, U.S. mainstream culture and Mexican culture. These fictional characters come to represent many of the tensions in the Mexican American culture, tensions that include an internal cultural conflict of love and fear. This conflict of emotion can be represented in three Mexican icons of mothers: La Virgen (the Virgin Mary), the mythic perfect mother; La Malinche (Cortés's mistress/translator, known as the raped one), mythic mother as well as actual historical figure, mother of the first Spanish and indigenous child; and La Llorona (the crier), a folk myth of a woman who loses or murders her children and hence, as penance, spends eternity grieving and looking for them. A close study of Helena María Viramontes's short story "Miss Clairol," Lucha Corpi's *Delia's Song*, Ana Castillo's *The Mixquiahuala Letters*, Sandra Cisneros's *The House on Mango Street* and *Woman Hollering Creek and Other Stories*, and Denise Chávez's *The Last of the Menu Girls* illustrates the range of emotional conflict represented by La Virgen, La Malinche, and La Llorona between characters and their mothers—a nurturing love that is both freeing and suffocating to the characters in the works.

La Virgen or the Virgin Mary is widely represented among Chicano authors as the perfect mother and hence the mother to be idealized and venerated. In the works by male Mexican American authors, the mother figure is often identified as Virgin-like and pictured in prayer. The religious iconography surrounding mother figures in the works by Chicanos is an accepted theme and one that represents a total veneration of the mother. Common in the Hispanic culture is the Mother-Son/Virgin-Christ mythos. Because of this common cultural icon, the mother-daughter relationship does not escape implications of the Virgin-Christ relationship. The veneration of the mother figure by the son represents the overwhelming cultural identification for the appropriate relationship between mother and child. If a member of the community, usually female, does not accept the traditional veneration for the mother, that individual faces conflict with the social value of motherhood, intimately entwined with the ultimate Mexican value of *la familia*. María Herrera-Sobek, in her ground-breaking work *The Mexican Corrido: A Feminist Analysis*, is one of the first critics to do a major study of Jungian archetypes, specifically the good mother and the terrible mother archetype. She posits the enormous influence upon the culture of these two images of motherhood, which she identifies within the form of the Mexican ballad known as the corrido. As Herrera-Sobek argues, the archetypal mother image is ubiquitous within the community, and most of its depictions are male centered and defined.

The authors included in this discussion are familiar with the traditional portrayal of mothers in the works of male Mexican American authors. That portrayal consistently informs and challenges the contemporary Mexican American woman writer. In order to gain legitimacy, she must challenge the male paradigms. The male authors, influenced by patriarchy and initially the legitimate producers of cultural products, recreated in their works a Virgin mother image that all must accept as representing the only valid relationship between mother and child, whether female or male child. A powerful cultural icon from the Hispanic world, the Virgin mother image remains a vital figure in the fiction of Mexican American males. By providing a few examples, one can see what in fact Chicana authors are responding to or reevaluating and revisioning for their own understanding of the relationship of mother and child and, specifically, mother and daughter.

Rudolfo Anaya in *Bless Me, Ultima*, an early classic by a Mexican American male author, portrays the main character's mother as a woman close to sainthood. She is a strong believer in Catholicism, unlike the husband. Mirroring the cultural value system where the female promotes appropriate family cultural mores and the father remains a distant, sometimes uncivilized and resistant cultural figure, the woman represents and teaches the values of the society. In Anaya's novel the mother figure is a stereotypical good mother whose character remains flat. This saintly but flat mother figure also appears in Richard Rodriguez's *Hunger of Memory*. Rodriguez dedicates his book to his parents and characterizes his mother as a good but not intelligent woman, who represents all the nurturing values of the society but has no real understanding of the culture she attempts to teach to her children. In Tomás Rivera's work (translated by Evangelina Vigil-Piñón) . . . *And the Earth Did Not Devour Him*, the story "A Prayer" presents the common occupation of mothers, which is to pray for their sons' lives, a mythic echo of the occupation of the Virgin Mary. The religious influence can never be dismissed or ignored.

Consistent throughout the works of these men is the shared concept that mothers both bestow and embody the values of the culture without fully understanding the meaning of those values. Mothers only do good but do not understand or have the wisdom to know good. The traditional view is that the male defines what is good and the female transmits the cultural values to the next generation without contributing to the meaning. Hence, it is up to the male to offer a critique of the social mores, albeit a simplistic critique in the form of direct opposition to the cultural authority of the female. It is also the male's prerogative to define the relationship between mother and child. Chicana authors challenge the cultural authority of the male by depicting mother and daughter relationships and at the same time removing the focus of the son from the mother-child relationship.

One early author does portray his mother as a fallen saint, and that text is important because it articulates for Chicana authors the duality of a patriarchal understanding of mothers without offering an understanding of the relationship between mother and child. The Chicana critique offers the following argument: the actual relationship portrayed by males in the dual images of the good and the bad mother is incomplete and destructive to women. José Villarreal in *Pocho* explains that the saintly mother stopped being a saint because she became more Americanized. The implication in this novel is that Hispanic women cannot be good mothers if they acculturate into mainstream American society. For Villarreal's novel, women in mainstream society are bad women, reinforcing the dualities of Mexican mothers as Virgin Mary–like and mainstream

American mothers as fallen women or sold-out women. For the Mexican American author the woman who becomes "Americanized" is represented by the mythic character of La Malinche, the betrayer of her race (Anzaldúa, 22).

This veneration of the mother, however, does not translate into the veneration of womanhood. What is often made distinct in these texts where one's mother is a saint is that all other women are less. Only one's mother is worthy of veneration; all other women are either evil or unworthy even of notice except as sexual objects submissive to their husbands. Ana Castillo identifies traditional male assumptions about the split between mothers and women: "My tía says my uncle confided in her once that he believes aside from his saintly mother, of course, all women are possessed by the devil" (14). It is a common cultural conception of women that except for the good mother all other women are bad and must be contained. The duality of the good and the destructive mother is represented in the image of La Malinche, Hernán Cortés's mistress and translator, the mythic mother of the Mexican and hence the Chicano. The male authors' traditional portrayal of motherhood and the relationship between mother and male child requires a reexamination from a different perspective. The Chicana author, by articulating a portrayal of the complexity in the mother-child and specifically mother-daughter relationship, responds to the narrowly defined understanding of motherhood within the Mexican American culture. In the texts by women, the image of La Virgen is displaced by La Malinche, a direct response to the male narratives.

It is the negligent mother that is often portrayed by Chicana writers representing the old myth of La Malinche and the old duality of mother (the Virgin) slash evil mother (La Malinche). Like Villarreal's failed mother figure who has become "Americanized" and hence sold-out to the invaders, repeating the La Malinche mythos, Chicana writers have also bought into the dual thinking and traditional cultural values that heavily punish one who is not completely loyal to the Mexican culture. Unafraid to acknowledge the failure to nurture, which in the traditional Hispanic community is a major sin because of the primacy of relationships, Chicana writers not only portray these wicked mothers, many of whom are promiscuous, but provide motives for their limited ability to nurture—motives different from those suggested by the male authors like Villarreal who offer "Americanization" as the culprit for the failure to nurture.

Helena María Viramontes depicts a failed mother in her short story "Miss Clairol." Arlene and her daughter Champ are in K-Mart looking for the perfect hair dye for Arlene: "For the last few months she has been a platinum 'Light Ash' blond, before that a Miss Clairol 'Flame' redhead, before that Champ couldn't even identify the color—somewhere between orange and brown, a 'Sun Bronze.' The only way Champ knows her mother's true color is by her roots which, like death, inevitably rise to the truth" (Herrera-Sobek and Viramontes, 101).

Arlene is preoccupied with a popular-culture definition of beauty. She is a foul-mouthed, coarse, and vulgar woman. She works in a factory, and there is no mention of a husband, just boyfriends who do not treat Arlene very well. Her only concern is to look like the mass media's models and attempt to live within the popular culture's concepts of what joy there is in life. It is the images of women produced in slick commercials that Arlene is attempting to teach her daughter: "When you get older I'll show you how you can look just as pretty—and she puts her head back, relaxes, like the Calgon commercials . . ." (103). As Arlene continues to prepare for her date, Champ, her prepubescent daughter, "is busy cutting out Miss Breck models from the stacks of old magazines Pancha found in the back of her mother's garage. Champ collects the array of honey colored haired women, puts them in a shoe box with all her other special things" (103). Afterward, Champ prepares her own meal of Campbell's soup. Viramontes is depicting stereotypes and not full characters. The aim of her text is to provide a cultural critique, not necessarily to develop realistic or full characters.

Viramontes's short story is an indictment of the society that produces images of beauty that both Champ and Arlene admire but do not represent. It is also part of the cultural stereotype that only Mexican women are good mothers and that women who attempt to acculturate into the American mainstream are bad mothers or promiscuous. Viramontes implies an indictment of motherhood similar to the indictment in Villarreal's *Pocho* of a woman who attempts to assimilate into a culture not originally her own; but, unlike Villarreal, Viramontes offers a feminist critique of both cultures' expectations for women—implying the debilitating effect that patriarchal cultures have upon women. The irresponsible behavior exhibited by Arlene toward Champ will only be replicated by Champ with her own children. A combination of poverty, ignorance, and influence by the mass media, according to Viramontes, produces the irresponsible and promiscuous mother: the image of La Malinche.

The daughter of this woman, it is assumed, will replicate the mother's life. The failure to nurture a daughter and provide some semblance of direction other than that offered by popular culture condemns the daughter to reenacting her mother's experience, a cycle not to be broken. Arlene is a woman whose life is limited, and her interaction with Champ limits her daughter's life as well. In her own way, Arlene loves Champ, but her total self-interest and failure to nurture leave Champ to the influence of the television. Champ, in the restricted consciousness she is allowed in the story, is portrayed as someone who will develop a limited critical view of the world because she was not nurtured. Sandra Cisneros implies a similar outcome for the unnurtured child in her stories.

In Cisneros's loosely connected stories from *The House on Mango Street*, another negligent mother is represented. The story "There Was an Old Woman She Had So Many Children She Didn't Know What to Do," an obvious play on the old Mother Goose rhyme, identifies the phenomenon of poor women whose children are uncontrollable. An important aspect here, different from both Viramontes and Villarreal, is that Cisneros does not judge the mother as completely culpable in her failure to nurture. It is simply that she is in an impossible position:

> Rosa Vargas' kids are too many and too much, It's not her fault you know, except she is their mother and only one against so many.
>
> They are bad those Vargas, and how can they help it with only one mother who is tired all the time from buttoning and bottling and babying, and who cries every day for the man who left without even leaving a dollar for bologna or a note explaining how come. (29)

The failure to nurture is due to being outnumbered. The children are out of control, and the neighborhood gives up on them because the Vargas children "are without respect for all things living, including themselves" (29). Once again, outside circumstances are the cause for a failure to nurture. The mother is not directly responsible for her bad children, both male and female, but is as much a victim of poverty and the irresponsibility of an absent father. Viramontes's short story and Villarreal's novel imply a similar victimization. Outside commercialization has warped the identity of the mother into one who is incapable of nurturing her children. The true culprit, hence, is not just an attempt at acculturation into mainstream American society but patriarchy as well.

While the victimization of the mother is obvious, the child is also victimized. Unlike the male child, who even if unnurtured realizes the value society places on him, the female child never receives the primacy value signal from society—if anything, she receives the opposite value signal. At least the male receives some acknowledgment from the society. A daughter receives both from her mother and from society the impression of unworthiness. Not only has her mother failed to nurture her, but society offers no validation for her existence as well. Hence, the daughter has been emotionally shortchanged, doomed to repeat her mother's existence and probably unable to develop a strong sense of self.

The victim's role is assigned to Doña Marina, Cortés's mistress and translator. The myths of La Malinche, known as the "raped one," have come to represent a victim of European conquest as well as someone who sold out her people to the Europeans. As the recognized mother of the mestizos, the indigenous and European mix, La Malinche is the mother/whore of the Mexican mythos. Hated for her apparent selling-out to the European conquerors and at the same time an actual historical figure who did bear Cortés a child, La Malinche represents the hatred for women and the cultural trauma of a people created by a rape (Sánchez, 147; Candelaria, 1). The victims of society—hence, the sold-out ones—are failed mothers like Arlene and Rosa Vargas. At the same time, they are the women who have bought into the cultural constructs created for them and their daughters and are doomed to a life of misery and poverty, and their daughters are doomed to repeat the cycle.

La Llorona, the crier, is a grieving mother, but she is also the mother who is allowed the range of human passions, both destructive and positive. Feminist writers can see the possibilities in this mother that are not available in the images of La Virgen and even La Malinche, who suffer in silence and are passive figures. The stories of La Llorona are told to children to get them to behave. Depending on the version, La Llorona is a woman who drowned her children or lost her children and is condemned to searching and grieving for eternity. As the moral of the myth exemplifies, if a child is out too late at night, La Llorona will come and claim that child as her own. An unimaginable death will be that child's fate. This folktale represents the fear of the suffocatingly nurturing mother and the eternal role of the grieving mother. Clarissa Pinkola Estés in her best-selling book *Women Who Run with the Wolves* provides the basic story line of the La Llorona folktale. She has some very different interpretations of the meaning of the story, claiming that "the theme remains the same: the destruction of the fertile feminine" (303). However, that interpretation is not necessarily true, because the image of La Llorona is defined by the community telling the story. The tale has a fairly consistent story line that continues to be told today.

A rich Hidalgo, nobleman, courts a beautiful but poor woman and wins her affections. She bears him two sons, but he deigns not to marry her. One day he announces that he is returning to Spain, where he will marry a rich woman chosen by his family, and that he will take his sons with him.

The young woman is crazed and acts in the manner of the great shrieking madwoman throughout time. She claws her own face, she tears at him, she tears at herself. She picks up the two small sons and runs to the river with them and there throws them into the torrent. The children drown, and *La Llorona* falls to the riverbank in grief and dies.

The *hidalgo* returns to Spain and marries the rich woman. The soul of *La Llorona* ascends to heaven. There the master of the gate tells her she may come to heaven, for she has suffered, but that she may not enter until she recovers the souls of her children from the river.

And that is why it is said today that *La Llorona*, the weeping woman, sweeps the riverbanks with her long hair, puts her long stickfingers into the water to drag the bottom for her children. It is also why living children must not go near the river after dark, for *La Llorona* may mistake them for her own children and take them away forever. (Estés, 302)

This version of the La Llorona story is the old standard one told to children and repeated in variations. The characterization of La Llorona can range from a typical spook, to a heroic fighter against patriarchy, to the retelling of the story of La Malinche: "Sometimes the *La Llorona* tale is told as a story about *Ce. Malinalli* or *Malinche*, the native woman said to have been translator and lover to the Spanish conqueror Hernán Cortés" (Estés, 301). For Estés, the story of La Llorona has evolved into a moral tale of the modern destruction of female fertility caused by patriarchal contamination of "wild beauty . . . in the inner world or in the outer world" (303). The story is also the violent and destructive response to patriarchy.

Irene Blea collapses the myths of La Malinche and La Llorona in her work *La Chicana and the Intersection of Race, Class, and Gender*. It is a very common assumption among those who look at Mexican folklore to equate La Malinche and La Llorona, their tales being similar. Blea implies a historical linearity in La Malinche's and La Llorona's relationship: "La Llorona has had more than four different names from four different periods. Malinalli, Malina, Malin, Malintzin, and Ixkakuk have appeared as her pre-Columbian names . . . , while Doña Marina and La Malinche are colonial period names. From the time of the U.S. war with Mexico to this day, she has existed as La Llorona" (27).

Collapsing the actual historical figure of La Malinche or Doña Marina, Cortés's translator and mistress, to La Llorona is not accurate. The myth of La Llorona is much older than the actual historical figure of La Malinche (Blea, 27; Estés, 301). But even more important is the fact that La Malinche serves a different function in the society than does La Llorona. La Malinche is the turncoat, the seller of her people, the "Americanized" or sometimes feminist woman who has accepted a set of values destructive to her cultural origins. She has turned away from the culture that is supposed to offer security and a codified role. La Llorona is a woman of passion, of emotion, of the mythic past represented in Aztec and Mayan cultures. While La Malinche has a specific politicized use, La Llorona serves the emotional fear of women because, unlike La Malinche, she is capable of enormous destruction. La Malinche does not have to be feared, just controlled. La Llorona is the uncontrollable. She has come to represent the overwhelmingly dangerous mother who is capable of destroying everything, while La Malinche simply is the failed nurturer, and La Virgen is the perfect nurturer.

The suffocatingly nurturing mother is one that the male writers have consistently created but not necessarily acknowledged as overwhelming—hence the images of La Virgen and La Malinche in their work. The critique of the overwhelmingly nurturing and destructive mother has been left to women. It is the grieving mother that has been represented by women. However, this mother, unlike La Virgen, who grieves for the suffering her male child must endure, grieves because of her own culpability in the suffering of all her children, both female and male. The image of La Llorona, who has, because of her passion, failed all her children and must grieve for them all, is more appropriate for women writers than for the male writers, who do not allow mothers human passions. For example, in Lucha Corpi's *Delia's Song*, Delia's two brothers have died, one because of drugs and the other in Vietnam. The character articulates in a stream of consciousness the conflict represented when society dictates that the male is the more valued child. A daughter can never replace the love a mother has for her sons:

> Why don't you love me Mother
> What must I do What can I do
> I wished I had died instead of them
> I live I live I love you Mother
> It isn't enough It'll never be enough for you
> Fill the emptiness Why did you abandon me
> What did I ever do to you I was a girl Was
> that it I wasn't a boy We never talk
> We don't even fight Silence between us
> Dark web you've crocheted to hold me there
> Speechless Why can't you love me
> Mother Why I'm not much but I'm all
> you've got All you've got (33)

The fundamental anger at a culture that values its male children above its female ones and its manifestation when a mother loves her sons more than her daughters is revealed in this stream of consciousness monologue by the character Delia. The novel itself is the tale of the search for identity. Delia is a good daughter, submissive and quiet. She goes to a California university, where she begins the process of revolting against the things her mother taught her were appropriate to being a good daughter. In the process of her developing an identity outside that of a "good daughter," Delia discovers her mother's favoritism toward her brothers. She also finds herself in an emotional quagmire because she no longer knows how to respond to her grieving mother. Her mother is no longer the easily recognizable Virgin Mary who loves and nurtures her children, but a woman who validates her sons and not her daughter. The traumatic realization pushes Delia to continue her development beyond the traditional gender role her family and society had assigned to her.

The mother who must grieve for her sons and, in doing so, admit to favoritism represents one of the issues feminist Chicanas have attempted to address in their writing. It is the spoiled sons of these women who raise the ire of Chicanas. These mothers are culpable for the disastrous relationships between male and female and the continued domination of women. As depicted by these feminist writers, these are mothers who played favorites and are now grieving in penance as represented in the myth of La Llorona for their limited ability to love beyond the patriarchal confines of society.

Ana Castillo in *The Mixquiahuala Letters* addresses the need to begin anew in the rearing of sons; in fact, the rearing of sons like daughters is the only salvation for the world. She has no advice for the raising of daughters, for clearly what she describes in the following excerpt is the traditional approach:

> The following day at the airport, i gave you a list of general instructions if Vittorio should ever become yours: he should be taught to look after himself, mend his own clothes, cook, clean up and do his share. He should be allowed to do whatever it was that little boys liked to do but he should also be sensitive . . .
>
> You smiled and gave me a peck on the cheek without looking into my eyes. i watched until you disappeared down the ramp. Next to you went a man you tried to teach all the things i had just told you Vittorio must learn if he was to grow up to be a decent companion to a woman. (130)

To Castillo, a daughter is raised by a mother to be a nurturing and caring person. The daughter is taught to care for the needs of others in the family and to believe in the ultimate value of the family. Included in this understanding of how a mother raises her daughter is the critique that showing favoritism to the son damages not only the daughter but also society. Feminists have been arguing for years that a mother who favors her sons over her daughters destroys the self-worth of the daughters. That search for self-worth becomes a theme in much of the work by Mexican American women authors. Castillo's novel is a search for identity. But unlike Corpi, who directly blames the mother for a weak sense of self-worth, Castillo only implies that something is amiss in the way a daughter is raised by her mother.

The response from authors like Corpi and Castillo to the traditional relationships between mothers and daughters is to demand that the sons be raised in the same way the daughters are raised. If that were to occur, some of the tensions in the relationship between mothers and daughters would be relieved. The sense of inferiority that becomes imbedded in a daughter's psyche from the cumulative inference of favoritism toward a son would be alleviated.

Sandra Cisneros in the story "Never Marry a Mexican" from *Woman Hollering Creek* implies a similar failed relationship between mother and daughter that has generational implications. The image of the mother in this story is of a woman who teaches her child not to trust men because of her own poisoned relationship with her husband. She is the La Llorona mother who is capable of destroying everything. In an almost classic retelling of the myth, Cisneros portrays the mother as a destructive emotional force, alienating and condemning her daughter to repeating her own mother's destructive powers.

Told from the daughter's perspective, the story blames the mother for the failed relationships they have had with men. Clemencia, the daughter, states the dictum she believes is responsible for her own destructive tendencies: "Never marry a Mexican, my ma said once and always. She said this because of my father. She said this though she was Mexican too. But she was born here in the U.S., and he was born there, and it's *not* the same, you know" (68). These first lines of the story set up the focus of her mother's destructive power upon her life. The outcome of her mother's dictum, according to Clemencia, is that "I'll *never* marry. Not any man" (68). Her mother taught her not to trust men, instilling a sense of distrust in relationships and a distrust in her own relationship with her mother. Trust is the issue Clemencia and her mother wrestle with and the force that will push their relationship into a schism neither will be able to cross.

Clemencia involves herself in affairs with men who are committing acts of infidelity. She has seen and participated in relationships that challenge concepts of trust between man and wife because she is "the other woman." She admits to this destructive tendency in herself when she accepts that she has caused deliberate pain to other women. Not oblivious to her own culpability in the destruction of trust between individuals, Clemencia rationalizes that this is the reason she will not marry. She "knows" men are untrustworthy, Mexican or otherwise. The failure to be able to trust is the rationalization Clemencia gives for her inability to marry but also for her ability to be cruel, destructive, and vindictive—and this, she claims, she learned from her mother. Her mother taught her specifically not to marry a Mexican: "Mexican men, forget it. . . . Not men I considered as potential lovers. Mexican, Puerto Rican, Cuban, Chilean,

Colombian, Panamanian, Salvadorean, Bolivian, Honduran, Argentine, Dominican, Venezuelan, Guatemalan, Ecuadorean, Nicaraguan, Peruvian, Costa Rican, Paraguayan, Uruguayan, I don't care. I never saw them. My mother did this to me" (69). Her mother has an enormous amount of power to be able to make a whole group of men disappear. That power, however, is limited to destructiveness.

As the La Llorona myth implies, the woman is given limited responsibility outside the family structure and finds herself trapped in a world that attempts to disempower her, a world known basically as the traditional patriarchal value system. It is the male who has forced her to do violent acts because that is her only outlet. In the original stories, La Llorona destroys her own children in a vindictive act against her lover—a crime of cataclysmic passion. The lover or husband represents the abuse of women by patriarchy. For Clemencia, her mother's dictum "kills" any possibility of trust with men or even her mother. She does give a reason for her mother's dictum and seems to understand why her mother has responded as she has: "I guess she did it to spare me and Ximena [her sister] the pain she went through. Having married a Mexican man at seventeen. Having had to put up with all the grief a Mexican family can put on a girl because she was from *el otro lado*, the other side, and my father had married down by marrying her" (69).

The understanding of her mother's pain does not release Clemencia from her anger for her mother's destructiveness. Clemencia is the voice of La Llorona's drowned children. The question posed by Cisneros is whether La Llorona's children could forgive the violence heaped upon them even if they understood the cause. For Clemencia, the answer is no. The emotional violence is unforgivable to the victim of the atrocity. For whatever his limitations, Clemencia's father is still her father and still a Mexican. One does not marry a Mexican. One does not love a Mexican. Her father is a Mexican, and, as the syllogism suggests, one does not love her father. As the family stands over his grave, Clemencia states, "I just stood there dry-eyed next to Ximena and my mother, Ximena between us because I wouldn't let her stand next to me" (74). Clemencia knows that her mother was seeing another man while her father was ill, and that is why she cannot forgive her mother (73).

Their relationship continues to dissipate when her mother remarries. Clemencia's description of their failed relationship represents the extension of the La Llorona myth:

> Once Daddy was gone, it was like my ma didn't exist, like if she died, too. My mother's memory is like that, like if something already dead dried up and fell off, and I stopped missing where she used to be. Like if I never had a mother. And I'm not ashamed to say it either. When she married that white man, and he and his boys moved into my father's house, it was as if she stopped being my mother. Like I never even had one. (73)

In the end, Clemencia implies the destruction of her mother. For her, there can be no forgiveness or reconciliation, no hope of salvaging a relationship between mother and daughter.

Of all the archetypal mother figures, La Llorona risks the most. Because of her passion and destruction, the relationship of the La Llorona mother and her daughter can end in total emotional disaster and estrangement. The mother who believes she is attempting simply to survive and the daughter who creates emotional havoc for others represent one of the possible outcomes of the relationship between La Llorona and her daughter.

There is no hope for reconciliation even when La Llorona attempts to explain the reason for her failure to her child. For Clemencia, it is not enough: "'Because I married so young, *mi'ja*,' she'd say. 'Because your father, he was so much older than me, and I never had a chance to be young. Honey, try to understand . . .' Then I'd stop listening" (73). For the child of La Llorona, there are not enough reasons for the destruction caused by the mother. And for Clemencia, who has decided to cause her own havoc on other people's lives, there is no possibility of redemption for her mother: "Ma always sick and too busy worrying about her own life, she would've sold us to the Devil if she could" (73).

Cisneros in "Never Marry a Mexican" has re-created the La Llorona myth and taken it to a logical extension of what the victims of La Llorona's passion would feel and how they might possibly react. The story itself also implies the continued cycle of victimization that happens to women when other women buy into only the destructive element of La Llorona without the redemptive powers of regret and attempts at reversing some of the destruction.

The La Llorona mother also takes the form of the mother who looks upon her daughter's opportunities with envy. Cisneros acknowledges, as do most contemporary Chicana authors, that it has only been the most recent generation of women who have had the opportunities to be other than wives and mothers. The longing for opportunity lost and the incomprehensibility of a life different from the traditional roles have also contributed to the inability to connect between mothers and daughters. The conflict between pride in the daughter and envy for her opportunities leads to an emotionally charged experience for the mother. La Llorona's response was to destroy her children rather than face the conflicts.

Denise Chávez's *The Last of the Menu Girls* includes the tension between mother and daughter, whose two very different lives contribute to the failure to communicate at times:

> "Now that's enough out of you, Rocio. That's enough. I never use the word, you know I never use the word, but shut up. Shut up!"
> "Okay, okay, I'll take the water."
> "SHUT UP!"
> "Just listen to me, Mother, you never listen."
> "You know me, Rocio, I only say things once. And that's that. YA."
> "Okay, Okay, . . ." (147)

The inability to relate to each other because they occupy two very different worlds is part of the conflict between mother and daughter. It does not take away from the actual love. It just makes it clear that the women do not understand each other. In Chávez's work, the love between mother and daughter is never questioned. In fact, at the end of the novel, it is Rocio's mother who encourages her to write the story she writes. It is this ability to nurture and not understand each other that haunts the stories. As in the La Llorona myth, the heavy expression of passions leads to conflicting values, pride in a daughter and envy in her, love and yet no understanding of each other. One generation had limited and few opportunities but at least was given a clear understanding of their role in society. The next generation had unlimited and diverse opportunities but unclear and often contradictory roles to perform in the society.

Cisneros in *The House on Mango Street* acknowledges the limited opportunities of the previous generation. Esperanza, the main character, is told by her mother to study and to learn to depend on herself and to take care of herself. One cannot depend upon husbands, her mother warns. The mother grieves for her lost opportunities: "I could've been somebody, you know? my mother says and sighs. She has lived in this city her whole life. She can speak two languages. She can sing an opera. She knows how to fix a T.V. But she doesn't know which subway train to take to get downtown. I hold her hand very tight while we wait for the right train to arrive" (90). Esperanza's mother cannot read. She quit school. She regrets the opportunities she gave up or never had. She looks to her daughter and tells her to study. She tells her that is the only way out and the only way to survive on her own. Grief is another major characteristic of the Hispanic mother. For Esperanza, however, her mother admitting to her own limited opportunities forces her to investigate her own opportunities.

Cisneros, in another story from *Woman Hollering Creek*, depicts a positive version of the La Llorona myth—that of a woman who has done what she wished to do and was willing to pay the price for it. This is a recuperation story, an attempt to retell and revalue the La Llorona myths and, for Cisneros, the creation of a new folktale. Like the story of La Llorona, the story of La Gritona (the female hollerer) concerns a body of water. In this particular case it is an actual creek that runs north to south, east of San Antonio. Its English title on the highway marker is "Woman Hollering Creek," La Gritona—"Such a funny name for a creek so pretty and full of happily ever after," thinks Cleofilas, the main character in the story (47). Cleofilas is a Mexican woman who marries a Mexican American and comes to live in Seguin, Texas, where she bears a child and is beaten frequently by her husband. Once again, the recurrent theme of abuse by the patriarchal system works as a literary technique and propels the story. When Cleofilas goes to the doctor for prenatal care of the second child, her black and blue body frightens the doctor into calling Felice (Spanish for happy) to take Cleofilas to San Antonio so she could head back to the safety of her father.

As they cross the creek, Felice yells out, surprising both Cleofilas and her son:

> Pues, look how cute. I scared you two, right? Sorry. Should've warned you. Every time I cross that bridge I do that. Because of the name, you know. Woman Hollering. Pues, I holler. She said this in a Spanish pocked with English and laughed. Did you ever notice, Felice continued, how nothing around here is named after a woman? Really. Unless she's the Virgin. I guess you're only famous if you're a virgin. She was laughing again. (55)

To Cleofilas this woman is very unusual. Felice represents her savior at the same time she is an agent of consciousness raising: "Everything about this woman, this Felice, amazed Cleofilas. The fact that she drove a pickup. A pickup, mind you, but when Cleofilas asked if it was her husband's, she said she didn't have a husband. The pickup was hers. She herself had chosen it. She herself was paying for it" (55).

This is the new myth of La Llorona: the nondestructive mother who leaves her husband, takes her children, escapes, and begins the process of becoming a self-reliant, responsible full human being. In this new story, the traditional mother figure must begin the process of being less dependent on others as well as begin to develop a new consciousness of self. Cisneros is describing the new Llorona as a mother who starts to take back from patriarchy the responsibility for self and child and has the willingness to accept the consequences of those actions. This is a new mother, who is exploring roles outside the traditional ones.

Cisneros has created a new myth, La Gritona—the hollerer instead of the crier. Where she will fit into the society of mothers is still unclear. La Gritona is a more positive image of La Llorona, who still carries the burden of destruction. La Gritona is a twin image of La Llorona—they both suffer, but La Gritona finds a response that is not totally destructive and one that does not completely close any opportunities for continued interaction between mother and daughter.

While La Virgen, La Malinche, and La Llorona may, in fact, depict the tortured relationships between mothers and daughters, they also depict one clear message: the relationship was not explored by the earlier Chicano authors. Mexican American women writers are expressing in their texts experiences that have been traditionally muted or ignored. The simple duality assigned to La Virgen or La Malinche mother images is inappropriate for Chicana authors, who are redefining, challenging, and remythologizing those images.

Works Cited

Anaya, Rudolfo A. *Bless Me, Ultima*. Berkeley: Quinto Sol, 1972.

Anzaldúa, Gloria. *Borderlands/La Frontera: The New Mestiza*. San Francisco: Spinsters/Aunt Lute, 1987.

Blea, Irene I. *La Chicana and the Intersection of Race, Class, and Gender*. New York: Praeger, 1992.

Candelaria, Cordelia. "La Malinche, Feminist Prototype." *Frontiers* 5, no. 2 (1980): 1–6.

Castillo, Ana. *The Mixquiahuala Letters*. Binghamton, N.Y.: Bilingual Press, 1986.

Chávez, Denise. *The Last of the Menu Girls*. Houston: Arte Público Press, 1986.

Cisneros, Sandra. *The House on Mango Street*. New York: Vintage, 1989.

———. *Woman Hollering Creek and Other Stories*. New York: Random House, 1991.

Córdova, Teresa, Norma Cantú, Gilberto Cardenas, Juan García, and Christine M. Sierra, eds. *Chicana Voices: Intersections of Class, Race, and Gender*. Albuquerque: University of New Mexico Press and National Association for Chicano Studies, 1990.

Corpi, Lucha. *Delia's Song*. Houston: Arte Público Press, 1989.

Del Castillo, Adelaida R. "Malintzin Tenépal: A Preliminary Look into a New Perspective." In Sanchez and Cruz, 124–149.

Estés, Clarissa Pinkola. *Women Who Run with the Wolves: Myths and Stories of the Wild Woman Archetype*. New York: Ballantine, 1992.

Herrera-Sobek, María. *The Mexican Corrido: A Feminist Analysis*. Bloomington: Indiana University Press, 1990.

Herrera-Sobek, María, and Helena María Viramontes, eds. *Chicana Creativity and Criticism: Charting New Frontiers in American Literature*. Houston: Arte Público Press, 1988.

Horno-Delgado, Asunción, Eliana Ortega, Nina M. Scott, and Nancy Saporta Sternbach, eds. *Breaking Boundaries: Latina Writings and Critical Readings*. Amherst: University of Massachusetts Press, 1989.

Miller, Beth, ed. *Women in Hispanic Literature: Icons and Fallen Idols*. Berkeley: University of California Press, 1983.

Ordóñez, Elizabeth. "The Concept of Cultural Identity in Chicana Poetry." *Third Woman* 2, no. 1 (1984): 75–81.

Rivera, Tomás. *. . . And the Earth Did Not Devour Him*. Trans. Evangelina Vigil-Piñón. Houston: Arte Público Press, 1987.

Rodriguez, Richard. *Hunger of Memory: The Education of Richard Rodriguez*. New York: Bantam, 1982.

Salinas, Judy. "The Image of Women in Chicano Literature." *Revista Chicana Riqueña* 4 (Oct. 1976): 139–148.

Sánchez, Marta E. *Contemporary Chicana Poetry*. Berkeley: University of California Press, 1985.

Sánchez, Rosaura, and Rosa Martínez Cruz, eds. *Essays on La Mujer*. Los Angeles: Chicano Studies Center, University of California, 1977.

Trujillo, Marcella. "The Dilemma of the Modern Chicana Artist and Critic." *Heresies* 2, no. 4 (1979): 5–10.

Vigil, Evangelina, ed. *Woman of Her Word: Hispanic Women Write*. Houston: Arte Público Press, 1983.

Villarreal, José Antonio. *Pocho*. New York: Doubleday, 1959.

Viramontes, Helena María. "Miss Clairol." In Herrera-Sobek and Viramontes, 101–105.

Mother-Daughter Relationships as Epistemological Structures

Leslie Marmon Silko's *Almanac of the Dead* and *Storyteller*

CHARLENE TAYLOR EVANS

So generation succeeds generation, the slow stream of mothers and daughters forming a current that carried with it husbands, sons, and grandsons.

A. J. KROEBER, *Zuni Kin and Clan* (1917)

For the past twelve thousand years, most cultures have practiced the tradition of passing on the explanation of "being" and "becoming" to their offspring. While this function is not gender specific, the recipient of this information must have full faith and confidence in the one who is teaching. In many cultures, women carry the ontologies to their offspring. According to Leslie Marmon Silko, the Native American woman has been "the tie that binds her people together, transmitting her culture through song and story from generation to generation" (Mainiero, 82–83).

In Silko's *Storyteller* (1981) and *Almanac of the Dead* (1991), grandmothers serve as mother-surrogates for Native American daughters. This grandmother-granddaughter pairing forms an intergenerational unit, sometimes supplanting the mother-daughter dyad. Native American women often bear the title "aunt" or "auntie" whether the familial relationship is grandmother, mother, aunt, sister, or neighbor. The grandmother or "auntie"-daughter relationship is taken quite seriously in American Indian culture; one of its major functions is to become the "histor" or repository of knowledge for Native Americans. The mother-daughter pair becomes an epistemology or "way of knowing." Mothers and daughters serve as the bridge of continuity for Native American posterity; thus they help preserve the embodiment of cultural values, of the past, and of the individual and collective identities of Native American people. The knowledge they transmit is essential to redemption or survival for a threatened or endangered society and helps maintain their true identity by providing the cultural underpinnings that counter the invasive and corrosive influences of Western culture.

Weaving ancestral/supernatural spirits into her narrative, Silko combines the oral tradition or literal "storytelling" (the past) into writing (the present), which are reconciled by a process of artistic development in her works. An offspring of this union is the highly intricate and almost protean relationship which exists between Native American mothers and daughters formulating myriad epistemological structures. The grandmother-granddaughter storytellers and their stories communicate, as accurately as the medium allows, the reality of the Native American existence.

Storytelling had always fascinated Silko as a child in the Laguna Pueblo district of Arizona. In a matrilineal community, especially the society in *Storyteller*, the female/mother is a powerful person who is oftentimes the storyteller. In her anthology, Silko establishes the significance of the "story" and discusses the transformation of the oral text to a written one.

Silko reminisces about her Aunt Susie, actually her great grandmother, Marie Anaya Marmon, and contends that at a certain point in the history of the American Indian "the atmosphere and conditions that had maintained the oral tradition had been irrevocably altered by the European intrusion" (*Storyteller*, 6). The onus lay on mothers/grandmothers to protect and to transmit to their daughters an accurate explanation or accounting of the Native American past. These stories were sometimes communicated through pictures, song, and dance. Silko heard her great-grandmother, Aunt Susie, saying "a'moo'ooh," a Laguna expression of endearment for a young child, and she and her sisters began calling her Grandma A'mooh. Grandma A'mooh spent much time with Silko and Wendy and Gigi, her sisters. The girls stayed with her while their mother worked; it was quite convenient since they lived next door to each other. Silko slept with her "in case she fell getting up in the night" (Grandma A'mooh was eighty years old at this time; *Storyteller*, 34) and was immensely influenced and nurtured in this relationship with her great-grandmother. Silko reveals in the *Storyteller* volume that Grandma A'mooh used "to tell me and my sisters about the good old days when they didn't have toothpaste and cleaned their teeth with juniper ash" (*Storyteller*, 35). She also notes that when she was only seven or eight years old Aunt Susie (Grandma A'mooh) was in her mid-sixties and listened to all of her questions and speculations. A seasoned practitioner of the oral tradition, Aunt Susie was the last of a generation at Laguna that passed an entire culture and history by word of mouth:

> . . . an entire vision of the world
> which depended upon memory
> and retelling by subsequent generations (*Storyteller*, 6)

In moving from orality to literacy or "technologizing the word," to use Walter Ong's phrase, Silko suggests that she attempts to use in her writing "certain phrases, certain distinctive words" that her Aunt Susie "used in her telling" (*Storyteller*, 7). Her writing emerges from the auditory and is a retelling:

> . . . I write when I still hear
> her voice as she tells the story
> . . . I remember only a small part.
> But this is what I remember
> . . . This is the way I remember. (*Storyteller*, 7)

The role of the grandmother is to "tell" and "re-tell," and the mother-daughter pair serves as a custodian of culture. In *Storyteller*, Silko accepts the challenge of being a storyteller as a part of the continuum. She is a "new age" storyteller in that she utilizes another medium—the written page. She also broadens her audience by switching from orality to literacy. Noting the loss in meaning when an oral culture is reduced to writing, Silko, along with numerous scholars and linguists, perceives the inadequacy and inaccuracy of the written word and uses individual portraits, landscape pictures, and other media to facilitate and enhance her story: "'Yes, that's the trouble with writing,' I said. 'You can't go on and on the way we do when we tell stories around here'" (*Storyteller*, 110).

It is the responsibility of the storyteller or grandmother/mother figure to preserve the integrity of the written text. In a 1986 interview with

Kim Barnes, Silko discusses other techniques she has used to minimize the loss of meaning in the written text: "I play around with the page by using different kinds of spacing or indentations or even italics so that the reader can sense, say, that the tone of the voice has changed. If you were hearing a story, the speed would increase at certain points" (87).

Silko's mothers and daughters occupy a symbiotic relationship as daughters thrive and flourish because of the knowledge passed on to them by their mothers/grandmothers, and mothers/grandmothers likewise thrive because of the knowledge they have transferred to their female offspring. In Grandma A'mooh's last years, she was sent to Albuquerque to live with her daughter, Aunt Bessie. Because Aunt Bessie worked, Grandma A'mooh "did not have anyone to talk to all day" (*Storyteller*, 35). "She might have lived without watering morning glories and without kids running through her kitchen but she did not last long without someone to talk to" (*Storyteller*, 35). The dyadic structure of mother-daughter relationships is essential to the "being"/survival of the Pueblo female. Silko describes the storytelling as a "whole way of being." "I mean a whole way of seeing yourself, the people around you, your life in the bigger context . . . in terms of what has gone on before, what's happened to other people" (Barnes, 86).

Personal ontologies and epistemologies are tied to the stories and the storytellers. The mothers and daughters are the fountains and reservoirs of knowledge as they interact and exchange on numerous levels. More importantly, the mothers and daughters transfer information for understanding who Native Americans are as a people. The highly revered position of the female as creator of life and preserver of culture is maintained from generation to generation:

> In the beginning was thought, and her name was Woman. The Mother, the Grandmother, . . . is celebrated in social structures . . . and the oral tradition. To her we owe our lives, and from her comes our ability to endure. . . . She is the Old Woman who tends the fires of life. She is the Old Woman Spider who weaves us together in a fabric of interconnection. She is the Eldest God, the one who Remembers and Re-members. (Allen and Ortiz, 11)

The matrix of life and being in the American Indian society is the female. Her role is paramount to God, as the first lines in the excerpt from *The*

Sacred Hoop are reminiscent of John 1:1: "In the beginning was the Word, and the Word was with God, and the Word was God."

The initial dedication of the *Storyteller* evokes an aspect of timelessness and circularity which also relates to a sense of being for the American Indian, especially the female. An understanding of this infinite relationship between the storyteller and the story, the present and the past, lays the foundation for individual ontologies. The reader can experience the fluidity of time; the past is omnipresent: "This book is dedicated to the storytellers as far back as memory goes and to the telling which continues and through which they all live and we with them" (title page).

Memory is an important variable on this historical continuum. Likewise, the storyteller and the story are inextricably linked. The focused and deliberate narratives in *Storyteller* depict the storyteller or "histor" as a highly revered member of society. Because the "telling" establishes a permanence and maintains the culture, the storytellers (grandmothers and daughters who will become mothers / grandmothers) have a unique relationship with the past. Silko's sense of the role of mother / daughter is very much like Rayna Green's expression of matrilineage in *That's What She Said*:

> The clay shapers, fiber twisters, picture makers, and storytellers—the ones who said what was and what will be—they've always been important in Indian Country. Whether it comes directly from the storyteller's mouth and She writes it down or someone writes it for her, the story has to be told. . . . Before European writing, there were voices to sing and speak, dances to make real the stories that the people told or to honor the retelling anew. There were hands that talked and drew and shaped. . . . They kept them [the stories] even when no one asked to hear them—even when the whiteeyes came and asked only the men what they knew. Thus the women have always kept the stories. . . . (3)

Having a spirit-centered culture, Native Americans search for alternative yet appropriate avenues of expression for their ontologies. Not being familiar with the Native American culture, Euro-Americans thought that men were the keepers of the information.

Preserving and maintaining the accuracy of the stories is an enormously difficult task. Silko's mothers and daughters extract from portraits or graphic "rememories" from the past to ensure accuracy. Sethe, the female protagonist in Toni Morrison's *Beloved,* remembers significant events from her past in colorful flurries of visual slides of meaning called "rememories." Although in an interview Silko denies any similarity to Morrison, Silko's "rememories" bear a striking resemblance to Sethe's visions in *Beloved.* They also place emphasis on recall and the vivid snapshots of life that tell all and remain eternally etched in one's mind. Silko associates these graphic visual memories with storytelling. Sensitivity to memory and remembering, an important attribute for the mothers and daughters, is illustrated in "Lullaby." Ayah, the protagonist, defines old age as a time of memories: "She [Ayah] felt peaceful remembering . . . and she could remember the morning her baby was born. She could remember whispering to her mother, who was sleeping on the other side of the hogan" (*Storyteller,* 44). This emphasis on the past and remembering, its relevance and relationship to the present (birth), illuminates the timelessness of the contexts that the mother-daughter dyads draw from as sources for the stories.

Native American literature is significantly different from Western literature, for the underlying assumptions about the cosmos and their experiential bases are different. According to Paula Gunn Allen and Roxanne Ortiz, Native Americans seek—through song, ceremony, legend, myths, and tales—to articulate and share reality, to bring the private self into harmony and balance with their Native American reality, to verbalize the sense of the majesty and reverent mystery of all things, and to actualize, in language, those truths that give humanity its greatest significance and dignity (55). As innocuous as the stories may sometimes appear to be, they are powerful weapons against assimilation. The emphasis is of course on the "telling," and remembering is a vital element of the telling and of survival, individually and collectively. Silko hallows the stories in *Almanac of the Dead* by characterizing the narratives as analogues for the actual experiences, which no longer exist, an embodiment or mosaic of memory and imagination. The past is embodied within the rememory: "An experience termed past may actually return if the influences have the same balances or proportions as before. Details may vary, but the essence does not change. The day would have the same feeling, the same character, as that day has been described having had before. The image of a memory exists in the present moment" (*Almanac of the Dead,* 575).

Frederic Jameson, a Marxist theorist and philosopher, suggests further that literary form (the story) is deeply engaged with a concrete reality: "narrative is not just a literary form or mode but an essential 'epistemological category'; reality presents itself to the human mind only in the form of stories" (Selden, 47). This again reinforces the idea of the omnipresence of the past (the story) and suggests that the story vivifies and objectifies experience. Just as females are lifegivers in the physical biological sense, they likewise generate, maintain, and sustain the lives of the Native American people through the narratives. Daughters inherit the stories and must tell and retell them to maintain and sustain their culture.

One of the major themes communicated by the mothers and daughters in *Storyteller* is the resilient and remarkable relationship between Native Americans and their natural physical environment. Individuals are an expression of the cosmos. Natural phenomena and objects in geophysical space are their kin. Complementing the idea of the past and its omnipresence is the idea of the natural environment being an integral part of the Native American ideology. In "Lullaby" Ayah, an old woman now, remembers the song she sang to her babies. "She could not remember if she had ever sung it to her children, but she knew that her grandmother had sung it and her mother had sung it" (*Storyteller*, 51). The song metaphorically asserts familial relationships between nature and Native Americans:

> The earth is your mother,
> she holds you.
> . . . .
> Sleep, sleep.
> We are together always
> There never was a time
> when this was not so. (*Storyteller*, 51)

The belief that American Indian children do not belong to their biological parents but to the land and to the heavens is also implied in the lyric. The last two lines of the song Ayah sings, "There never was a time / when this was not so," suggest an ancient and infinite relationship between the earth (Mother) and the Native American. The people are the earth and the earth is "being," as all creatures are "being." The life-sustaining forces are female in gender. The land (Mother) and the people (mothers) are the same (Allen and Ortiz, 119).

Within the web of other familial relationships, mothers and daughters deliver the blueprint for the survival of their culture to the Native Americans. Exactly ten years after the publication of *Storyteller*, *Almanac of the Dead* addresses the desecration and violation of the land (the Americas) and the Native American people by Euro-Americans and depicts the mother-daughter unit as the interpreter and purveyor of the American Indian past. American Indians' overriding concern to regain tribal lands is expressed in Silko's assertion of the Indian connection to the resistance movement against Euro-American oppression of people of color in *Almanac of the Dead*: "Sixty million Native Americans died between 1500 and 1600. The defiance and resistance to things European continue unabated. The Indian Wars have never ended in the Americas. Native Americans acknowledge no borders; they seek nothing less than the return of all tribal lands" (epigraph). The climate of turmoil is exacerbated by the Native Americans' unwillingness to assimilate into the Euro-American culture. *Almanac of the Dead* chronicles the moral deterioration of the Native Americans brought on by the onslaught of alien aggressors. There is a nostalgia for the past and the restoration of their former lifestyles. Mother-daughter units (combinations of Old Yoeme, the grandmother, and Zeta and Lecha, her twin granddaughters) quietly brace themselves for war and make attempts to protect and preserve their epistemologies.

An example of the protean or shape-shifting nature of the American Indian mothers and daughters is their becoming literal caretakers of Native American history. A chapter entitled "Stone Idols" in *Almanac of the Dead* affirms the significance and reverence the Native American females, in particular, have for their past (represented by stone figures). The narrator notes that the care and protection of stone figures passed from generation to generation to an elder clanswoman. Readily accepting their responsibility, women are the recipients and conscientious caretakers of these figures; many precious objects belonging to the Indian culture were destroyed by Europeans or sold by weakhearted Native Americans. These stones are valued for their intrinsic spiritual life force and are extensions of the supernatural beings they represent. Feeding these objects a mixture of cornmeal and pollen sprinkled with rainwater, the women lift the stone figures as tenderly as they had lifted their own babies and call them "esteemed and beloved ancestors" (*Almanac*, 31). The use of cornmeal is an important part of the birth ritual in the Laguna Pueblo culture (Babcock, 70). Clearly, reverence and dedication are illustrated in these mother/offspring or characteristically feminine actions.

George Lakoff and Mark Johnson support the idea of the investment of meaning in objects into their essay "Ontological Metaphors": "Understanding our experiences in terms of objects and substances allows us to pick out parts of our experience and treat them as discrete entities or substances of a uniform kind. . . . We can refer to them, categorize them, group them, and quantify them—and, by this means, reason about them" (25). Certain objects in the Native American culture are spiritual embodiments which take on "life" or "being." These objects also serve as epistemologies and may be referred to, grouped, and quantified as Lakoff and Johnson suggest. Because many of these figures/objects are extensions of supernatural beings, the mother-daughter dyad takes on, of necessity, a supernatural aspect.

In *Almanac of the Dead,* Silko's mother-daughter units delve into the supernatural. Old Yoeme (the grandmother-figure) and Lecha and Zeta, her twin granddaughters, defy categorization and illustrate the supernatural influences of the surrogate mother-daughter unit. Yoeme is an important influence in the self-definition and moral development of both of her granddaughters, and she preoccupies herself with the guardianship of the epistemology or the ancient, arduously preserved journals that contain the history of her own people—a Native American Almanac of the Dead. The ancient prophecies maintain that all things European will disappear from the Americas and that a decipherment of the ancient tribal texts of the Americas foretells the future of all Americans. The future is encoded in arcane symbols and old narratives. It is Zeta's duty to seek, interpret, and tell Lecha, her sister, what to add to the growing epistemology. This spiritually powerful female triumvirate is more than capable of the tedious and painful task of transmitting and preserving the sacred history and future plans for the American Indian culture.

The powerful and supernatural influence of Yoeme over her granddaughters cannot shield them from the hypocrisy and dangers presented by the contemporary American society in which they live. Silko's panoramic view of the Native American diaspora highlights an insidious yet forceful and highly programmed assault by Euro-Americans on the American Indian way of life. Shackled by restrictions and demands for mandatory assimilation, the Native American woman does not respond to this oppression in the weak and reactionary manner in which the Euro-American society has stereotyped her male counterpart. She does not resort to alcoholism or silence. Instead the mother-daughter unit is about the business of fortifying its ranks by enlightening the Indian masses. Old Yoeme speaks to Zeta and charges her with the responsibility of interpreting and keeping the notebooks containing information about the past which is integral to their future. She warns Zeta that nothing must be added to the manuscript that was not already there. Because of the assault on the American Indian culture, the need for secrecy is clearly transmitted from mother to daughter. Again there is the implication of the inaccuracy and distrust of the written word. The window of opportunity to embellish and distort the text is present, yet it must not be considered. Consequently, to assure that they are guarding and transmitting truth, Yoeme and Zeta must be in direct communication with ancestral spirits and the dead.

Yoeme teaches Zeta to communicate and to rely on the big bull snake. The notebook of the snakes is the key to understanding the rest of the old almanac. Yoeme had always consulted "the big bull snake out behind the adobe woodshed" (*Alamanac*, 131). The mystical and ritualistic conferences with the snake conjure elemental truths of being for the Native American:

> [Yoeme] had her own picture of things. Snakes crawled under the ground. They heard the voices of the dead; actual conversations, and lone voices calling out to loved ones still living. . . . Snakes moved through the branches of trees. They saw and heard a good deal. . . . It [talking to the bull snake] was something Zeta did alone with her grandmother. (*Almanac*, 131)

Zeta learns from her grandmother Yoeme that death is not final or the end of life; it is a part of the universal cycle. This circular orientation encompasses reincarnation. People do not die unless descendants lose memory of them. In the fall Zeta had watched her grandmother Yoeme pick up the big bull snake while it sunned itself behind the woodshed. Cradling the snake against her chest, Zeta understood that the big snake recognized Yoeme "because he lay quietly, only his tongue moving slowly in and out at Zeta" (131). Zeta never discusses this with Lecha because words cannot explain how one talks to snakes. Because the snake does not actually speak, the information is transmitted in a higher, more spiritual form. The telepathy between the woman and the serpent contributes to the epistemology. Much of the information is already in the notebooks in code; the snake validates and provides information for the void. Communicating with the serpent empowers the mother-daughter pair supplying information for the survival of Native American culture. This operates counter to the Judeo-Christian myth of the serpent corrupting Eve in the Garden; rather than bringing sin and death into the world, this snake supplies positive knowledge for the Indian peoples through the women—mothers and daughters.

Once the notebooks are transcribed, Lecha feels that she will figure out how to use the old almanac. Then she will be able to foresee months and years to come. Interestingly, when Yoeme tells Lecha a story on the beach, Lecha writes the story on the blank pages of the notebook in English. Afterward, Yoeme demands to see it, for she is uncertain about Zeta's competence and intentions. Zeta waits for Yoeme to break into a fury, but instead she sighs with pleasure: this is the sign the keepers of the notebooks had long awaited. Transcribing this information into English marks the fusion of the present with the past.

Lecha recognizes that the almanac is a great legacy, and Yoeme and others believe the almanac has living power within it to unite all the tribal people of the Americas to retake the land. Finally, Lecha feels the life, energy, and power of the words; she recognizes her power and authority as female interpreter and purveyor of life. In "Discourse in the Novel," Mikhail Bakhtin discusses the world of "authoritative discourse," which is represented in *Almanac of the Dead* as the old almanac:

> The authoritative word demands that we acknowledge it, that we make it our own; it binds us, quite independently of any power it might have to persuade us internally; we encounter it with its authority already fused into it. The authoritative word is located in a distanced zone, organically connected with a past that is felt to be hierarchically higher. . . . It is a *prior* discourse. . . . It is akin to taboo. . . . It demands our unconditional allegiance. (Bakhtin, 342–343)

Because Yoeme believes that power resides within certain stories, the power ensures the retelling of the story, and with "each retelling a slight but permanent shift [takes] place" (*Almanac*, 581). The story is given to the daughter so that she can know and actualize her role of histor; the importance of the story and its relationship to life is succinctly stated in the final entry of Old Yoeme's notebook addressed to Native American posterity: "One day a story will arrive in your town. There will always be disagreement over direction; whether the story came from the southwest or the southeast. The story may arrive with a stranger . . . or brought by an old friend. . . . But after you hear the story, you and others prepare by the new moon to rise up against the slave masters" (*Almanac*, 578).

Convinced of the authenticity of the notebooks and the prophecy, Lecha becomes a conscientious guardian of that history. She is now acutely aware of her function in the mother-daughter dyad. After receiving much notoriety and money from her psychic predictions, the old and now cancerous Lecha hires the blond mixed blood Seese to help type the notebook. The fragments from the sacred notebooks address the importance of the narrative which facilitates the perpetuation of the American Indian culture. The mother-daughter pairing symbolizes the merging of past and present and undermines or minimizes the assault of the Western culture on the Native American people.

In *Almanac of the Dead*, Silko makes continual reference to the African American/Native American relationship. The Native American and African American cultures share striking similarities in many areas. Historically, the griot figure (histor) in the African society was male, and he transmitted knowledge of the past orally to subsequent generations. Like the Native American, the African followed a pattern of oppression and dispossession in America. The African male histor was replaced by an African American female. Understanding one's past is an essential element of empowerment, and both cultures understand the significance of the past and work to eradicate myths, distortions, and omissions in their respective histories. Most importantly, the common mission and agenda of the African American and Indian American peoples coalesce as a part of the final prophecy in Leslie Silko's *Almanac of the Dead*. In a section of the text called "Africa," Clinton, the central character, identifies the histor or African griot-figures in his life. Interestingly, they are also women speaking to other women/daughters. Clinton recalls the elderly women talking about the branches of their family, including intermarriages with whites and American Indians. One whole branch in Tennessee had married "Native Americans" (*Almanac*, 415).

Throughout this section of the novel, Clinton validates the link between the African American and Native American female histor:

Clinton remembered those old granny women sitting with their pipes or chew, talking in low, steady voices about in-laws and all the branches of the family. . . . [He] remembered the old grannies arguing among themselves to pass time. The older they got, the more they talked about the past; and they had sung songs in languages Clinton didn't recognize. . . . (418–420)

It is important to note this similarity because Silko notes the interconnectedness of missions for the Native American and African American peoples. *Almanac of the Dead* with its heavily symbolic and highly allusive style presents five discrete narrative lines. Both African American and Native American cultures are represented by Damballah and Quetzalcoatl, two giant snakes. Quetzalcoatl is the winged serpent and god of amalgamation or expansion. The following is the sacred prophecy guarded by the Native American mothers and daughters:

In Africa and in the Americas too, the giant snakes, Damballah and Quetzalcoatl, have returned to the people. I have seen the snakes . . . they speak to the people of Africa, and they speak to the people of the Americas; they speak through dreams. The snakes say this: From out of the south the people are coming, like a great river flowing restless with the spirits of the dead who have been reborn again and again all over Africa and the Americas, reborn each generation more fierce and more numerous. Millions will move instinctively; unarmed and unguarded, they begin walking steadily north, following the twin brothers. (*Almanac*, 735)

Silko refers to Native Americans and African Americans symbolically as snakes and "twin brothers." Native Americans and the earth (Mother) are also kin and have been ravaged by the Europeans. The parallels between both cultures and the earth are obvious, and the conclusion of the novel states the final prophecy and a call to action for a united effort by American Indians and African Americans.

To borrow Zora Neale Hurston's "mules of the world" metaphor, the tremendous burden on women gives rise to and necessitates a mother-daughter relationship of incomprehensible proportions. Using the appropriate media for maintaining and transmitting their sacred and important history, the designated female units in the Native American society labor to provide a pipeline for the people. One of the basic unspoken feminist assumptions—that women are essentially powerless—is debunked within Silko's texts, for the mothers and daughters are bastions of the American Indian society in times of great crisis. They hold the fortress after the male power has failed. In *The Sacred Hoop,* Allen and Ortiz present a society controlled by women: "In a system where all persons in power are called Mother Chief and where the supreme deity is female, and social organization is matrilocal, matrifocal, and matrilineal, gyarchy is happening. However, it does not imply domination of men by women as patriarchy implies domination by ruling class males of all aspects of a society" (223).

Unlike Western society, a struggle for dominance between the sexes does not exist in Native American culture. The various ontologies and epistemologies depicted in Silko's *Storyteller* and *Almanac of the Dead* exhibit a strong sense of the reality of the Native American experience. Unfortunately, Native American culture has not been kept completely intact by the stories transmitted by and in the care of these tenacious mothers and daughters. The acculturation of the Native American into Western society has been a rather slow and painful process. Native Americans have courageously resisted total assimilation into Western culture and struggled to survive near extinction. For millennia the social system of the Native Americans has been based on ritual, spirit-centered, woman-focused world views (Allen and Ortiz, 2). Consequently, Western culture has difficulty making sense of "who" these people are. The mother-daughter units constitute the complex and fluid Native American relationships which provide representative visions and voices "invoking the inestimable power of the earth and all the forces of the universe" (*Almanac of the Dead,* 723) to resolve and complete the Indian American mission of survival.

Works Cited and Consulted

Allen, Paula Gunn, and Roxanne Dunbar Ortiz. *The Sacred Hoop: Recovering the Feminine in American Indian Traditions.* Boston: Beacon Press, 1986.

Babcock, Barbara A. *Pueblo Mothers and Children: Essays by Elsie Clews Parsons, 1915–1924.* Sante Fe, N.M.: Ancient City Press, 1991.

Baillie, James. *Problems in Personal Identity.* New York: Paragon House, 1993.

Bakhtin, Mikhail M. *The Dialogic Imagination.* Austin: University of Texas Press, 1981.

Barnes, Kim. "A Leslie Marmon Silko Interview." *Journal of Ethnic Studies* 13, no. 4 (1986): 83–105.

Bartlett, Mary Dougherty. *The New Native American Novel.* Albuquerque: University of New Mexico Press, 1986.

Bataille, Gretchen, and Kathleen Sands. *American Indian Women Telling Their Lives.* Lincoln: University of Nebraska Press, 1984.

Beaty, Jerome, and J. Paul Hunter. *New Worlds of Literature.* New York: W. W. Norton, 1989.

Berkhoffer, Robert F., Jr. *The White Man's Indian: Images of the American Indian from Columbus to the Present.* New York: Alfred A. Knopf, 1978.

Boaz, Franz. *Race, Language, and Culture.* New York: Macmillan, 1953.

Cortés, Carlos. *Three Perspectives on Ethnicity—Blacks, Chicanos, and Native Americans.* New York: Putnam, 1976.

Felski, Rita. *Beyond Feminist Aesthetics.* London: Hutchinson Radius, 1989.

Green, Rayna, ed. *That's What She Said: Contemporary Poetry and Fiction by Native American Women.* Bloomington: Indiana University Press, 1984.

Hawkesworth, M. E. *Beyond Oppression: Feminist Theory and Political Strategy.* New York: Continuum Publishing, 1990.

Hertzberg, Hazel W. *The Search for an American Indian Identity: Modern Pan Indian Movement.* New York: Syracuse University Press, 1971.

Jacob, Wilbur R. *Dispossessing the American Indian.* Norman: University of Oklahoma Press, 1985.

Katz, Jane B. *I Am the Fire of Time: The Voices of Native American Women.* New York: E. B. Dutton, 1977.

Krause, Corinne Azea. *Grandmothers, Mothers, and Daughters: Oral Histories of Three Generations of Ethnic American Women.* Boston: Twayne Publishers, 1990.

Lakoff, George, and Mark Johnson. *Metaphors We Live By*. Chicago: University of Chicago Press, 1980.

Lerner, Andrea, ed. *Dancing on the Rim of the World*. Tucson: University of Arizona Press, 1990.

Mainiero, Lina, ed. *American Women Writers*. New York: Frederick Ungar, 1982.

Niethhammer, Carolyn. *Daughters of the Earth*. New York: Collier, 1977.

Ong, Walter J. *Orality and Literacy: The Technologizing of the Word*. New York: Methuen, 1982.

Ortiz, Simon J. *Woven Stone*. Tucson: University of Arizona Press, 1992.

Peyer, Bernd C., ed. *The Singing Spirit*. Tucson: University of Arizona Press, 1989.

Selden, Raman. *Contemporary Literary Theory*. 2nd ed. Lexington: University of Kentucky Press, 1989.

Shoemaker, Sydney. *Self-Knowledge and Identity*. Ithaca, N.Y.: Cornell University Press, 1963.

Silko, Leslie Marmon. *Almanac of the Dead*. New York: Simon and Schuster, 1991.

———. *Ceremony*. New York: Viking Press, 1977.

———. *Storyteller*. New York: Seaver Books, 1981.

St. Clair, R., and W. Leap, eds. *Language Renewal among American Indian Tribes: Issues, Problems, and Prospects*. Rosslyn, Va.: National Clearinghouse for Bilingual Education, 1982.

Wade, Edwin L. *The Arts of the North American Indian: Native Traditions in Evolution*: New York: Hudson Hills Press, 1986.

Wright, Anne, ed. *The Delicacy and Strength of Lace: Letters between Leslie Silko and James Wright*. Saint Paul, Minn.: Graywolf Press, 1985.

Disrupted Motherlines

Mothers and Daughters in a Genderized, Sexualized, and Racialized World

ELIZABETH BROWN-GUILLORY

A close reading of texts by women of color invariably leads to the discovery of mothers who go to extremes to protect their children, particularly daughters, from forces in society that would destroy them. The idea of women who kill their children to keep them safe is a recurring motif in diasporic literature, particularly African American literature. Toni Morrison's 1973 novel *Sula* includes the story of Eva Peace's pouring gasoline on her son Plum to keep him from further destroying his own life with drugs and alcohol. She explains to Hannah that she couldn't stop Plum from crawling back into her womb, so she set him free. Eva's comment about the womb suggests that she had tried to mother Plum as best she could but had somehow failed to instill in him the independence he needed to survive on his own. In an act of desperation, motivated by absolute love for her son, Eva takes his life. Morrison's 1987 Pulitzer prize–winning novel, *Beloved*, also calls attention to this phenomenon of mothers killing their children to protect them. Sethe murders her daughter, Beloved, when the lecherous owner tries to take them back into slavery. Marianne Hirsch in *The Mother/Daughter Plot* insightfully characterizes Sethe's taking of her daughter's life as "more than judgment" (7). Hirsch argues that the novel contains "stories that form and surround the relationship of mother and daughter during slavery and in post-abolition times. It contains stories both of maternal sorrow, guilt, and pain and of maternal joy and pleasure" (7). The act is a complex one, and

Morrison delves deeply into the circumstances which bring a mother to such desperation.

Morrison joins a long line of black writers who have chosen as their subjects women who take desperate steps to keep their children safe. One such account of this desperation is described by the pivotal black writer Olaudah Equiano, who wrote both about his African homeland and about his experiences in the United States. Equiano's 1789 text *The Interesting Narrative of the Life of Olaudah Equiano, or Gustavus Vasa, the African* describes incidences of women who threw themselves overboard from slave-ships when they discovered they were pregnant by white seamen.

This perplexing phenomenon of women killing their children is given clarification by a host of black women playwrights who wrote between the 1789 and 1987 publication dates of landmark books by Equiano and Morrison. Angelina Weld Grimke, Georgia Douglas Johnson, Shirley Graham, Lorraine Hansberry, and Alice Childress are five black playwrights who mirror the tensions and conflicts between mothers and daughters as they attempt to communicate with each other in what Toni Morrison views as a "genderized, sexualized and wholly racialized world" (*Playing in the Dark*, 4). Mary Helen Washington in "Black Women Image Makers" notes that while black women suffer from race, class, and gender biases, they are undeniably preoccupied with keeping their children safe and with making life better for themselves and their families. She posits, "To outsiders, she is the one-dimensional Rock of Gibraltar—strong of back, long of arm, invincible. But to those writers whose perceptions are shaped by their own Black womanhood, who can take us into the dark recesses of the soul, she is an individual—profound, tragic, mysterious, sacred, and unfathomable—strong in many ways, but not in all" (13). As Kathy Perkins notes in *Black Female Playwrights*, "The central focus in these women's plays was usually on the children, with the mother being overly protective because of the times in which they lived" (2). While times may have changed, the same obstacles which black mothers encountered in plays written between 1916 and 1971 continue to be reflected in literature written by such contemporary literary daughters as Alice Walker, Toni Morrison, Amy Tan, Maxine Hong Kingston, Cherríe Moraga, and Leslie Marmon Silko.

Grimke, Johnson, and Graham are among the most insightful and frank playwrights of the 1920s through 1940s, as noted in *Their Place on the Stage: Black Women Playwrights in America*:

> These sages wrote for the sheer joy of capturing and preserving the essence of Black life for future generations. They were able to turn theaters into nurseries where the Black race is given roots, nurtured, tested, healed, and provided with the spirit to survive. They are, indeed, the missing pieces to a multifaceted puzzle of Black life during the decades when Blacks were becoming aware, and awakening to their own self-worth, and struggling for an identity robbed them as a result of mutilated African roots. (Brown-Guillory, 5)

The plays by black women discussed here amplify the conditions under which women of color struggle to nurture their families and illustrate the role that race plays in the rearing of females.

Angelina Weld Grimke's treatment of mother-daughter relationships is especially germane to any discussion of the writings of contemporary women of color. Grimke's 1916 play *Rachel* became the "first twentieth-century full-length play written, performed, and produced by blacks" (Perkins, 8). *Rachel* examines the devastating effects of racism on an innocent child and his surrogate mother. When the play was published in 1917, inflamed critics accused Grimke of advocating genocide. However, a counter to her critics can be found in Grimke's papers in the Moorland-Spingarn Research Center at Howard University. Grimke justifies writing *Rachel* by saying that the play was directed as much at whites as it was at blacks. She was particularly interested in reaching white women, who are "the worst enemies with which the colored race has to contend" (quoted in Perkins, 9). Grimke's intentions in *Rachel* are elucidated when she says:

> My belief was then that if I could find a vulnerable point in their armour, if I could reach their hearts, even if only a little, then perhaps instead of being active or passive enemies they might become, at least, less inimical and possibly friendly. Did they have a vulnerable point and if so what was it? I believed it to be motherhood. . . . If anything can make all women sisters underneath the skins, it is motherhood. If, then, I could make the white women of this country see, feel, understand just what [effect] their prejudice and the prejudice of their fathers, brothers, husbands, and sons were having on the souls of the colored mothers everywhere, and upon the mothers that are to be, a great power to affect public opinion would be set free and the battle would be half won. (quoted in Perkins, 9)

While Grimke notes that she was partly trying to appeal to white women, there is evidence that she was also seriously concerned with mothering practices in the black community. Grimke scholars have tended to focus on *Rachel* as an antilynching play, not an unlikely subject since Walter White in *Rope and Faggot* estimated that 3,389 blacks, including 76 women, were lynched between 1882 and 1927 (229). Grimke was, indeed, concerned that white women seemed oblivious to the plight of black women, including their pain of witnessing the lynching of their sons, husbands, and brothers. In a 1992 essay, Judith L. Stephens argues that "in *Rachel,* Angelina Grimke threw the image of idealized motherhood back at white women in an attempt to make them see what meaning this so-called 'revered institution' might hold for black women. . . . Grimke was attempting to make white women question the desirability of motherhood from a black woman's perspective at a time when lynchings were at an all-time high" (333–334).

A closer reading of Grimke's play, however, reveals a key issue which has not been explored in critical studies. Grimke clearly points out that Rachel's own mother, Mrs. Loving, has not adequately prepared her for mothering. Grimke suggests that Rachel's depression and feelings of alienation could have been prevented had her mother adequately prepared her for a hostile world. While Grimke certainly protests against lynching practices in America in this play, she, more importantly, makes the point that mothers must tell their daughters the truth about the obstacles in the world which they will probably face and instruct them to survive with strength and dignity. Grimke suggests that black mothers must model for their daughters the various ways to reach inside to find courage to live triumphantly in a world in which they must ultimately face and overcome race and gender barriers. Rachel, who becomes Jimmy's legal guardian when his parents die of smallpox, is ill-equipped to mother because her own mother has sheltered her from the harsh realities of the world, which, in turn, short-circuits her ability to nurture little Jimmy properly. When Jimmy comes home crying to Rachel that he has been called a "nigger" and has had stones thrown at him, Rachel's mother tries to comfort Jimmy and the distraught Rachel. Rachel is devastated because of her inability to give Jimmy a satisfactory explanation of what it means to be subaltern and to be treated with derision because of race biases. She feels powerless to protect her child and becomes overwhelmed by his confusion and pain. While Rachel never blames her own mother for not teaching her how to cope with racism, it seems clear that Grimke is leveling precisely that indictment in her development of Rachel, who becomes increasingly neurotic during the course of the play. Patricia Hill Collins in *Black Feminist Thought* underscores Grimke's view of black motherhood: "African-American mothers place a strong emphasis on protection, either by trying to shield their daughters as long as possible from the penalties attached to their race, class, and gender status or by teaching them skills of independence and self reliance so that they will be able to protect themselves" (126).

Grimke indicts Mrs. Loving for sheltering Rachel, thereby fostering her dependence. She uses her play to caution black women that too much protection can be destructive. Mrs. Loving's delayed revelation that Rachel's father and brother had been lynched in the South some ten years prior, causing the Loving family to flee to the North for refuge, backfires and traumatizes Rachel instead of helping her to understand Jimmy's dilemma. Mrs. Loving's silence about the two lynchings is held up by Grimke as unfortunate and unwise, particularly since her silence prevents Rachel from understanding her own mother's idiosyncratic behavior for so many years. While Mrs. Loving's storytelling is meant to bolster Rachel and foster courage in her because of her father's valiant attempts at staving off an angry white mob before the lynching, this revelation only serves further to erode Rachel's already low self-esteem. She is incapacitated by her mother's overprotection. Furthermore, Mrs. Loving's story does nothing to reassure Rachel that life will be any better in the North for her son, who has just experienced a violent initiation into the real world. In fact, the positioning of the story of the lynchings convinces Rachel that there is no hope for a better world for poor black children. Mrs. Loving breaks silence too late to militate against Rachel's perception of herself as a failed mother. Rachel expresses her fear at mothering other children in the future:

> Everywhere, everywhere, throughout the South, there are hundreds of dark mothers who live in fear, terrible suffocating fear, whose rest by night is broken, and whose joy by day in their babies on their hearts is three parts—pain. . . . Why—it would be more merciful—to strangle the little things at birth. And so this nation—this white Christian nation—has deliberately set its curse upon the most beautiful—the most holy thing in life—motherhood! (149)

Note Rachel's pain as she vows that she will never give birth: "You god!—You terrible, laughing God! Listen! I swear—and my soul be damned to all eternity, if I do break this oath—I swear—that no child of mine shall ever lie upon my breast, for I will not have it rise up, in the terrible days that are to be—and call me cursed" (161). Helene Keyssar in "Rites and Responsibilities: The Drama of Black American Women" views Rachel's promise never to marry and have babies as an act of abortion: "For Rachel abortion, as she conceives it, is the only act that will authenticate her double existence as woman and black person. Any other act would, for her, be a false resolution of her hybrid self" (228). Contrary to Keyssar's interpretation, Rachel's vow never to have babies has less to do with Grimke's offering abortion as a viable option and more to do with illustrating that women sometimes erroneously consider desperate and destructive measures when mothering practices are disrupted. Racist cultural practices coupled with a black mother's attempts to veil the truth, according to Grimke, prevent children, daughters in particular, from learning how to cope with racial injustices which they must inevitably face. Grimke seems to be suggesting that black mothers and daughters pay a high price when mothers shield their daughters from racial hostility. She clearly makes the point that children lose their equilibrium when they go out into the world unprepared and that naive daughters become naive mothers who have great difficulty nurturing and empowering their children. This play makes it clear that when daughters are not taught survival skills by their mothers, they are forced to learn from the world, which can be a callous teacher.

Grimke's vision is in direct opposition to those blacks who believe that it is not important to tell their children about slavery or other race-related atrocities because they are an ugly part of their past. In her play *Rachel* Grimke addresses the need not only for mothers to educate their daughters (i.e, tell their stories of struggle and survival), but for daughters to listen to their mothers' stories and find healing and courage. In short, Grimke's play fulfills Mary Helen Washington's call for black women writers to reach back "into their black and female past for the authority to rename their experiences" ("New Lives and New Letters: Black Women Writers at the End of the Seventies," 10). Rachel learns too late of her mother's stories of struggle, but Grimke holds Rachel up as a lesson to daughters and mothers beyond the text who do not communicate, who do not hear each other. Rachel's choice never to have babies is a sacrifice that results from a daughter not being mothered properly. Grimke's play, then, can be viewed as one which calls for mothers to prepare their daughters for a hostile world by teaching them coping strategies early in life and by reinforcing those strategies at every stage of development in a female's life.

Another play which examines the extreme sacrifices that a black mother makes is Georgia Douglas Johnson's 1929 play, *Safe*. Like *Rachel*, *Safe* typically is critiqued as an antilynching play, as noted by Jeanne-Marie A. Miller in "Georgia Douglas Johnson and May Miller: Forgotten Playwrights of the New Negro Renaissance" (356). Given the astronomical number of blacks lynched in the United States between 1882 and 1927, it is not surprising that Johnson chose to write about the horrors of lynching. A revisionist analysis of *Safe*, however, reveals that Johnson is pointing not only to the horrific experiences of blacks at the hands of racists but to the inexcusable manner in which women allow the politics of race to destroy them and their children. Johnson's play portrays a mother who does not recognize her own power to teach her child to circumvent and survive the worst possible odds. Instead, she decides that she can protect him only by taking his life and sparing him from a possible lynching. Johnson's heroine in *Safe* embodies Glenda Dickerson's concept of black womanhood in "The Cult of True Womanhood: Toward a Womanist Attitude in African-American Theatre." Dickerson argues, "The depiction and perception of the African-American woman in this country through stereotypes has garbled her voice and distorted her image. The real tragedy is that the African-American woman herself has too frequently bought that distortion" (179). Johnson portrays her protagonist as a woman who feels voiceless and invisible and chooses a resistance strategy that is destructive instead of lifegiving.

Safe is a powerful play about a young black mother, Liza, who after witnessing the lynching of Sam, an upstanding, hardworking, devoted son, suffocates her newborn boy to prevent him from growing up to face a similar fate. As Sam is being dragged through the streets, he screams out to his mother, begging her not to let them hang him. Liza, traumatized by this lynching, envisions Sam as her child. Essentially, Liza experiences maternal feelings not just for the child she is carrying but also for Sam and, by extension, all black children. She hysterically cries, "Oh, my God, did you hear that boy crying for his mother? He's jest a boy—jest a boy—jest a little boy" (29). Later she cries, "Oh that poor boy—poor little nigger boy!" (30). Mandy, Liza's mother, tries to comfort and console her daughter about the lynching. However, Liza quickly becomes consumed with despair. She whispers, "I been setting here thinking 'bout that poor boy Sam—him working hard to take kere of his widder mother, doing the best he kin, trying to be a man and stan up for hisself. . . . What's little nigger boys for anyhow? I show hopes mine will be a girl. I don't want no boy baby to be hounded down and kicked 'round. No, I don't want to ever have no boy chile" (28). This merging of delusions and reality alarms Liza's mother, who fears that Liza will lose the child she is carrying. She cautions Liza to focus on her own child that is battling to come into the world. As Liza's labor intensifies, she increasingly becomes obsessed with giving birth to a girl baby. When the doctor tells her that she has given birth to a fine baby boy, she chokes it to death with her bare hands.

When Liza tries to protect her male offspring in the only way she knows how, she essentially plays God. While she is portrayed sympathetically, Johnson clearly illustrates that this young mother believes she has no options. Liza's perceptions of powerlessness are linked to her mother's values and teachings. Georgia Douglas Johnson demonstrates that unless all members of the community, particularly the mothers, unite by seeing all black children as their own and taking responsibility for empowering all black children, the community will dissipate. Patricia Hill Collins in "The Meaning of Motherhood in Black Culture and Black Mother-Daughter Relationships" insightfully points out that mothering as a collective responsibility is very familiar in African and African American cultures. She suggests that mothering in black communities often involves "othermothers," women who assist biological mothers by sharing mothering responsibilities, taking public responsibility for all black children (5).

Sara Ruddick in *Maternal Thinking: Toward a Politics of Peace* corroborates Collins's perceptions of the dangers of mothering by exclusion. Ruddick argues that a construction of motherhood which requires the mother to love her children at the exclusion of all others and to place her own children above other children is harmful to both mothers and children (56–57). Liza's mother by implication suggests to her that her child is better than or more special than other black children. Cautioning Liza to forget about Sam and to think of her own baby sends mixed signals to Liza. In her moment of epiphany when she sees Sam being lynched, Liza recognizes that her child has as much chance of facing lynching as any other black child of the time. This realization flies in the face of her mother's teachings. One poignant case in point is Mandy's instruction to Liza to try to forget what is taking place in the streets and concentrate on birthing her own son. Liza asks, "Did you hear him cry for his mother? Did you?" (30) Mandy's response is crucial—it is the response which quickens Liza's realization that the child she is carrying, if it is a boy, is no less at risk than the young man being lynched. Johnson suggests that Mandy gives bad advice when she tells Liza, "Yes, honey chile, I hear him, but you mustn't think about that now. Ferget it. Remember your own little baby—you got him to think about. You got to born him safe!" (30).

Johnson juxtaposes Liza's maternal feelings for Sam, her feelings for the child she is about to bear, and her mother's advice to divorce herself from what is happening to Sam in the streets and, by extension, to the masses of black men in America. The more insistent Mandy becomes that Liza forget about Sam's plight, the more Liza sees her child's destiny as synonymous with Sam's. The division she experiences adds to her confusion. She wants to save Sam, but can't. She transfers this helplessness to her own son. The end result is that Liza's maternal feelings are disrupted. Instead of recognizing that her son has options, albeit limited ones, she loses the type of maternal feeling that drives a mother to empower her child to battle life's obstacles, regardless of the severity of the conditions. Johnson clearly demonstrates that if black mothers teach their daughters to value their own children above others in their community, the children will suffer because mothers in African American communities can't reconcile the sense of disconnectedness which is linked to this type of mothering.

To some extent, Mandy is guilty of the same errors in judgment as Mrs. Loving in *Rachel*. Mrs. Loving suppresses the most important story of her life, the lynching of her husband and firstborn son. Mandy, similarly, tries to suppress the lynching of Sam, almost treating the murder as if it is an anomaly in the community instead of a frequent occurrence. Johnson poignantly mirrors Liza's devastation, confusion, and ultimate destruction of the son she believes she is powerless to protect or to provide life-sustaining options.

A third literary foremother whose writings shed light on the works of contemporary women writers of color is Shirley Graham, second wife of the legendary W. E. B. Du Bois. Graham's 1940 play *It's Mornin'* revolves around a mother, Millie, who goes to extreme lengths to protect Cissie, her daughter, from impending degradation. Set on the eve of the Emancipation Proclamation, the play portrays the horrors of slavery, including the repeated abuse of Millie, who was high-spirited and once loved to sing. Members of her community discuss the overseer's repeated beating and raping of Millie until her spirit is broken. When a new master comes to negotiate for Cissie with the mistress of the plantation, Millie is overwhelmed with rage. She is certain that the master intends to break her sixteen-year-old daughter's spirit by making her his concubine, particularly since she witnesses him fondling Cissie's breasts at the auction. After the rage subsides, Millie calmly plans a celebration party, much to everyone's surprise, for Cissie to say good-bye to her community. After much singing, eating, and dancing, Millie takes Cissie to her sleeping quarters. When she hears what appears to be the master approaching to take Cissie away, Millie slices her daughter's throat and emerges from the shack with a dead Cissie in her arms. The irony of the play is that it is not the new master; it is, in fact, a Union soldier bearing news of freedom. Graham sets up a devastating moment as Millie realizes her mistake. What falls from her lips is an unforgettable whisper: "Hit's mawnin'!" (95). Graham writes in the stage instructions, "Then from her throat there comes a cry of anguish as she falls on her knees. Above her, on the door, a single spray of mistletoe sways in the morning breeze and then falls gently on the upturned face of the child" (95).

Graham's play centers around the powerlessness experienced by blacks, particularly women. Graham cogently argues that black women in the South have no protection from the lust of white men. Her view of black women slaves is echoed by Barbara Christian in "Creating a Universal Literature: Afro-American Women Writers," who notes that "female slaves were both valued and devalued for their capacity to breed slaves and mother their master's children. They were valued and devalued for their supposedly incredible sexuality in a society where a true woman was not supposed to have sexuality. They were valued and devalued for their physical and psychological strength in a society where strength was a masculine word, for their lack of beauty in a society where beauty was equated with woman" (161). *It's Mornin'* is a particularly painful play because of the desperation that Millie feels. Indeed, it seems to Millie that she has no options but to murder her daughter to keep her safe—safe from the same types of horrendous abuses she experienced at the hands of a lustful and power-hungry overseer.

On one level, this play addresses the injustices of slavery. On a deeper level, it is a play which indicts patriarchy for the abuses heaped upon women, particularly black women. While Graham characterizes Big Missy sympathetically, portraying her as powerless and as a victim in a system manipulated by white men, the central issue of the play is the victimization of black women. Graham's indictment of white American men for the rape of black women is very much in keeping with the censure leveled by W. E. B. Du Bois in *Darkwater:*

> I shall forgive the South much in its final judgement day: I shall forgive its slavery, for slavery is a world-old habit; I shall forgive its fighting for a well-lost cause, and for remembering that struggle with tender tears; I shall forgive its so called 'pride of race,' the passion of its hot blood, and even its dear, old laughable strutting and posing; but one thing I shall never forgive, neither in this world nor in the world to come; its wanton and continued and persistent insulting of the black womanhood which it sought and seeks to prostitute to its lust. (172)

Du Bois's wife also viewed the oppression of black women as institutional racism. Graham's indictment of the slave system calls attention to the corrupting forces which demeaned blacks and blurred their vision to the possibilities of life.

Graham's exploration of the impact of slavery on mother-daughter relationships in *It's Mornin'* has yet to be explored in any critical study. Her play examines the role that the damaged "othermother" plays on the central character. Millie's biological mother does not appear in the play; however, Grannie Lou, believed to be a conjurer by some and a lunatic by others, serves as Millie's surrogate mother. It is Grannie Lou who gives Millie the idea to thwart the master's plans by killing Cissie. Grannie Lou tells Millie about an African woman who killed her three sons rather than have them sold away from her and says that the African woman's act was courageous and heroic. Grannie Lou's story has been passed down to her by her ancestral mothers, and she retells it with pride:

> Ah ain't so ole dat Ah don' membah! Ain't Ah nebbah tole you bout dat 'oman long time gone? Dey say she straight from jungles in da far off Af'ica. She nevah say. Dat war a 'oman—straight lak a tree, an' tall, swift as a lion an' strong as any ox. Da sugah cane wen' down fo' huh big knife lak cotton stalks under da fierce's gale. No man could wok wid huh . . . An sing! She ustah sing out in da fields. . . . (90)

Millie's interest is aroused when she hears Grannie Lou speak with such pride about an African foremother, someone who apparently had done something courageous to protect her child. When challenged by skeptics, Grannie Lou continues her story:

> Dat 'oman dar do mo' den sing! Lissen—she hab t'ree sons, dey black an' tall lak she. An' one day come dat dey sole des sons down ribbah . . . dey bring good price. She say dey nebbah go. Da white folk laf, but niggahs dassent laf . . . dey see huh face. She don' say not'in mo', but go away. An' early in da mawnin' call she boys, an' when dey come, she tell 'em to stan' close an' watch da sun come up out ob da hill. Dey sort ob smile at huh an' look, an' den dat 'oman lift huh big cane knife, she cry out sompin' in a wild, strange voice, an' wid one sweep she cut off all dey heads—dey roll down at she feet. All t'ree ob dem! (90)

Shortly after she hears this story, Millie finds a knife and determines that she, too, will keep her child safe.

A strong case can be made that Graham intended Grannie Lou to be viewed as someone severely damaged because of the ravages of slavery. The practice of disrupting families by selling away its members wreaked havoc on the African American family. Grannie Lou has only memories of stories told to her by her foremothers about acts of heroism by black women. Because the mothering process was disrupted as part of the slave system, bonding between mother and children was damaged in many cases. What Grannie Lou reads as heroic, Graham wants her audience to see as a tragic example of what happens when mothers and daughters are denied an opportunity to bond and nurture each other. What Grannie Lou passes down to Millie is a damaged view of motherhood: when life seems hopeless, it is a mother's right and responsibility—by any means necessary—to remove her children from harm's way. The African woman who killed her three sons believed she was doing the right thing, the only thing she could do for her children to keep them safe from slavery.

Graham, however, suggests that slavery so corrupted some of its victims that they were blinded by their own degradation, a belief she shared with Frederick Douglass. Graham, who wrote a Douglass biography and was therefore intimately familiar with all of his works, takes the same position as does Douglass in his essay "The Right to Criticize American Institutions," where he comments on the debilitating effects of slavery:

> But in regard to American slavery . . . it is such a giant crime, so darkening to the soul, so blinding in its moral influence, so well calculated to blast and corrupt all the humane principles of our nature, so well adapted to infuse its own accursed spirit into all around it, that the people among whom it exists have not the moral power to abolish it. . . . I stated these facts to show to the British public how difficult it is for a coloured man in this country to do anything to elevate himself or his race from the state of degradation in which they are plunged; how difficult for him to be virtuous or temperate, or anything but a menial outcast. (61, 63)

Douglass posits that slavery not only blinded slaveowners to their own morality but imposed on blacks a hopelessness that sometimes manifested itself in horrendous acts of reclamation. Graham suggests that Millie's decision to kill her child results from transference of negative mothering from Grannie Lou and a history of violated ancestral mothers.

It is important to consider the lack of options that the women characters perceived in plays by Angelina Weld Grimke, Georgia Douglas Johnson, and Shirley Graham. A close reading of these three plays suggests that early scholarship about these works neglected to examine closely the mother-daughter relationships and their impact on the communities in which they lived. All three playwrights call attention to the mothering process and suggest that when a black community, and by extension the entire African American community, seems to be dissipating, one needs to look closely at the factors which disrupt the mothering process. Women learn to mother from their mothers, either biological or surrogate, and when that learning process is obstructed, feelings of hopelessness and powerlessness are transferred from mothers to daughters. Marianne Hirsch in *The Mother/Daughter Plot* cogently argues, "If mothers cannot 'own' their own children or even themselves, they experience separation and loss all the more intensely" (6).

Both Lorraine Hansberry in *A Raisin in the Sun* (1959) and Alice Childress in *Mojo* (1971) add to the dialogue of a mother's responsibility to her children. Like Grimke, Johnson, and Graham, Hansberry and Childress level an indictment against women whose acts of reclamation may be perceived by some as heroic or courageous. Both playwrights suggest that black mothers who choose abortion or who give up their children for adoption break with historical mothering practices in the black community. While adoption is sometimes in the best interest of the child, the choice, according to Childress, is often made too hastily. They argue that these women invariably suffer emotional trauma when they make such choices. While this break with mothering practices in the black community may bolster individual self-esteem temporarily, texts by Hansberry and Childress suggest that long-term, deep-seated, corrosive pain results when such practices are disrupted.

Historically, black mothers, because of genocide and centuries of racial oppression, have resisted abortions and opted to rear their children even amidst abject poverty and other forms of degradation. They have chosen to give life to and nurture their babies because of a close identification with a community of women who modeled for them that a black mother rarely gives up on her babies, regardless of the difficulties of nurturing under oppressive conditions. Millions of black women have stared poverty in the face and fought back with unconditional love. Black mothers historically have shunned the notion that a woman's body is solely hers, to do with it as she pleases. Instead, many black women, not out of ignorance but because of institutional racism and an African survival spirit and spirituality, have not been open to abortion or have avoided mothering practices which shifted responsibilities away from themselves, their mates, and members of their extended family. While abortion continues to be a highly controversial subject, many black women live with a collective memory of their children who were sold away, raped, lynched, denied an education, and ghettoized in urban America. This memory serves as a reverberating consciousness which reminds black mothers of their importance in fostering strong children who will survive and survive whole.

Angela Davis in "Reflections on the Black Woman's Role in the Community of Slaves" argues that the black woman historically has been "assigned the mission of promoting the consciousness and practice of resistance" (5) and that "she was, therefore, essential to the survival of the community. Not all people have survived enslavement; hence her survival-oriented activities were themselves a form of resistance" (7). When Davis speaks of resistance, she is referring to insurrectionist acts which black women orchestrated during slavery, such as poisoning the food, setting fire to the houses of their masters, or playing an active role in rebellions (9). Black mothers, who are at once powerful and powerless, continue to be guided by an African principle which acknowledges the black mother as a beacon of hope and as the crucial link in preserving and fostering the black survival spirit. As Angela Davis notes, black women are "heirs to a tradition of supreme perseverance and heroic resistance" (15).

Both Hansberry and Childress suggest that something has gone awry in the mothering process when black mothers abandon or abort their babies to keep them safe. Their view of motherhood is echoed by Patricia Hill Collins, who argues that African American women's "innovative and practical approaches to mothering under oppressive conditions often bring power and recognition" (*Black Feminist Thought*, 133). Hansberry portrays a mother who teaches her daughter-in-law that having an abortion violates their five generations of families in the United States, and Childress depicts a woman's angst resulting from placing her child up for adoption.

Hansberry's *A Raisin in the Sun* is primarily a play about mothering. Mary Louise Anderson in "Black Matriarchy: Portrayals of Women in Three Plays" notes that "Mama's dreams, her reasons for existence, are her family" (93). Lena Younger during the course of the play admits that she has made mistakes in mothering her son, Walter Lee, Jr., particularly since she accepts responsibility for his plan to sell out to the white neighborhood association that wants to block the Younger family from moving into the segregated community. Hansberry not only uses Lena to show that mothering brings with it errors in judgment, but also uses her as a "motherline," to borrow from Susan Willis in *Specifying* (6), to teach Ruth that black mothers must not abort their babies simply because times are hard. Lena becomes the motherline to Ruth when she helps her recognize that her own destiny is intricately linked to the decision she makes with regard to her unborn child. In the presence of her son, Mama invokes ancestral spirits to guide both Ruth and Walter Lee, Jr.:

> Well—son, I'm waiting to hear you say something. . . . (She waits) I'm waiting to hear how you be your father's son. Be the man he was . . . (Pause. The silence shouts) Your wife say she going to destroy your child. And I'm waiting to hear you talk like him and say we a people who give children life, not who destroys them—(She rises) I'm waiting to see you stand up and look like your daddy and say we done give up one baby to poverty and that we ain't going to give up nary another one . . . I'm waiting. (75)

Though Ruth sees nothing but hardship ahead, she ultimately accepts the reasoning of her motherline, Lena Younger. Ruth essentially embodies Mary Helen Washington's concept of black womanhood in "The Black Woman's Search for Identity," where she argues that "one of the few miracles in this world is the survival of love and loyalty among Black people in America, despite the inhuman definitions of manhood and womanhood that have been forced upon us" (68). Ruth chooses to keep her child, after she realizes that a place can and will be carved for this child, who will survive because of love and loyalty. While post-1960s feminists might attack Hansberry for what might be perceived as antifeminist notions about womanhood, many black women critics would argue that Hansberry was more concerned with the future of black children and the survival of the black family than she was with pro-choice. *A Raisin in the Sun*, written in the late 1950s, reflects a black woman's consciousness predicated upon strong links to a black community not yet influenced by the women's movement of the 1960s and 1970s.

Childress's *Mojo* portrays Irene as a woman whose choice of putting her daughter up for adoption makes her a participant in her own misery. Irene recalls that she left her husband, Teddy, because their relationship was violent and because she did not want to bring up a child in a home filled with turmoil. She leaves without even telling Teddy that she is pregnant, for fear that he might try to interfere with a decision she believed was solely hers to make. Irene quips, "Didn't think it was too much any of your business . . . because you didn't seem to love me like I loved you" (69). In showing the overwhelming pain which results when mothers abdicate their responsibilities, Childress clearly indicts such choices. Childress, who strongly believed in the viability of black men and women working together to make a better future for their children, criticizes Irene for depriving Teddy of his right and opportunity to nurture their child. She suggests that Irene's pain stems from a selfish choice. Irene recalls that every time she saw a raggedy child on the streets, she worried that it was her daughter. Note Irene's pain when she says, "Instead of one child. . . . I had thousands. Years of lookin at strange, raggedy-ass children runnin round the streets" (72). She tells how she began to imagine that every baby-faced prostitute she saw on the street was her daughter. She rationalizes that her daughter's future was marred because she gave her up for adoption without considering all of the ramifications. Irene's remorse is intense as she cries, "God oughtta kill me for my sins" (78). She confides in her husband that she fears that their child might be in jail with the other Civil Rights activists or maybe has been beaten or killed in the streets of Harlem.

Childress seems to suggest that Irene's choice to give up her child for adoption stems from alienation from her own mother and other women in her community. Patricia Hill Collins substantiates this view by arguing:

> In African-American communities, fluid and changing boundaries often distinguish biological mothers from other women who care for children. Biological mothers, or bloodmothers, are expected to care for their children. But African and African-American communities have also recognized that vesting one person with full responsibility for mothering a child may not be wise or possible. As a result, othermothers—women who assist bloodmothers by sharing mothering responsibilities—traditionally have been central to the institution of Black motherhood. (*Black Feminist Thought*, 119)

Irene neglects to make use of the resources, the othermothers, of her community; consequently, she lives the best years of life viewing herself as a failed mother and a woman who has great difficulty surmounting obstacles which occur frequently in a racialized and racist world. In "Learning from the Outsider Within: The Sociological Significance of Black Feminist Thought" Collins elucidates Childress's vision when she argues, "If Black women simultaneously use all resources available to them—their roles as mothers, their participation in churches, their support of one another in Black female networks, their creative expression—to be self-defined and self-valuating and to encourage others to reject objectification, then Black women's everyday behavior itself is a form of activism" (24). Childress, like Hansberry, posits that even intolerable conditions should strengthen a mother's resolve to inculcate in her children the determination to survive. After all, many black mothers have taught their children to circumvent obstacles even when they themselves have not had those skills. Jeanne-Marie A. Miller in "Images of Black Women in Plays by Black Playwrights" argues, "In Black-authored dramas depicting ghetto lifestyles, Black women hold on to life, however harsh it may be, and sometimes work for a better future" (507).

Childress poignantly shows what can happen to black women who do not seriously contemplate a variety of options. According to her, black mothers experience a sense of power when they help their children to meet life's challenges and often feel guilt when they choose to relinquish the rearing of their children to someone else. While Childress does not argue that adoption is never or even rarely an option women should exercise, she does seem to suggest that there is a heavy price that goes along with making such a choice. Childress argues that black women should try to find ways to rear and empower their children. They can opt to seek out othermothers to assist them while continuing to play a significant role in their children's lives. Patricia Hill Collins notes in *Black Feminist Thought* that "mothering is an empowering experience for many African-American women" (137). She also asserts, "But what cannot be overlooked in work emphasizing mothers' influences on their children is how Black children affirm their mothers and how important that affirmation can be in a society that denigrates Blackness and womanhood" (137). While Childress was certainly pro-woman, her play *Mojo* suggests that she believed that black women and men must take responsibility for their actions. The fact that Irene returns to admit her mistakes and to ask her ex-husband's forgiveness suggests that Childress envisioned a world where black men and women must work together to save their children.

Grimke, Johnson, Graham, Hansberry, and Childress explore the consequences of mothering in a society where many obstacles are placed between mothers and daughters as they try to nurture each other. These black women playwrights recognized the suffering that accompanies motherhood in a world where race, class, and gender barriers often obfuscate the judgment of mothers. While some critics might accuse these playwrights of blaming the victims, a close reading will not substantiate such a claim. The black women playwrights included in this study point to a path which might empower women, namely, the strengthening of motherlines. These plays strongly suggest that hope was and still is the single most important strength inherited by black Americans from their African ancestors. It is hope that black mothers must continue to offer their children. When there is a sense of hopelessness, mothers commit desperate acts which have far-reaching consequences for both mothers and children. These playwrights suggest that mothers, with the help of othermothers, ultimately can save their daughters (and sons too) by teaching them to persevere at making a place for themselves in society, despite difficult or even impossible odds.

Works Cited

Anderson, Mary Louise. "Black Matriarchy: Portrayals of Women in Three Plays." *Negro American Literature Forum* 10, no. 3 (Fall 1976): 93–95.

Brown-Guillory, Elizabeth. *Their Place on the Stage: Black Women Playwrights in America*. Westport, Conn.: Greenwood Press, 1988.

Childress, Alice. *Mojo*. *Black World* 20 (April 1971): 54–82.

Christian, Barbara. "Creating a Universal Literature: Afro-American Women Writers." In *Black Feminist Criticism*, ed. Gloria Bowles and Renate Duelli-Klein, 159–163. New York: Pergamon Press, 1985.

Collins, Patricia Hill. *Black Feminist Thought*. New York: Routledge, 1990.

———. "Learning from the Outsider Within: The Sociological Significance of Black Feminist Thought." *Social Problems* 33 (December 1986): 14–32.

———. "The Meaning of Motherhood in Black Culture and Black Mother-Daughter Relationships." *Sage* 4, no. 2 (1987): 3–10.

Davis, Angela. "Reflections on the Black Woman's Role in the Community of Slaves." *Black Scholar* 3 (December 1971): 3–15.

Dickerson, Glenda. "The Cult of True Womanhood: Toward a Womanist Attitude in African-American Theatre." *Theatre Journal* 40, no. 2 (May 1988): 178–187.

Douglass, Frederick. "The Right to Criticize American Institutions." In *Afro-American Writing*, ed. Richard A. Long and Eugenia Collier, 58–66. University Park and London: Pennsylvania State University Press, 1985.

Du Bois, W. E. B. *Darkwater: Voices from within the Veil*. New York: AMS Press, 1969.

Graham, Shirley. *It's Mornin'*. In *Wines in the Wilderness: Plays by African-American Women from the Harlem Renaissance to the Present*, ed. Elizabeth Brown-Guillory, 84–95. Westport, Conn.: Greenwood Press, 1990.

Grimke, Angelina Weld. *Rachel*. In *Black Theater U.S.A.: Forty-five Plays by Black Americans, 1847–1974*, ed. James V. Hatch and Ted Shine, 139–172. New York: Free Press, 1974.

Hansberry, Lorraine. *A Raisin in the Sun*. New York: Signet, 1959.

Hirsch, Marianne. *The Mother/Daughter Plot: Narrative, Psychoanalysis, Feminism*. Bloomington: Indiana University Press, 1989.

Johnson, Georgia Douglas. *Safe*. In *Wines in the Wilderness: Plays by African-American Women from the Harlem Renaissance to the Present*, ed. Elizabeth Brown-Guillory, 26–32. Westport, Conn.: Greenwood Press, 1990.

Keyssar, Helene. "Rites and Responsibilities: The Drama of Black American Women. In *Feminine Focus: The New American Playwrights*, 226–240. Oxford: Oxford University Press, 1989.

Miller, Jeanne-Marie A. "Georgia Douglas Johnson and May Miller: Forgotten Playwrights of the New Negro Renaissance." *CLA Journal* 33 (June 1990): 349–366.

———. "Images of Black Women in Plays by Black Playwrights." *CLA Journal* 20 (June 1977): 494–507.

Morrison, Toni. *Playing in the Dark: Whiteness and the Literary Imagination*. New York: Vintage Books, 1993.

Perkins, Kathy A., ed. *Black Female Playwrights: An Anthology of Plays before 1950*. Bloomington and Indianapolis: Indiana University Press, 1989.

Ruddick, Sara. *Maternal Thinking: Toward a Politics of Peace*. Boston: Beacon Press, 1989.

Stephens, Judith L. "Anti-Lynch Plays by African-American Women: Race, Gender, and Social Protest in American Drama." *African-American Review* 26 (Summer 1992): 329–339.

Washington, Mary Helen. "The Black Woman's Search for Identity." *Black World* 21 (August 1972): 68–75.

———. "Black Women Image Makers." *Black World* 23 (August 1974): 10–18.

———. "New Lives and New Letters: Black Women Writers at the End of the Seventies." *College English* 43 (January 1981): 1–11.

White, Walter. *Rope and Faggot: A Biography of Judge Lynch*. New York: Alfred A. Knopf, 1929.

Willis, Susan. *Specifying: Black Women Writing the American Experience*. Madison: University of Wisconsin Press, 1987.

Voice, Mind, Self

Mother-Daughter Relationships in Amy Tan's *The Joy Luck Club* and *The Kitchen God's Wife*

M. MARIE BOOTH FOSTER

In *The Joy Luck Club* and *The Kitchen God's Wife,* Amy Tan uses stories from her own history and myth to explore the voices of mothers and daughters of Chinese ancestry. Each woman tells a story indicative of the uniqueness of her voice. Mary Field Belensky, in *Women's Ways of Knowing,* argues that voice is "more than an academic shorthand for a person's point of view. . . . it is a metaphor that can apply to many aspects of women's experience and development. . . . Women repeatedly used the metaphor of voice to depict their intellectual and ethical development; . . . the development of a sense of voice, mind, and self were intricately intertwined" (18). In Tan's fiction, the daughters' sense of self is intricately linked to an ability to speak and be heard by their mothers. Similarly, the mothers experience growth as they broaden communication lines with their daughters. Tan's women are very much like the women Belensky portrays in *Women's Ways of Knowing*: "In describing their lives, women commonly talked about voice and silence: 'speaking up,' 'speaking out,' 'being silenced,' 'not being heard,' 'really listening,' 'really talking,' 'words as weapons,' 'feeling deaf and dumb,' 'having no words,' 'saying what you mean,' 'listening to be heard'" (18). Until Tan's women connect as mothers and daughters, they experience strong feelings of isolation, a sense of disenfranchisement and fragmentation. These feelings often are a result of male domination, as Margery Wolf and Roxanne Witke describe in *Women in Chinese Society* (1–11).

A photo that is in part a pictorial history of Tan's foremothers is the inspiration for many of her portrayals of women. Tan writes in "Lost Lives of Women" of a picture of her mother, grandmother, aunts, cousins:

> When I first saw this photo as a child, I thought it was exotic and remote, of a faraway time and place, with people who had no connection to my American life. Look at their bound feet! Look at that funny lady with the plucked forehead. The solemn little girl was in fact, my mother. And leaning against the rock is my grandmother, Jing mei. . . . This is also a picture of secrets and tragedies. . . . This is the picture I see when I write. These are the secrets I was supposed to keep. These are the women who never let me forget why stories need to be told. (90)

In her remembrances, Tan presents Chinese American women who are forging identities beyond the pictures of concubinage and bound feet, women encountering new dragons, many of which are derived from being "hyphenated" American females. She views mother-daughter relationships in the same vein as Kathie Carlson, who argues, "This relationship is the birthplace of a woman's ego identity, her sense of security in the world, her feelings about herself, her body and other women. From her mother, a woman receives her first impression of how to be a woman" (xi).

The Joy Luck Club and *The Kitchen God's Wife* are studies in balance—balancing hyphenation and the roles of daughter, wife, mother, sister, career woman. In achieving balance, voice is important: in order to achieve voice, hyphenated women must engage in self-exploration, recognition and appreciation of their culture(s), and they must know their histories. The quest for voice becomes an archetypal journey for all of the women. The mothers come to the United States and have to adapt to a new culture, to redefine voice and self. The daughters' journeys become rites of passage; before they can find voice or define self they must acknowledge the history and myth of their mothers—"her-stories" of life in China, passage to the United States, and assimilation. And each must come to grips with being her mother's daughter.

The Joy Luck Club is a series of stories by and about narrators whose lives are interconnected as a result of friendship and membership in the Joy Luck Club: Suyuan and Jing-mei Woo, An-mei Hsu and Rose Hsu Jordan, Lindo and Waverly Jong, and Ying-ying and Lena St. Clair. The stories illuminate the multiplicity of experiences of Chinese women who are struggling to fashion a voice for themselves in a culture where women are conditioned to be silent. The stories are narrated by seven of the eight women in the group—four daughters and three mothers; one mother has recently died of a cerebral aneurysm. Jing-mei, nicknamed June, must be her mother's voice. The book is divided into four sections: Feathers from a Thousand Li Away, The Twenty-six Malignant Gates, American Translation, and Queen Mother of the Western Skies. Each chapter is prefaced with an introductory thematic tale or myth, all of which tend to stress the advice given by mothers.

Tan tells her mother's stories, the secret ones she began to tell after the death of Tan's father and brother in *The Kitchen God's Wife*. Patti Doten notes that Tan's mother told stories of her marriage to another man in China and of three daughters left behind when she came to the United States in 1949 (14), a story that is in part remembered in *The Joy Luck Club* with An-mei's saga. In *The Kitchen God's Wife*, a mother and daughter, Winnie Louie and Pearl Louie Brandt, share their stories, revealing the secrets that hide mind and self—and history—and veil and mask their voices. Winnie Louie's tale is of the loss of her mother as a young girl, marriage to a sadistic man who sexually abused her, children stillborn or dying young, a patriarchal society that allowed little room for escape from domestic violence (especially against the backdrop of war), and her flight to America and the love of a "good man." Daughter Pearl Louie Brandt's secrets include her pain upon the loss of her father and the unpredictable disease, multiple sclerosis, that inhibits her body and her life.

Tan's characters are of necessity storytellers and even historians, empowered by relating what they know about their beginnings and the insufficiencies of their present lives. Storytelling—relating memories—allows for review, analysis, and sometimes understanding of ancestry and thus themselves. The storytelling, however, is inundated with ambivalences and contradictions which, as Suzanna Danuta Walters argues, often take the form of blame in mother-daughter relationships (1).

Voice balances—or imbalances—voice as Chinese American mothers and daughters narrate their sagas. Because both mothers and daughters share the telling, the biases of a singular point of view are alleviated. Marianne Hirsch writes, "The story of female development, both in fiction and theory, needs to be written in the voice of mothers as well as in that of daughters. . . . Only in combining both voices, in finding a double voice that would yield a multiple female consciousness, can we begin to envision ways to live 'life afresh'" (161). Tan's fiction presents ambivalences and contradictions in the complicated interactions of mothers' and daughters' voices.

Regardless of how much the daughters try to deny it, it is through their mothers that they find their voice, their mind, their selfhood. Voice finds its form in the process of interaction, even if that interaction is conflict. "Recognition by the daughter that her voice is not entirely her own" comes in time and with experiences (one of the five interconnecting themes referred to by Nan Bauer Maglin in *The Literature of Matrilineage* as a recurring theme in such literature [258]). The experiences in review perhaps allow the daughters to know just how much they are dependent upon their mothers in their journey to voice. The mothers do not let them forget their own importance as the daughters attempt to achieve self-importance.

As Jing-mei "June" Woo tells her story and that of her deceased mother, the importance of the mother and daughter voices resonating, growing out of and being strengthened by each other, is apparent in her state of confusion and lack of direction and success. Perhaps her name is symbolic of her confusion: she is the only daughter with both a Chinese and an American name. As she recalls life with her mother, Jing-mei / June relates that she is constantly told by her mother, Suyuan Woo, that she does not try and therefore cannot achieve success. June's journey to voice and balance requires self-discovery—which must begin with knowing her mother. June has to use memories as a guide instead of her mother, whose tale she tells and whose saga she must complete. She must meet the ending to the tale of life in China and daughters left behind that her mother has told her over and over again, a story that she thought was a dark fairy tale.

The dark tale is of a previous life that includes a husband and daughters. Suyuan's first husband, an officer with the Kuomintang, takes her to Kweilin, a place she has dreamed of visiting. It has become a war refuge, no longer idyllic. Suyuan Woo and three other officers' wives start the Joy Luck Club to take their minds off the terrible smells of too many people in the city and the screams of humans and animals in pain. They attempt to raise their spirits with mah jong, jokes, and food.

Warned of impending danger, June's mother leaves the city with her two babies and her most valuable possessions. On the road to Chungking, she abandons first the wheelbarrow in which she has been carrying her babies and her goods, then more goods. Finally, her body weakened by fatigue and dysentery, she leaves the babies with jewelry to provide for them until they can be brought to her family. America does not make Suyuan forget the daughters she left as she fled. June Woo secretly views her mother's story as a fairy tale because the ending always changed. Perhaps herein lies the cause of their conflict: neither mother nor daughter listens to be heard, so each complains of not being heard. June Woo's disinterest and lack of knowledge of her mother's history exacerbate her own voicelessness, her lack of wholeness.

At a mah jong table where, appropriately, June takes her mother's place, she is requested by her mother's friends to go to China and meet the daughters of her mother. Thus her journey to voice continues and begins: it is a journey started at birth, but it is only now that she starts to recognize that she needs to know about her mother in order to achieve self-knowledge. She is to tell her sisters about their mother. The mothers' worst fears are realized when June asks what she can possibly tell her mother's daughters. The mothers see their daughters in June's response, daughters who get irritated when their mothers speak in Chinese or explain things in broken English.

Although it startles her mother's friends, June's question is a valid one for a daughter whose relationship with her mother was defined by distance that developed slowly and grew. According to June, she and her mother never understood each other. She says they translated each other's meanings: she seemed to hear less than what was said, and her mother heard more. It is a complaint leveled by mothers and daughters throughout *The Joy Luck Club* and later in *The Kitchen God's Wife*. Both women want to be heard, but do not listen to be heard. They must come to understand that a voice is not a voice unless there is someone there to hear it.

Jing-mei is no longer sitting at the mah jong table but is en route to China when she summons up memories of her mother that will empower her to tell the daughters her mother's story. In the title story and in the short story "A Pair of Tickets," she occupies her mother's place in the storytelling, much as she occupies it at the mah jong table, and she is concerned with the responsibilities left by her mother. In her own stories, "Two Kinds" and "Best Quality," she is concerned with her selves: Jing-mei and June—the Chinese and the American, her mother's expectations and her belief in herself. Her stories are quest stories, described by Susan Koppelman in *Between Mothers and Daughters* as "a daughter's search for understanding" of her mother and herself (xxii). As June makes soup for her father, she sees the stray cat that she thought her mother had killed, since she had not seen it for some time. She makes motions to scare the cat and then recognizes the motions as her mother's; the cat reacts to her just as he had to her mother. She is reminded that she is her mother's daughter.

According to Judith Arcana in *Our Mothers' Daughters*, "we hold the belief that mothers love their daughters by definition and we fear any signal from our own mother that this love, which includes acceptance, affection, admiration and approval does not exist or is incomplete" (5). It does not matter to Jing-mei that she is not her mother's only disappointment (she says her mother always seemed displeased with everyone). Jing-mei recalls that something was not in balance and that something always needed improving for her mother. The friends do not seem to care; with all of her faults, she is their friend. Perhaps it is a "daughter's" expectations that June uses to judge her mother. Suyuan tells the rebellious June that she can be the best at anything as she attempts to mold her child into a piano-playing prodigy. She tells June she's not the best because she's not trying. After the request by the Joy Luck Club mothers June, in really listening to the voice of her mother as reserved in her memory, discovers that she might have been able to demonstrate ability had she tried: "for unlike my mother I did not believe I could be anything I wanted to be. I could only be me" (154). But she does not recognize that the "me" is the one who has made every attempt to escape development. The pendant her late mother gave her is symbolic. It was given to her as her life's importance. The latter part of the message is in Chinese, the voice of wisdom versus the provider of American circumstances.

In archetypal journeys, there is always a god or goddess who supports the "traveler" along his or her way. In *The Kitchen God's Wife*, Lady Sorrowfree is created by Winnie Louie, mother of Pearl, when the Kitchen God is determined by her to be an unfit god for her daughter's altar, inherited from an adopted aunt. The Kitchen God is unfit primarily because he became a god despite his mistreatment of his good wife. A porcelain figurine is taken from a storeroom where she has been placed as a "mistake" and is made into a goddess for Pearl, Lady Sorrowfree. Note Winnie's celebration of Lady Sorrowfree:

> I heard she once had many hardships in her life. . . . But her smile is genuine, wise, and innocent at the same time. And her hand, see how she just raised it. That means she is about to speak, or maybe she is telling you to speak. She is ready to

listen. She understands English. You should tell her everything. . . . But sometimes, when you are afraid, you can talk to her. She will listen. She will wash away everything sad with her tears. She will use her stick to chase away everything bad. See her name: Lady Sorrowfree, happiness winning over bitterness, no regrets in this world. (414–415)

Perhaps Tan's mothers want to be like Lady Sorrowfree; they are in a sense goddesses whose altars their daughters are invited to come to for nurturance, compassion, empathy, inspiration, and direction. They are driven by the feeling of need to support those daughters, to give to them "the swan" brought from China—symbolic of their her-stories and wisdom, and the advantages of America, like the mother in the preface to the first round of stories. In the tale, all that is left of the mother's swan that she has brought from China after it is taken by customs officials is one feather; the mother wants to tell her daughter that the feather may look worthless, but it comes from her homeland and carries with it all good intentions. But she waits to tell her in perfect English, in essence keeping secrets. The mothers think that everything is possible for the daughters if the mothers will it. The daughters may come willingly to the altar or may rebelliously deny the sagacity of their mothers.

The mothers struggle to tell their daughters the consequences of not listening to them. The mother in the tale prefacing the section "Twenty-six Malignant Gates" tells her daughter not to ride her bike around the corner where she cannot see her because she will fall down and cry. The daughter questions how her mother knows, and she tells her that it is written in the book *Twenty-six Malignant Gates* that evil things can happen when a child goes outside the protection of the house. The daughter wants evidence, but her mother tells her that it is written in Chinese. When her mother does not tell her all twenty-six of the Malignant Gates, the girl runs out of the house and around the corner and falls, the consequence of not listening to her mother. Rebellion causes conflict—a conflict Lady Sorrowfree would not have to endure. June Woo and Waverly Jong seem to be daughters who thrive on the conflict that results from rebellion and sometimes even the need to win their mother's approval. June trudges off every day to piano lessons taught by an old man who is hard of hearing. Defying her mother, she learns very little, as she reveals at a piano recital to which her mother has invited all of her friends. June notes the blank look on her mother's face that says she has lost everything. Waverly wins at chess, which pleases her mother, but out of defiance she stops playing until she discovers that she really enjoyed her mother's approval. As an adult she wants her mother to approve of the man who will be her second husband; mother and daughter assume the positions of chess players.

Tan's mothers frequently preach that children are to make their mothers proud so that they can brag about them to other mothers. The mothers engage in fierce competition with each other. Suyuan Woo brags about her daughter even after June's poorly performed piano recital. All of the mothers find fault with their daughters, but this is something revealed to the daughters, not to the community.

Much as Lindo Jong credits herself with daughter Waverly's ability to play chess, she blames herself for Waverly's faults as a person and assumes failures in raising her daughter: "It is my fault she is this way—selfish. I wanted my children to have the best combination: American circumstances and Chinese character. How could I know these things do not mix?" (289). Waverly knows how American circumstances work, but Lindo can't teach her about Chinese character: "How to obey parents and listen to your mother's mind. How not to show your own thoughts, to put your feelings behind your face so you can take advantage of hidden opportunities. . . . Why Chinese thinking is best" (289). What she gets is a daughter who wants to be Chinese because it is fashionable, a daughter who likes to speak back and question what she says, and a daughter to whom promises mean nothing. Nonetheless, she is a daughter of whom Lindo is proud.

Lindo Jong is cunning, shrewd, resourceful; Waverly Jong is her mother's daughter. Waverly manages to irritate her mother when she resists parental guidance. Judith Arcana posits that "some daughters spend all or most of their energy trying futilely to be as different from their mothers as possible in behavior, appearance, relations with friends, lovers, children, husbands" (9). Waverly is a strategist in getting her brother to teach her to play chess, in winning at chess, in gaining her mother's forgiveness when she is rude and getting her mother's acceptance of the man she plans to marry. Lindo proudly reminds Waverly that she has inherited her ability to win from her.

In literature that focuses on mother/daughter relationships, feminists see "context—historical time and social and cultural group" as important (Rosinsky, 285). Lindo relates in "The Red Candle" that she once sacrificed her life to keep her parents' promise; she married as arranged. Chinese tradition permits Lindo's parents to give her to Huang Tai for her son—to determine her fate—but Lindo takes control of her destiny. On the day of her wedding, as she prepares for the ceremony, she schemes her way out of the planned marriage and into America, where "nobody says you have to keep the circumstances somebody else gives to you" (289).

It takes determination to achieve voice and selfhood, to take control of one's mind and one's life from another, making one's self heard, overcoming silence. Lindo does not resign herself to her circumstances in China. Waverly reveals that she learns some of her strategies from her mother: "I was six when my mother taught me the art of invisible strength. It was a strategy for winning arguments, respect from others, and eventually, though neither of us knew it at the time, chess games" (89). Therein lies Lindo's contribution to her daughter's voice.

Lindo uses the same brand of ingenuity to play a life chess game with and to teach her daughter. Adrienne Rich writes in *Of Woman Born:* "Probably there is nothing in human nature more resonant with charges than the flow of energy between two biologically alike bodies, one which has lain in amniotic bliss inside the other, one which has labored to give birth to the other. The materials are there for the deepest mutuality and the most painful estrangement" (226). Lindo has to contend with a headstrong daughter: "'Finish your coffee,' I told her yesterday. 'Don't throw your blessings away.' 'Don't be old-fashioned, Ma,' she told me, finishing her coffee down the sink. 'I'm my own person.' And I think, how can she be her own person? When did I give her up?" (290).

Waverly is champion of the chess game, but she is no match for her mother in a life chess game. She knows her chances of winning in a contest against her mother, who taught her to be strong like the wind. Waverly learns during the "chess years" that her mother was a champion strategist. Though she is a tax attorney able to bully even the Internal Revenue Service, she fears the wrath of her mother if she is told to mind her business: "Well, I don't know if it's explicitly stated in the law, but you can't ever tell a Chinese mother to shut up. You could be charged as an accessory to your own murder" (191). What Waverly perceives as an impending battle for her mother's approval of her fiancé is nothing more than the opportunity for her mother and her to communicate with each other. She strategically plans to win her mother's approval of her fiancé, Rick, just as if she is playing a game of chess. She is afraid to tell her mother that they are going to be married because she is afraid that her mother will not approve. The conversation ends with her recognition that her mother also needs to be heard and with her mother's unstated approval of her fiancé. Waverly Jong recognizes her mother's strategies in their verbal jousts, but she also recognizes that, just like her, her mother is in search of something. What she sees is an old woman waiting to be invited into her daughter's life. Like the other mothers, Lindo views herself as standing outside her daughter's life—a most undesirable place.

Sometimes Tan's mothers find it necessary to intrude in order to teach the daughters to save themselves; they criticize, manage, and manipulate with an iron fist. An-mei Hsu and Ying-ying St. Clair play this role. "My mother once told me why I was so confused all the time," says Rose Hsu during her first story, "Without Wood" (212). "She said that I was without wood. Born without wood so that I listened to too many people. She knew this because she had almost become this way" (212). Suyuan Woo tells June Woo that such weaknesses are present in the mother, An-mei Hsu: "Each person is made of five elements. . . . Too little wood and you bend too quickly to listen to other people's ideas, unable to stand on your own. This was like my Auntie An-mei" (19). Rose's mother tells her that she must stand tall and listen to her mother standing next to her. If she bends to listen to strangers, she'll grow weak and be destroyed. Rose Hsu is in the process of divorce from a husband who has labeled her indecisive and useless as a marriage partner. She is guilty of allowing her husband to mold her. He does not want her to be a partner in family decisions until he makes a mistake in his practice as a plastic surgeon. Then he complains that she is unable to make decisions: he is dissatisfied with his creation. Finding it difficult to accept divorce, she confusedly runs to her friends and a psychiatrist seeking guidance.

Over and over again her mother tells her to count on a mother because a mother is best and knows what is inside of her daughter. "A psyche-atricks will only make you hulihudu, make you heimongmong" (210). The psychiatrist leaves her confused, as her mother predicts. She becomes even more confused as she tells each of her friends and her psychiatrist a different story. Her mother advises her to stand up to her husband, to speak up. She assumes the role of Lady Sorrowfree. When Rose does as her mother advises, she notices that her husband seems scared and confused. She stands up to him and forces him to retreat. She is her mother's daughter. She listens to her mother and finds her voice—her self.

Like the other mothers, An-mei demonstrates some of the qualities of "Lady Sorrowfree." An-mei is concerned that her daughter sees herself as having no options. A psychologist's explanation is "to the extent that women perceive themselves as having no choice, they correspondingly excuse themselves from the responsibility that decision entails" (Gilligan, 67). An-mei was "raised the Chinese way": "I was taught to desire nothing, to swallow other people's misery, to eat my own bitterness" (241). She uses the tale of the magpies to indicate that one can either make the choice to be in charge of one's life or continue to let others be in control. For thousands of years magpies came to the fields of a group of peasants just after they had sown their seeds and watered them with their tears. The magpies ate the seeds and drank the tears. Then one day the peasants decided to end their suffering and silence. They clapped their hands and banged sticks together, making noise that startled and confused the magpies. This continued for days until the magpies died of hunger and exhaustion from waiting for the noise to stop so that they could land and eat. The sounds from the hands and sticks were their voices. Her daughter should face her tormentor.

An-mei tells stories of her pain, a pain she does not wish her daughter to endure. Memory is, in part, voices calling out to her, reminding her of what she has endured and of a relationship wished for: "it was her voice that confused me," "a familiar sound from a forgotten dream," "she cried with a wailing voice," "voices praising," "voices murmuring," "my mother's voice went away" (41–45). The voices of her mothers confused her. She was a young girl in need of a mother's clear voice that would strengthen her circumstances and her context. The voices remind her, in "Scar," of wounds that heal but leave their imprint and of the importance of taking control out of the hands of those who have the ability to devour their victims, as in the story "Magpies." A scar resulting from a severe burn from a pot of boiling soup reminds her of when her mother was considered a ghost: her mother was dead to her family because she became a rich merchant's concubine. With time the scar "became pale and shiny and I had no memory of my mother. That is the way it is with a wound. The wound begins to close in on itself, to protect what is hurting so much. And once it is closed, you no longer see what is underneath, what started the pain" (40). It is also the way of persons attempting to assimilate—the wounds of getting to America, the wounds of hyphenation, close in on themselves and then it is difficult to see where it all began.

An-mei remembers the scar and the pain when her mother returns to her grandmother Poppo's deathbed. Upon the death of Poppo, she leaves with her mother, who shortly afterward commits suicide. Poppo tells An-mei that when a person loses face, it's like dropping a necklace down a well: the only way you can get it back is to jump in after it. From her mother An-mei learns that tears cannot wash away sorrows; they only feed someone else's joy. Her mother tells her to swallow her own tears.

An-mei knows strength and she knows forgetting. Perhaps that is why her daughter tells the story of her loss. It is Rose Hsu who tells the story of her brother's drowning and her mother's faith that he would be found. She refuses to believe that he is dead; without any driving lessons, she steers the car to the ocean side to search once more for him. After her son Bing's death, An-mei places the Bible that she has always carried to the First Chinese Baptist Church under a short table leg as a way of correcting the imbalances of life. She gives her daughter advice on how to correct imbalances in her life. The tale prefacing the section "Queen of the Western Skies" is also a fitting message for Rose Hsu. A woman playing with her granddaughter wonders at the baby's happiness and laughter, remembering that she was once carefree before she shed her innocence and began to look critically and suspiciously at everything. She asks the babbling child if it is Syi Wang, Queen Mother of the Western Skies, come back to provide her with some answers: "Then you must teach my daughter this same lesson. How to lose your innocence but not your hope. How to laugh forever" (159).

Like all the other daughters, Lena must recognize and respect the characteristics of Lady Sorrowfree that are inherent in her mother, Ying-ying. Ying-ying describes her daughter as being devoid of wisdom. Lena laughs at her mother when she says "arty-tecky" (architecture) to her sister-in-law. Ying-ying admits that she should have slapped Lena more as a child for disrespect. Though Ying-ying serves as Lena's goddess, Lena initially does not view her mother as capable of advice on balance. Ying-ying's telling of her story is very important to seeing her in a true mothering role; her daughter's first story makes one think that the mother is mentally unbalanced.

Evelyn Reed in *Woman's Evolution* writes: "A mother's victimization does not merely humiliate her, it mutilates her daughter who watches her for clues as to what it means to be a woman. Like the traditional foot-bound Chinese woman, she passes on her affliction. The mother's self-hatred and low expectations are binding rags for the psyche of the daughter" (293). Ying-ying, whose name means "Clear Reflection," becomes a ghost. As a young girl she liked to unbraid her hair and wear it loose. She recalls a scolding from her mother, who once told her that she was like the lady ghosts at the bottom of the lake. Her daughter is unaware of her mother's previous marriage to a man in China twenty years before Lena's birth. Ying-ying falls in love with him because he strokes her cheek and tells her that she has tiger eyes, that they gather fire in the day and shine golden at night. Her husband opts to run off with another woman during her pregnancy, and she aborts the baby because she has come to hate her husband with a passion. Ying-ying tells Lena that she was born a tiger in a year when babies were dying and because she was strong she survived. After ten years of reclusive living with cousins in the country, she goes to the city to live and work. There she meets Lena's father, an American she marries after being courted for four years, and continues to be a ghost. Ying-ying says that she willingly gave up her spirit.

In Ying-ying's first story, "The Moon Lady," when she sees her daughter lounging by the pool she realizes that they are lost, invisible creatures. Neither, at this point, recognizes the importance of "listening harder to the silence beneath their voices" (Maglin, 260). Their being lost reminds her of the family outing to Tai Lake as a child, when she falls into the lake, is rescued, and is put on shore only to discover that the moon lady she has been anxiously awaiting to tell her secret wish is male. The experience is so traumatic that she forgets her wish. Now that she is old and is watching her daughter, she remembers that she had wished to be found. And now she wishes for her daughter to be found—to find herself.

Lena, as a young girl, sees her mother being devoured by her fears until she becomes a ghost. Ying-ying believes that she is already a ghost. She does not want her daughter to become a ghost like her, "an unseen spirit" (285). Ying-ying begins life carefree. She is loved almost to a fault by her mother and her nursemaid, Amah. She is spoiled by her family's riches and wasteful. When she unties her hair and floats through the house, her mother tells her that she resembles the "lady ghosts . . . ladies who drowned in shame and floated in living people's houses with their hair undone to show everlasting despair" (276). She knows despair when the north wind that she thinks has blown her luck chills her heart by blowing her first husband past her to other women.

Lena, Ying-ying's daughter, is a partner in a marriage where she has a voice in the rules; but when the game is played, she loses her turn many times. Carolyn See argues that "in the name of feminism and right thinking, this husband is taking Lena for every cent she's got, but she's so demoralized, so 'out of balance' in the Chinese sense, that she can't do a thing about it" (11). In the introductory anecdote to the section "American Translation," a mother warns her daughter that she cannot put mirrors at the foot of the bed because all of her marriage happiness will bounce back and tumble the opposite way. Her mother takes from her bag a mirror that she plans to give the daughter as a wedding gift so that it faces the other mirror. The mirrors then reflect the happiness of the daughter. Lena's mother, as does Rose's mother, provides her with the mirror to balance her happiness; the mirror is a mother's advice or wisdom. It is Lena's mother's credo that a woman is out of balance if something goes against her nature. She does not want to be like her mother, but her mother foresees that she too will become a ghost; her husband will transform her according to his desires. Ying-ying recalls that she became "Betty" and was given a new date of birth by a husband who never learned to speak her language. Her review of her own story makes her know that she must influence her daughter's "story" that is in the making. Lena sees herself with her husband in the midst of problems so deep that she can't see where the bottom is. In the guise of a functional relationship is a dysfunctional one. Her mother predicts that the house will break into pieces. When a too-large vase on a too-weak table crashes to the floor, Lena admits that she knew it would happen. Her mother asks her why she did not take steps to keep the house from falling, meaning her marriage as well as the vase.

The goddess role becomes all important to Ying-ying as she becomes more determined to prevent her daughter from becoming a ghost. She fights the daughter that she has raised, "watching from another shore" and "accept[ing] her American ways" (286). After she uses the sharp pain of what she knows to "penetrate [her] daughter's tough skin and cut the tiger spirit loose," she waits for her to come into the room, like a tiger waiting between the trees, and pounces. Ying-ying wins the fight and gives her daughter her spirit, "because this is the way a mother loves her daughter" (286). Lady Sorrowfree helps her "charge" achieve voice.

From the daughter with too much water, to the mother and daughter with too much wood, to the tiger ghosts and just plain ghosts, to the chess queens, Tan's women in *The Joy Luck Club* find themselves capable of forging their own identities, moving beyond passivity to assertiveness—speaking up. They are a piece of the portrait that represents Amy Tan's family history—her own story included; they are, in composite, her family's secrets and tragedies. Tan is unlike some Asian American writers who have had to try to piece together and sort out the meaning of the past from shreds of stories overheard or faded photographs. As in her stories, her mother tells her the stories and explains the photographs. Bell Gale Chevigny writes that "women writing about other women will symbolically reflect their internalized relations with their mothers and in some measure re-create them" (80). From Tan's own accounts, her interaction with her mother is reflected in her fiction.

Tan's women with their American husbands attempt often without knowing it to balance East and West, the past and the future of their lives. A level of transcendence is apparent in the storytelling, as it is in *The Kitchen God's Wife*. Mothers and daughters must gain from the storytelling in order to have healthy relationships with each other.

In *The Kitchen God's Wife*, Winnie Louie and her daughter Pearl Louie Brandt are both keepers of secrets that accent the distance that characterizes their relationship. Pearl thinks after a trip to her mother's home: "Mile after mile, all of it familiar, yet not this distance that separates us, me from my mother" (57). She is unsure of how this distance was created. Winnie says of their relationship: "That is how she is. That is how I am. Always careful to be polite, always trying not to bump into each other, just like strangers" (82). When their secrets begin to weigh down their friends who have known them for years, who threaten to tell each of the other's secrets, Winnie Louie decides that it is time for revelation. The process of the revelation is ritual: "recitation of the relationship between mother and daughter," "assessment of the relationship," and "the projection of the future into the relationship" (Koppelman, xxvii). At the same time revelation is a journey to voice, the voice that they must have with each other. Again, voice is a metaphor for speaking up, being heard, listening to be heard. No longer will stories begin as Pearl's does: "Whenever my mother talks to me, she begins the conversation as if we were already in the middle of an argument" (11). That they argue or are in conflict is not problematic; it is the "talks to" that should be replaced with "talks with." As much as Pearl needs to know her mother's secrets,

Winnie Louie needs to tell them in order to build a relationship that is nurturing for both mother and daughter.

Pearl's secret is multiple sclerosis. At first she does not tell her mother because she fears her mother's theories on her illness. What becomes her secret is the anger she feels toward her father, the inner turmoil that began with his dying and death. Sometimes the mother's voice drowns the voice of the daughter as she attempts to control or explain every aspect of the daughter's existence. "If I had not lost my mother so young, I would not have listened to Old Aunt," says Winnie Louie (65) as she begins her story. These might also be the words of her daughter, though Pearl's loss of mother was not a physical loss. The opportunity for the resonating of mother and daughter voices seems to be the difference between balance and imbalance. American circumstances are to be blamed for the distance; the need to keep secrets grows out of the perceived necessity of assimilation and clean slates. Because her mother was not there, Winnie "listened to Old Aunt" (65). Winnie Louie's dark secret begins with her mother, who disappeared without telling her why; she still awaits some appearance by her mother to explain. Her mother's story is also hers: an arranged marriage—in her mother's case, to curb her rebelliousness; realization that she has a lesser place in marriage than purported; and a daughter as the single lasting joy derived from the marriage. The difference is that Winnie's mother escaped, to be heard from no more.

Winnie's family abides by all of the customs in giving her hand in marriage to Wen Fu: "Getting married in those days was like buying real estate. Here you see a house you want to live in, you find a real estate agent. Back in China, you saw a rich family with a daughter, you found a go-between who knew how to make a good business deal" (134). Winnie tells her daughter, "If asked how I felt when they told me I would marry Wen Fu, I can only say this: It was like being told I had won a big prize. And it was also like being told my head was going to be chopped off. Something between those two feelings" (136). Winnie experiences very little mercy in her marriage to the monstrous Wen Fu.

Wen Fu serves as an officer in the Chinese army, so during World War II they move about China with other air force officers and their wives. Throughout the marriage, Winnie knows abuse and witnesses the death of her babies. She tries to free herself from the tyranny of the marriage, but her husband enjoys abusing her too much to let her go. Her story is a long one, a lifetime of sorrow, death, marriage, imprisonment, lost children, lost friends and family. Jimmie Louie saves her life by helping her to escape Wen Fu and to come to the United States. She loves Jimmie Louie and marries him. The darkest part of her secret she reveals to Pearl almost nonchalantly: Pearl is the daughter of the tyrant Wen Fu.

The daughter asks her mother: "Tell me again . . . why you had to keep it a secret." The mother answers: "Because then you would know. . . . You would know how weak I was. You would think I was a bad mother" (398). Winnie's actions and response are not unexpected. She is every mother who wants her daughter to think of her as having lived a blemish-free existence. She is every mother who forgets that her daughter is living life and knows blemishes. Secrets revealed, the women begin to talk. No longer does Winnie have to think that the year her second husband, Jimmie Louie, died was "when everyone stopped listening to me" (81). Pearl knows her mother's story and can respect her more, not less, for her endurance. She is then able to see a woman molded by her experiences and her secrets—a woman who has lived with two lives. With the tiptoeing around ended, the distance dissipates. By sharing their secrets, they help each other to achieve voice. The gift of Lady Sorrowfree is symbolic of their bonding; this goddess has all of the characteristics of the nurturing, caring, listening mother. Her imperfections lie in her creation; experiences make her. She has none of the characteristics of the Kitchen God.

The story of the Kitchen God and his wife angers Winnie Louie; she looks at the god as a bad man who was rewarded for admitting that he was a bad man. As the story goes, a wealthy farmer, Zhang, who had a good wife who saw to it that his farm flourished, brought home a pretty woman and made his wife cook for her. The pretty woman ran his wife off without any objection from the farmer. She helped him use up all of his riches foolishly and left him a beggar. He was discovered hungry and suffering by a servant who took him home to care for him. When he saw his wife, whose home it was, he attempted to hide in the kitchen fireplace; his wife could not save him. The Jade Emperor, because Zhang admitted he was wrong, made him Kitchen God with the duty to watch over people's behavior. Winnie tells Pearl that people give generously to the Kitchen God to keep him happy in the hopes that he will give a good report to the Jade Emperor. Winnie thinks that he is not the god for her daughter. How can one trust a god who would cheat on his wife? How can he be a good judge of behavior? The wife is the good one. She finds another god for her daughter's altar, Lady Sorrowfree. After all, she has already given her a father.

Even as Winnie tells her story, one senses that the women are unaware of the strength of the bond between them that partly originates in the biological connection and partly in their womanness. Storytelling/revealing secrets gives both of them the opportunity for review; Winnie Louie tells Pearl that she has taught her lessons with love, that she has combined all of the love that she had for the three she lost during the war and all of those that she did not allow to be born and has given it to Pearl. She speaks of her desire "to believe in something good" (152), her lost hope and innocence: "So I let those other babies die. In my heart I was being kind. . . . I was a young woman then. I had no more hope left, no trust, no innocence" (312). In telling her story, she does not ask for sympathy or forgiveness; she simply wants to be free of the pain that "comes from keeping everything inside, waiting until it is too late" (88).

Perhaps this goddess, Lady Sorrowfree, to whom they burn incense will cause them never to forget the importance of voice and listening. On the heels of listening there is balance as both Winnie and Pearl tell their secrets and are brought closer by them. East and West, mother and daughter, are bonded for the better. Arcana notes that "mother/daughter sisterhood is the consciousness we must seek to make this basic woman bond loving and fruitful, powerful and deep . . ." (34). It ensures that women do not smother each other and squelch the voice of the other or cause each other to retreat into silence.

In exploring the problems of mother-daughter voices in relationships, Tan unveils some of the problems of biculturalism—of Chinese ancestry and American circumstances. She presents daughters who do not know their mothers' "importance" and thus cannot know their own; most seem never to have been told or even cared to hear their mothers' history. Until they do, they can never achieve voice. They assimilate; they marry American men and put on American faces. They adapt. In the meantime, their mothers sit like Lady Sorrowfree on her altar, waiting to listen. The daughters' journeys to voice are completed only after they come to the altars of their Chinese mothers.

Works Cited and Consulted

Arcana, Judith. *Our Mothers' Daughters*. Berkeley: Shameless Hussy Press, 1979.

Belensky, Mary Field, et al. *Women's Ways of Knowing*. New York: Basic Books, 1986.

Blicksilver, Edith. *The Ethnic American Woman: Problems, Protests, Lifestyle*. Dubuque, Ia.: Kendall/Hunt Publishing, 1978.

Carlson, Kathie. *In Her Image: The Unhealed Daughter's Search for Her Mother*. Boston: Shambhala, 1990.

Chevigny, Bell Gale. "Daughters Writing: Toward a Theory of Women's Biography." *Feminist Studies* 9 (1983): 79–102.

Chodorow, Nancy. *Feminism and Psychoanalytic Theory*. New Haven: Yale University Press, 1989.

Doten, Patti. "Sharing Her Mother's Secrets." *Boston Globe*, June 21, 1991, E9–14.

Friday, Nancy. *My Mother/My Self*. New York: Delacorte Press, 1977.

Gardiner, Judith Kegan. "Mind Mother: Psychoanalysis and Feminism." In *Making a Difference: Feminist Literary Criticism*, ed. Gayle Greene and Coppélia Kahn, 113–145. New York: Methuen, 1985.

Gilligan, Carol. *In a Different Voice*. Cambridge, Mass.: Harvard University Press, 1982.

Hirsch, Marianne. *The Mother-Daughter Plot: Narrative, Psychoanalysis, Feminism*. Bloomington: Indiana University Press, 1989.

Hirsch, Marianne, and Evelyn Fox Feller. *Conflicts in Feminism*. New York: Routledge, 1990.

Kim, Elaine H. *Asian American Literature: An Introduction to the Writings and Their Social Context*. Philadelphia: Temple University Press, 1982.

Koppelman, Susan. *Between Mothers and Daughters, Stories across a Generation*. New York: Feminist Press at the City University of New York, 1985.

Maglin, Nan Bauer. "The Literature of Matrilineage." In *The Lost Tradition: Mothers and Daughters in Literature*, ed. Cathy N. Davidson and E. M. Broner, 257–267. New York: Frederick Ungar, 1980.

Marbella, Jean. "Amy Tan: Luck But Not Joy." *Baltimore Sun*, June 30, 1991, E-11.

"Mother with a Past." *Maclean's* (July 15, 1991): 47.

Reed, Evelyn. *Woman's Evolution*. New York: Pathfinder Press, 1975.

Rich, Adrienne. *Of Woman Born: Motherhood as Experience and Institution*. New York: Norton, 1976, 1986.

Rosinsky, Natalie M. "Mothers and Daughters: Another Minority Group." In *The Lost Tradition: Mothers and Daughters in Literature*, ed. Cathy N. Davidson and E. M. Broner, 281–303. New York: Frederick Ungar, 1980.

See, Carolyn. "Drowning in America, Starving in China." *Los Angeles Times Book Review*, March 12, 1989, 1, 11.

Spence, Jonathan D. *The Search for Modern China*. New York: W. W. Norton, 1990.

Tan, Amy. *The Joy Luck Club*. New York: Ivy Books, 1989.

———. *The Kitchen God's Wife*. New York: G. P. Putnam's Sons, 1991.

———. "Lost Lives of Women." *Life* (April 1991), 90–91.

Walters, Suzanna Danuta. *Lives Together/Worlds Apart: Mothers and Daughters in Popular Culture*. Berkeley: University of California Press, 1992.

Wolf, Margery, and Roxanne Witke. *Women in Chinese Society*. Stanford: Stanford University Press, 1975.

Yamada, Mitsuye. "Invisibility Is an Unnatural Disaster: Reflections of an Asian American Woman." In *This Bridge Called My Back: Writings of Radical Women of Color*, ed. Cherríe Moraga and Gloria Anzaldúa, 35–40. Latham, N.Y.: Kitchen Table / Women of Color Press, 1982.

To Make Herself

Mother-Daughter Conflicts in Toni Morrison's *Sula* and *Tar Baby*

LUCILLE P. FULTZ

A girl has got to be a daughter first.
TONI MORRISON

Few feminist issues generate so much angst as the mother-daughter dyad. This symbiotic merging of consciousness and subjectivities, bonding and alienation, is marked by tenderness and tension, love and resentment, sacrifice and inadequate appreciation. What occurs between mother and daughter during the daughter's emergent consciousness most often determines the daughter's attitude toward the mother and motherhood. African American daughters have had no paucity of courageous, self-sacrificing mothers. The alliances between African American mothers and daughters have not been easy, however. Rather they have been ambivalent on one hand and deeply appreciative on the other. African American mothers alternately long for their daughters' independence and acknowledgment of their mothers' influence and sacrifice with the concomitant recognition of their mothers' failure to achieve their own desires, which ultimately enabled the daughters' achievements. Such desires would suggest that the daughter "cannot stir without the [m]other" (Irigaray, 60, 67), thereby compelling the daughter to admit her dependence upon her mother and the mother to seek vicarious achievement through her daughter.

The African American mother-daughter relationships are multivalent and multiconfigured. Economic conditions for many African American women require their working outside the home and spending many hours away from their children, thereby making it impossible to provide proper care during their absence. Added to the economic factor is the interconnectedness of race, gender, and class, the axes on which power and influence turn, resulting in a triple jeopardy, especially for African American women. And if one adds the melanin dimension, that jeopardy is quadrupled. African American women observing their mothers struggling with and against a hostile world realize quite early that some popular notions of motherhood do not assimilate to their mothers' lived experiences. These daughters discover early on that in place of tenderness and demonstrative affection they must frequently settle for physical care and protection. They come to understand love not as a verbal expression or affective gesture but rather as sacrificial acts and stays against illness and death.

One might be tempted to select from the many texts by African American women writers those which valorize the mother. However, a close scrutiny of the African American mother-daughter dyad illustrates the complexity of womanhood for African American females. This putatively "normative" sphere is the site where the mother and daughter encounter each other as gendered subjects. It is here that the mother in her role as nurturer and enabler prepares the daughter, through example and precept, for her role as woman and mother. Because mothers are expected to socialize daughters to become mothers, one might ask to what extent African American mothers serve as effective role models for their daughters and to what degree daughters emulate and/or resist their mothers' examples. In her seminal text *Of Woman Born*, Adrienne Rich argues that women are "growing into a world so hostile to us [that we] need a very profound kind of loving in order to love ourselves"—not the "old, institutionalized sacrificial, 'mother-love' which men have demanded: we want courageous mothering" (246). African American women have no paucity of courageous mothers, but they also have a superabundance of "sacrificial" mothers. This dynamic enters a number of texts by African American women: Toni Morrison's novels are especially illuminating.

Morrison's use of "contrastive parallelism and antithetical character development" offers a useful paradigm for examining mother-daughter relationships in *Sula*,[1] which demonstrates, among other things, how to be a "bad" mother or how to engender a daughter's hatred. The tension produced by the emotional and psychological distance between mothers and daughters is at the core of this novel. This disruptive element in the mother-daughter relationship is presaged by other disruptions in the novel. The prologue posits an oppositional world, a community that has already disappeared—a community nostalgically reconstructed: "In that place . . . there was once a neighborhood" (3). One is asked to enter two fictions: a fictional narrative of a place called the Bottom, the locus of action; and a narrative fiction (the perverted promise that inaugurates this neighborhood). Additionally, the characters encountered are not what they seem. Shadrack, a key force in the community's sense of itself in time and space, has been mentally shattered by war and is so disoriented when one first meets him that he does not trust his hands to be at the end of his arms. But Shadrack's disordered psyche is counterpoised by an external structure that orders his life. The novel posits other disruptions as well. For example, Eva Peace, perhaps the most powerful and manipulative character in the novel, has lost a leg under mysterious circumstances. The reader meets three markedly different boys with a single identity: "the deweys." Elizabeth Abel notes that *Sula* "repeatedly assaults our expectations by planting its narration in an existential context in which the nature of identity is problematic" (427).

In this inverted world Morrison posits two maternal narratives which, like everything else in the novel, appear to be diametrically opposed. Eva Peace's house with its many rooms randomly added over five years and situated on Carpenter Road "sixty feet" from the "one-room cabin" (35), where her husband had abandoned her and their three small children, is a veritable whirlwind of people and activities. It is a "household of throbbing disorder constantly awry with things, people, voices and the slamming of doors" (52). Helene Wright's house is, by contrast, the paragon of order and cleanliness, a charming house with a brick porch and elegant lace curtains at the windows.

Nel and Sula, who grow up in these respective households, are drawn to each other like polar opposites. Sula "felt comfortable" in Nel's house and "would sit on the red-velvet sofa for twenty minutes at a time—still as dawn." Nel, on the other hand, "preferred Sula's woolly house, where a pot of something was always cooking on the stove" (29). Within their respective households Sula and Nel experience quite different upbringings, yet they both are denied a necessary aspect of childhood—affection. Nel "became obedient and polite" under her mother's scrupulous guidance (18), while Sula's mother "never scolded or gave directions" (29). "The high silence of her mother's incredibly orderly house" thrusts Nel into daydreams, while Eva's "household of throbbing disorder" causes Sula to seek shelter in her own imagination (51–52).

Their mothers' failure to meet their emotional needs brings these solitary girls together. Abel sees Nel's rejection of her mother's values as "an essential step in Nel's orientation toward a peer relationship" with Sula and Nel's attraction to her grandmother, a prostitute, as "an alternative object of identification" (427). However, Sula and Nel's friendship can be viewed as a reaction to their emotional distance from their mothers. Hannah Peace and Helene Wright are largely responsible for their daughters' rejection. Intergenerational maternal tensions are at issue in *Sula*.

In 1937 when Sula returns to Medallion after a ten-year absence, Eva asks her when is she going to get married, have babies, and settle down. Eva's question and admonition are at once a critique of Sula's behavior and a traditional view of gender. According to Eva, Sula needs to get married in order to have babies and she needs stability. Eva's pronouncement contradicts her experiences as a mother—Eva has been no illuminating example of the type of motherhood / womanhood she is espousing for her granddaughter, since her decision to settle down and have children with BoyBoy left her (un)settled with three children. And Hannah's settling in Eva's house and her de facto abandonment of her daughter Sula certainly are no indications that she is an exemplary model of motherhood by Eva's definition. If Sula has learned anything of men and children from her mother and grandmother, it is that men can be counted on for sex, that they are sometimes cruel and grossly irresponsible, and that women cannot always rely upon them for sustenance and child support.

When Sula tells Eva, "I don't want to make somebody else. I want to make myself," Eva calls her "selfish. . . . Ain't no woman got no business floatin' around without no man" (92). Sula reminds Eva that neither she nor Hannah had settled down with men, but Eva tells her it was not by choice. Yet Hannah's free and easy sexual play contributes to Sula's resistance to Eva's urgent push toward marriage and children. Sula's argument suggests that the daughter must reject the mother's choices in order to give birth to herself, that she must eschew marriage and childbirth in order to save herself. Martha Giminez argues that "motherhood, if conceived as a taken-for-granted dimension of women's normal adult role, becomes one of the key sources of women's oppression" (287). Moreover, as Rich observes, "A female child needs to be told, very early, the practical difficulties females have to face even in trying to imagine 'what they want to be'" (247). Thus Eva's advice is incomplete. Her urging Sula toward marriage and motherhood should be accompanied by descriptions of Eva's own experiences as well as Hannah's. Rich notes that as women "we bring something other than children into the world, we engender something other than children: love, desire, language, art, the social, the political, the religious, for example" (249).

In positing an alternative role for herself, Sula registers a radically different desire, which reinforces the narrator's earlier assessment of Sula's and Nel's possibilities limited by the fact "that they were neither white nor male . . . they had set about creating something else to be" (52). Nel, of course, submits to tradition; she becomes "one of them." Sula almost surrenders to the system after she meets Ajax. But in the final analysis, Sula emerges as an imaginative, independent, self-assured creature who does not feel compelled to please anybody else "unless their pleasure pleased her" (120). The closeness/the inseparableness Sula shared with Nel—"They were two throats and one eye"—ultimately comes down to separate subjectivities. Sula insists upon her right to create herself, even though it is a self at odds with her community and larger societal norms. To borrow from Adrienne Rich: "we have no familiar, ready-made name for a woman who defines herself, by choice, neither in relation to children nor to men, who is self-identified, who has chosen herself" (249) or, in Sula's words, who "make[s] [her]self." Hortense Spillers notes that Sula "lives for Sula"; she is "woman-for-the-self," not "woman-for-the-other" (28).

Behind Eva's question, however, lies a desire for posterity and stability. More important is Eva's desire for assurance that Sula's sexual and maternal experiences will be more traditional than hers and Hannah's. Still, Eva's insistence upon marriage and children posits a female identity limited to a traditional familial role—motherhood—and a fixed space—the home. Implicit in Eva's argument is the assumption that women must be economically dependent on men and that a "good" mother stays home, where she creates a nurturing environment for her husband and children. Sula will have none of this. Moreover, she has shown a fundamental disregard for such fixities—witness her affair with her best friend's husband and her consternation that Nel would take offense. Sula, again to borrow from Adrienne Rich, "may have looked at the lives of women with children and felt that, given the circumstances of motherhood, she must remain childless if she is to pursue any other hopes or aims" (250). Some years earlier Sula had overheard her mother discussing with two neighbors the problems and pains of child-rearing. What arrests and shocks Sula is Hannah's response to one of the women's comments: "'Well, Hester grown now and I can't say love is exactly what I feel.' 'Sure you do. You love her, like I love Sula. I just don't like her. That's the difference'" (57). "Bewilder[ed]" by her mother's pronouncement, Sula "flies up the stairs" into "dark thoughts" (57) that surely must have found expression in her teasing and furiously hurling Chicken Little to his accidental death.

The shape of Hannah's sentence implies an ironic commentary. The comma forces a pause: "You love her," Hannah asserts, but this comes after the other woman's assertion: "I can't say love is exactly what I feel." Hannah insists that there is no difference between her feelings for Sula and the other woman's feelings for her daughter Hester. Hannah's "I just don't like her" goes deeper since it conveys distance and disapproval. Hannah suggests that love is a given, but, as the other woman says, "likin' them is another thing" (57). This other thing is precisely what Sula and Nel desire and what their mothers do not and cannot give them. Hannah's inability to like her daughter may be linked to her own mother's inability or failure to give Hannah the feeling of being liked. Hannah has no experiential knowledge or maternal role model for this aspect of the mother-daughter bond.

In contrast to the three generations in the Peace household, Nel represents the fourth generation of Sabat women with four Virgin Marys. Yet the Virgin, the symbol of ideal womanhood—chastity and motherhood—in a larger sense fails to protect the Sabat women in their hour of sorest need. Cecile dies before Helene arrives; Rochelle succumbs to prostitution; Helene is humiliated by a racist system despite her efforts toward bourgeois values; and Nel, in spite of her claims that she belongs to herself and no one else, follows her mother's example by marrying and having children.

Morrison sets up the intergenerational tensions among the Sabat women first, by allowing Nel to see her mother through the gaze of other people. Watching her mother reduced to "custard" under the gaze of a white conductor and black men helps to distance Nel from Helene and forces her to question her mother as a role model. The trip to New Orleans and the subsequent meeting with her grandmother and great-grandmother offer Nel glimpses into her female ancestry. More importantly, this encounter provides the reader with a larger commentary on Helene's flight toward bourgeois values and her estrangement from her mother, Rochelle.

A closer examination of the scene in New Orleans yields a shocking commentary on motherhood and the effect of the mother's behavior upon the daughter. Rochelle's beauty, as the narrative suggests, has been her downfall. Her creole physiognomy has made her ripe for prostitution. Observing that Helene at sixteen has a striking resemblance to Rochelle and eager to protect Helene from the Sun Down House of prostitution that marks her mother's life, Cecile arranges a marriage with an older cousin—Wiley Wright, who takes Helene to Medallion, far from the site of her mother's "sooty" lifestyle. The narrative underscores the irony of Helene's repulsion of Hannah's "sooty" lifestyle, which is strikingly like Helene's own mother's.

Helene is threatened by Nel's attraction to Rochelle, whose influence she has spent all her life trying to escape. After being hugged by Rochelle, Nel observes to Helene, "She smelled so nice. And her skin was soft." To which Helene replies, after "soap[ing] Nel from head to toe," "Much handled things are always soft" (27).

The mothers in both Nel's and Sula's families do not know how to show affection, particularly in Sula's case. Sula's rejection of Hannah, like Nel's strained relations with Helene, originates in Hannah's lack of an affective relationship with Eva. This absence of maternal affection is played out between Hannah and Eva the day before Hannah dies. Hannah's adult-child wants reassurance that she has been loved: "Mama, did you ever love us?" (67). Hannah's posture reinforces the urgency of her childlike plea as she "knelt to spread a newspaper on the floor" and "tucked [a basket of snap beans] in the space between her legs," poised and waiting like a child eager for her mother's reassuring answer.

Eva braces herself—her "hand moved snail-like down her thigh toward her stump, but stopped short of it to realign a pleat"—a gesture that invokes the phantom leg and all it signifies in the novel: Eva's mysterious absence for nearly two years, the mystique surrounding the missing leg, and the narratives it engenders. She then begins a definitive answer that seems both to understand and to misread Hannah's intention: a question motivated by desire for articulation of maternal love and perhaps by

Hannah's need to understand her relationship with her own daughter. But Eva reads Hannah's question as accusation and condemnation, because she perceives her role as provider, nurturer, and protector, a staying power against hunger and death: "'You settin here with your healthy-ass self and ax me did I love you. Them big old eyes in your head would a been two holes full of maggots if I hadn't. . . . Play? Wasn't nobody playin' in 1895. . . . Soon as I got one day done here come the night'" (68–69). For Eva motherhood is also replete with sacrifice and horrific choices: "You want me to tickle you under the jaw and forget 'bout them sores in your mouth? Pearl was shittin' worms and I was supposed to play rang-around-the-rosie?" (69). Hannah pleads her cause by telling her mother that she did not mean to upset her. Nonetheless, Eva's anger is unabated.

This eruption of anger marks Eva's guilt in the face of Hannah's longing to hear her mother speak her love. But Hannah's desire is unfulfilled. According to Eva, love is expressed in deeds. Hannah keeps trying: "I know you fed us and all. I was talking about something else." "But, Mamma, they had to be some time when you wasn't thinkin' 'bout . . . [taking care of us?]." Eva insists there was "no time. . . . Not none" (69).

Hannah's question is a commentary on the psyche of the adult deprived of affection as a child, and Eva's answer is a commentary on the material conditions that interfere with the maternal expression of love in affective ways. Yet the text does not present a facile solution to Hannah's desire, nor does it give Eva a loophole of retreat. Rather, it underscores the toll exacted upon mothers and children when fathers desert their families and mothers are burdened by poverty. As one sociologist puts it, "When mothers are deserted, mistreated, or made destitute, so too are their children" (Polakow, 20).

Hannah's gesture toward reaching Eva on this crucial issue of mother-love suggests not only the intergenerational tensions—the mother's unwillingness/inability to face the daughter's desire and/or the daughter's failure to comprehend a mother who found no time to love her children—but also the guilt and anger a question like Hannah's evokes. One might argue that the polar opposition that characterizes Sula and Nel exists simultaneously in Eva. Eva's complex nature is manifested in her love for her children, a love that both sustains and kills. It is this contradictory love that Hannah cannot understand: "But what about Plum? What'd you kill Plum for, Mamma?" (70). The question goes to the heart of Eva's complex nature. Why did she make such profound sacrifices to keep Plum alive only to destroy him brutally later? Hannah's question engenders a dual-voiced response: "Two voices. Like two people were talking at the same time, saying the same thing, one fraction of a second behind the other" (71). The question causes Eva to rehearse the moment before Plum's murder: "Eva couldn't see Hannah clearly for the tears, but she looked up at her anyway and said, by way of apology or explanation or perhaps just by way of neatness, 'But I held him close first. Real close. Sweet Plum. My baby boy'" (72). A few pages later the reader understands the urgency of Hannah's questions. The next day she dies, but not before discovering that her mother is capable of tenderness.

Further analysis of this moment between Hannah and Eva reveals Morrison's symbolic play with the maternal. Hannah is snapping beans for the evening meal. The language captures the musicality and complexity of the moment through Hannah's motions: "What with the sound of the cracking and snapping her swift fingered movements, she seemed to be playing a complicated instrument" (68). The language here encodes the complexity of Hannah's question and the "cracking" of Eva's armor of the sacrificial mother. The question causes Eva to "snap" back at Hannah's recognition that despite all Eva's maternal sacrifices she had failed her daughter in one very important area—she had denied her the closeness, the physical love she clearly desired.

Eva is a mother "more afraid of what is behind her than of what is in front of her" and must perforce "create the New World and with it a new way of life" (Braxton, 302). Enraged by Hannah's question, Eva tells her, "Girl I stayed alive for you can't you get that through your thick head or what is between your ears, heifer?" (69). For Eva, motherhood is a reminder of the terror of the winter of 1895—signifying a mother's strength in overcoming the forces that would overwhelm her ability to care for her children. This notion of motherhood is clearly grounded in the material conditions of 1895. And while she now is the matriarch of a house full of disparate people, Eva's consciousness holds on to the old house, the old time of hardships—trying to care for three children without their father. At this juncture when she responds to Hannah's question, Eva's definition of motherhood is grounded in the reality of cold, hard experience. Hannah cannot identify with Eva's memory of the past; she can only "discern" a mother who did not/does not hold her, did not/does not "tell her how wonderful she is" (Rich, 245). But Eva cannot say her love; she can only show it through her sacrificial act of saving Hannah from starvation and death.

The Eva Peace model posits an African American motherhood marked by what Gloria Wade-Gayles has aptly termed "the halo and the hardships" (57–113). This hallowed black mother, as Hortense Spillers observes, is one who "protects her children and forgives her men for their failure to share in the responsibility of protecting and caring for their children" (28).

In her seminal study of black feminist thought Patricia Hill Collins posits an Afro-centric model that encompasses and validates a wide range of mother figures, which she problematizes by raising the issue of African American mothers who simultaneously encourage their daughters to be independent and admonish them to get married and raise children. This apparent cognitive dissonance emerges from these mothers' attempts to create buffers for their daughters against a hostile world and at the same time pass along a legacy of love and service (126). Such a mixed message is what defines the mother-daughter relationship in *Tar Baby*. If motherlove is called into question in *Sula*, the reverse is true in *Tar Baby*, where the surrogate mother challenges the daughter's love and service.

The dilemma for African American mothers and daughters circulates around the issue of "physical survival [within] systems of oppression" and "serious challenges to oppressive situations" (Collins, 123–124). Collins terms this a "troubling dilemma" (124). But the daughter's break with and escape from the mother's experience are not always clean and facile accomplishments. Moreover, the African American daughter may never quite fully escape her mother's influence because the mother often sees herself as enabler and her daughter as the agent of promise and change. Julia Kristeva convincingly argues that "a woman rarely . . . experiences passion—love or hate—for another woman, without at some point taking the place of her own mother—without becoming a mother herself and, even more importantly, without undergoing the lengthy process of learning to differentiate herself from her daughter, her simulacrum whose presence she is forced to confront" (116).

In *Tar Baby* the mother / daughter relationship is expanded to embrace the "othermother."[2] Jadine Child's aunt fulfills the role of othermother when Jadine's mother dies—a role the aunt takes most seriously. Ondine Child's notion of motherhood is expansive: it encompasses both familial and extensive relationships. Ondine posits a broader model for mother-daughter relationships. She is pained when she feels she has not given Jadine the proper guidance owed a daughter by her mother, a concern that is lost on Jadine, for whom her aunt "mattered a lot," but what Ondine "thought did not" (49). Ondine apologetically articulates her failure as a surrogate mother: "Jadine, we done what we could for you because—well, what I mean to say is you don't owe us nothing. But, well, I never told you nothing. I never told you nothing at all and I take full responsibility for that" (280–281). What Ondine fails to tell Jadine is how to be a woman, not woman as social construct, but woman as defined through the lived experiences of older African American women. Ondine apparently feels guilty for isolating Jadine in a white world and not exposing her to the African American community. And the contempt with which Ondine and Sydney treat the black servants from the islands is testimony to the arrogance and superiority Jadine has learned from them and accounts in part for Jadine's behavior toward Son and his relatives in Eloe.

Having failed to teach Jadine important lessons about her culture, Ondine feels the urgency of telling her "something now." She offers Jadine a lesson in familial and communal loyalty, a commitment to family and community, a lesson Jadine totally misconstrues: "You want me to pay you back. You worked for me and put up with me. Now it's my turn to do it for you, that's all you're saying" (281). Jadine feels pressured, cornered; she believes that she is expected to sacrifice her future plans in order to support her aunt. But for Jadine, Ondine's wishes are not even an issue: if it comes to taking care of Ondine at the expense of her career and marriage, she will abandon her aunt.

For Ondine the opposite is true. She belongs to the generation of African American mothers who place their children's welfare above their own desires. Having worked thirty years as a household servant so that her feet are now badly swollen, Ondine expects no remuneration from Jadine—nothing by way of money or personal sacrifice—but rather respect for and appreciation of her struggles to guarantee Jadine an education and a future strikingly different from her own. When Jadine misunderstands her aunt's maternal discourse of angst and desire, Ondine becomes the outraged mother impelled to give her niece/daughter a lesson on daughterhood and womanist responsibility—not duty or obligation. "This ain't no game of bid whist," Ondine tells her—no quid pro quo. It is a legacy from mother to daughter: "Jadine, a girl has to be a daughter first. She have to learn that. And if she can't never learn how to be a daughter she can't never learn how to be a woman. I mean a real woman: a woman good enough for a child; good enough for a man—good enough for other women" (280).

Yet Ondine refuses to exonerate herself for failing to fulfill what she perceives to be her gendered role—the responsibility to pass along a womanist sensibility: "You don't need your own natural mother to be a daughter. All you need is to feel a certain . . . careful way about people older than you are. Don't mistake me now. I don't mean you have to love all kinds of mean old people, and if it's in your mind that I'm begging you for something, get it out. I ain't" (281).

A cursory reading of Ondine's text may suggest that she is speaking to the moment, is concerned about Jadine's affair with Son and her decision to return to Paris and hopes that Jadine will stay around to take care of her in her old age. Closer scrutiny, however, reveals a subtext that embraces the larger text surrounding Jadine's flight from her natal culture and community. Unlike Son, who wishes to keep Jadine trapped in Eloe, Florida, Ondine desires that Jadine excel in whatever she undertakes, but that she not forget her "ancient properties"—the long line of Africanist women who paved the way for her moment of achievement as an internationally recognized fashion model. Ondine's speech is part of a continuum of *mise-en-scènes* which Jadine misreads because she reads them through the eyes of one outside her natal culture.

Morrison scatters throughout *Tar Baby* a series of signs which suggest that Jadine is, indeed, a cultural orphan. The Africanist women insinuate their presence through traditional female signs: the African woman "with skin like tar" balancing three eggs "between earlobe and shoulder" (45), who "had made her feel lonely . . . and inauthentic" (48); the bare-breasted women who "looked down from the rafters of trees," aware of "their value, their exceptional femaleness"; Ondine through her role as enabler; Therese, in her rejection of Western culture, which Jadine counters in her rejection of African culture quite early in the novel as she contemplates her pending marriage to a Frenchman:

I guess the person I want to marry is him, but I wonder if the person he wants to marry is me or a black girl? And if it isn't me he wants, but any black girl who looks like me, talks and acts like me, what will happen when he finds out that I hate ear hoops, that I don't have to straighten my hair, that Mingus puts me to sleep, that sometimes I want to get out of my skin and be only the person inside—not American—not black—just me? (48)

Aside from the African woman who makes Jadine feel "inauthentic," Alma Estée is perhaps the best embedded commentary on Jadine's orphaned condition. In her red wig Alma Estée is Jadine's travestied double, a mocking epigone. She stands before Jadine admiring and desiring her bourgeois trappings. Alma Estée reminds the reader that Jadine is herself an Africanist in Western clothes, her Africanist sensibility shrouded by her adopted Western mannerisms. Alma Estée has some urgency for Jadine, who looks sneeringly at her ridiculous wig with "black pearls of hair . . . visible at the wig's edge" (289). The reader's gaze, however, is deflected from Alma Estée to Jadine, who fails to see the woman behind the wig and by extension herself. Jadine instead sees another "Mary"—the name used by Ondine and Sydney for all the female servants who worked at L'Arbe de la Croix—a woman unworthy of subjectivity. Jadine's artificiality is refracted through Alma Estée, and her Africanist sensibility is shrouded by the superimposition of bourgeois capitalism. Jadine suddenly reaches into her traveling bag and drops a few francs into the girl's plastic pail. This is a brilliant stroke. In objectifying Alma Estée, Jadine calls attention to herself as an object of scrutiny. Through this juxtaposition Morrison brings into relief the overarching issue of the novel—Jadine's inability to see herself as an imitation of bourgeois values, as an orphan within her native culture. It is this orphaned state that Ondine strives to impress upon Jadine; she asks not that Jadine give up the advantages of her Western education, but that she embrace her Africanist female heritage: the community of "bare-breasted women" which includes "her own mother for God's sake and *Nan*adine!" (258).

This vision of bare-breasted women might be glossed as those who nurtured Jadine and prepared the way for her entry into previously forbidden territory. But Jadine cannot understand their roles in her development ("I have breasts too" [58]) because her gaze is that of an outsider, of one so thoroughly Westernized that it would be a mistake to see her as alienated from her community. Jadine has never been properly enculturated to the African community, despite her claim that she "knew the life [she] was leaving" (74). Her education has brought her to the flawed conviction that the "Ave Maria" is "better than gospel singing" and that

"Picasso *is* better than an Itumba mask. The fact that he was intrigued by them is proof of his genius, not the mask-maker's" (74).

Ondine inveighs against precisely this hegemonic poseur: "a daughter is a woman that cares about where she comes from and takes care of them that took care of her. . . . I want you to care about me for [your sake]" (281). This failure to appreciate "where she comes from" engenders Jadine's embarrassment at "those black art shows mounted two or three times a year" (74). It is the white patron's properties and gifts that repeatedly resonate in Jadine's conversations with Son: "He [Valerian Street] put me through school" (263). Son's bitter retort brings the issue of motherhood to the fore: "Did he do anything for you? Did he give up anything important for you?" (263). Son's questions recall Ondine's commentary on her sacrificial investment in Jadine: "I would have stood on my feet all day and all night to put her through that school. And when my feet were gone, I would have cooked on my knees. . . . She crowned me, that girl did. No matter what went wrong or how tired I was, she was my crown" (193).

"The quality of the mother's life—however embattled and unprotected—is her primary bequest to her daughter, because a woman who can believe in herself, who is a fighter, and who continues to struggle to create a livable space around her, is demonstrating to her daughter that these possibilities exist" (Rich, 247). As Collins observes, "Black daughters must learn [from their mothers] how to survive in interlocking structures of race, class, and gender oppression while rejecting and transcending those very structures." And black mothers must assist their daughters in these struggles by "demonstrat[ing] varying combinations of behavior devoted to ensuring their daughters' survival [by] helping [them] go farther than mothers themselves were allowed to go" (Collins, 124). Toni Morrison's novels give voice to both mothers and daughters. She permits both to speak directly out of their own convictions and through their own discourses. Morrison's novels open up maternal silences by allowing mothers to speak out of their experiences and to confront their daughters head to head and conversely for daughters to interrogate their mothers' choices. The mother's crown for years of sacrifice is the daughter's transcendence over race, gender, and class and her acknowledgment of the mother's role in that transcendence.

Notes

1. Monika Hoffarth-Zelloe, "Resolving the Paradox?: An Interlinear Reading of Toni Morrison's *Sula*," 120, 125*n*12. Hoffarth-Zelloe traces Nel's and Sula's characters along parallel/divergent axes, but her formulations are useful in discussing the parallel and contrastive mother-daughter couplets along inter- and intragenerational trajectories.
2. Patricia Hill Collins defines "othermothers" as "women who assist blood mothers by sharing mothering responsibilities. . . . Grandmothers, sisters, aunts, cousins act as other mothers by taking on child-care responsibilities for one another's children" (*Black Feminist Thought*, 119–120).

Works Cited

Abel, Elizabeth. "(E)Merging Identities: The Dynamics of Female Friendship in Contemporary Fiction by Women." *Signs: Journal of Women in Culture and Society* 6 (1981): 413–435.

Braxton, Joanne M. "Ancestral Presence: The Outraged Mother Figure in Afra-American Writing." In *Wild Women in the Whirlwind,* ed. Joanne M. Braxton and Andree Nicola McLaughlin, 299–315. New York: Routledge, 1990.

Collins, Patricia Hill. *Black Feminist Thought: Knowledge, Consciousness, and the Politics of Empowerment.* New York: Routledge, 1990.

Gimenez, Martha E. "Feminism, Pronatalism, and Motherhood." In *Mothering: Essays in Feminist Theory,* ed. Joyce Trebilcot, 287–314. Totowa, N.J.: Rowman and Allenheld, 1983.

Hoffarth-Zelloe, Monika. "Resolving the Paradox?: An Interlinear Reading of Toni Morrison's *Sula.*" *Journal of Narrative Technique* 22 (1992): 114–127.

Irigaray, Luce. "And the One Doesn't Stir without the Other." *Signs: Journal of Women in Culture and Society* 7 (1981): 60–67.

Kristeva, Julia. "Stabat Mater." In *The Female Body in Western Culture,* ed. Susan Suleiman, 98–118. Cambridge: Harvard University Press, 1986.

Morrison, Toni. *Sula.* New York: New American Library, 1973.

———. *Tar Baby.* New York: New American Library, 1981.

Polakow, Valerie. *Lives on the Edge: Single Mothers and Their Children in Other America.* Chicago: University of Chicago Press, 1993.

Rich, Adrienne. *Of Woman Born: Motherhood as Experience and Institution.* New York: Norton, 1976, 1986.

Spillers, Hortense J. "A Hateful Passion, A Lost Love." In *Modern Critical Studies: Toni Morrison,* ed. Harold Bloom, 27–54. New York: Chelsea House, 1990.

Wade-Gayles, Gloria. *No Crystal Stair: Visions of Race and Sex in Black Women's Fiction.* New York: Pilgrim Press, 1984.

Index

Index

Index

Printed and bound by CPI Group (UK) Ltd, Croydon, CR0 4YY

13/04/2025

14656494-0002